A heartbreaking, searing exposé of ███████ of the Roman Catholic Church ███ to the resilience and power of a mother's love. Chrissie's passionate commitment to her daughters and to the principles of truth and justice jump off every page.

If the Pope wants to understand the true impact of clergy sexual abuse on all of its victims, he need only read this book.

Colm O'Gorman, author of *Beyond Belief*

Chrissie Foster's courageous and utterly devastating book, while intensely personal, is a wake-up call for us all. We can no longer collectively sit by as the crime of child sexual assault decimates our children, as systems of power perpetuate the victimisation, as lives are irreparably damaged, as faith is destroyed and morality mocked. Each child abuse statistic represents the imposed hell of stolen innocence and the lived horror of everyday families like Emma's and Katie's. Together we must protect our children, bring the perpetrators of these crimes to justice and address the systems that perpetuate them.

Dr Cathy Kezelman
Chairperson, ASCA, Adults Surviving Child Abuse

This is an awful yet compelling story of the rape of children and the complicity of the church. Every journalist interviewing a senior member of the Catholic Church must now ask one question: 'Are you, telling the truth, or are you using "mental reservation", trying to lie without lying?'

This is the extraordinary story of children raped by priests, and the organised behaviour of the church hierarchy to silence the helpless victims and intimidate their families. These children deserve a Royal Commission.

Professor Chris Goddard
Child Abuse Prevention Research Australia, Monash University

CHRISSIE FOSTER
with PAUL KENNEDY

Hell on the Way to Heaven

*An Australian mother's love. The power of the Catholic Church.
A fight for justice over child sexual abuse.*

BANTAM
SYDNEY • AUCKLAND • TORONTO • NEW YORK • LONDON

Some of the names of people in this book have been changed to protect their privacy.

A Bantam book
Published by Random House Australia Pty Ltd
Level 3, 100 Pacific Highway, North Sydney NSW 2060
www.randomhouse.com.au

First published by Bantam in 2010
This edition published in 2011

Copyright © Chrissie Foster and Paul Kennedy 2010

The moral right of the author has been asserted.

Addresses for companies within the Random House Group can be found at
www.randomhouse.com.au/offices

National Library of Australia
Cataloguing-in-Publication Entry

Foster, Chrissie.
Hell on the way to heaven/Chrissie Foster and Paul Kennedy.

ISBN 978 1 74275 304 1 (pbk).

Foster family.
Catholic Church – Australia.
Abused children – Australia – Biography.
Child sexual abuse – Religious aspects – Catholic Church.

Other Authors/Contributors: Kennedy, Paul.

362.76092

Cover design by Blue Cork
Internal design and typesetting by Midland Typesetters, Australia
Printed in Australia by Griffin Press, an accredited ISO AS/NZS 14001:2004
Environmental Management System printer

THE

HIERARCHY

OF THE

ROMAN CATHOLIC CHURCH HAVE

ONLY

THEMSELVES

TO BLAME

FOR ME

WRITING

THIS

BOOK.

THEY MADE IT NECESSARY

To my beautiful daughters, Emma, Katie and Aimee
— written in the hope that other parents may see what we did not.
And to Lu, Emma's soul mate.

Contents

'The parish priest from my childhood was being accused of being a pedifoil. I didn't suspect it — I knew he was.'

Emma Foster, age 13

Prologue
Saturday 19 October 1996
Melbourne, Australia

Attending Archbishop George Pell's Melbourne Forum, a response to the Catholic Church's Sex Abuse Crisis

M y voice embarrassed me.

It fell apart whenever I was stressed or nervous. The words formed perfectly in my mind. They were strong invincible words, of forceful sentences, containing the irrefutable truth. But when it came time to speak, they broke and stumbled from my mouth, cracked, high-pitched and shaking. This angered me, although not nearly as much as the other injustices in my life.

In the mid-1990s, when I was starting my unholy battle against the Catholic Church, I recorded a message of anguish, pouring my feelings out into a sound room microphone and recorder, to be played at a historic forum of victims of clergy sexual abuse, before their families, friends and leaders of the Church. I wondered how my croaky voice would sound broadcast to a packed hall, boomed above the quiet tension by public address speakers.

I chose with great care what I wanted to say.

'It used to be that I read the Bible every day . . .'

Would my many years of Christian devotion make the Church representatives take me seriously?

'People are dying . . .'

Would they believe me?

'We have been so deeply betrayed.'

Would my voice humiliate me? Or worse? Would it be so weak that the Church would not hear me at all? I was about to find out.

The church was insisting it was not in crisis. But in the four years between 1992 and 1996, thirty-two Australian paedophile priests and brothers had been arrested, charged and had pleaded guilty, or were found guilty in court, of sexual assaults. Twenty-two of them had been jailed for their criminal assaults. This alone was scandalous. But it was just the beginning. There were so many more to be uncovered and prosecuted. The hierarchy had a reasonable understanding of the potential scale of the problem because it had taken out a multi-million-dollar insurance policy against victims' claims. It must have felt vulnerable. The Church's actions in moving offenders from parish to parish, hiding their crimes, denying paedophilia existed and refusing to be accountable were being heavily scrutinised by the media. The forum we were here to attend would, by any definition, be best described as a crisis meeting – even if the hosts did not use the 'C' word.

We were seated inside the Catholic Church headquarters, east of the city's biggest buildings, a short stroll from one of the most majestic cathedrals in town, which overlooked the state's Parliament House. Anthony, my husband, and my mother sat next to me. Beside and around us were my aunt, uncle and a number of friends from Oakleigh. Soon victims of sexual assault, their families and friends were filling up the rest of the seats, all facing the stage in anticipation. The atmosphere inside was subdued and solemn, as people sat alone in silence or in small groups, speaking quietly to each other. Each person or family had unique experiences and pain, but we all had the same secret hope that justice and understanding were only moments away.

I knew all of us would rather not have been there, would prefer our loved ones were as they should have been, without the suffering. The unholy hand of paedophilia and sexual assault within the Church had touched all three hundred and fifty members of the audience. The man who was hosting the forum, George Pell, the new Archbishop of Melbourne, entered the room. Our eyes followed him and he was accompanied by a foreboding silence as he took his seat on the stage, looking down on us.

We had a full arsenal of questions. Had they finally heard us? Did they now care? Did they believe us? Were they going to open their hearts and minds to victims?

Chapter 1
My religious origins

Way off the western coast of Scotland, past the Inner Hebrides, past the Outer Hebrides, out in the Atlantic Ocean is a dot of an island called St Kilda, flanked by rock pinnacles, styled by the waves of centuries. The lonely archipelago, lashed by violent salt air, must be the windiest and most isolated place on earth that isn't made of ice. These days, low-lying quilt clouds and thousands of majestic seabirds are the cliffs' only friends. But people used to live there. My ancestors.

I come from a long line of Scots on my father's side. They were Presbyterians but this was never mentioned. In our life there were only Catholics or non-Catholics.

St Kilda wasn't named after a saint. Rather, it came from the word 'skildir', meaning shield, which is what the islands resembled to the Vikings on their ships.

The people of St Kilda lived in a simple but fascinating way, through a community of hardship. Sadly, only one in ten babies survived. It was traditional for an old woman to visit all newborn infants with a sheep's stomach-bag full of oil. The old woman would rub the babies' cords with the special brew. It was a crude ritual. The bag and its oil contained tetanus and most newborns died of lockjaw within days. It was so common that the mothers carried tiny coffins with them when they went to give birth.

My family name on that side was MacQueen. I used to try to identify relatives in old photos, until I realised they were *all* relatives, not just those bearing the name MacQueen. The island men had red hair and all the women had black hair, just like mine.

In 1852, thirty-six of the one hundred and ten islanders sailed for Melbourne, Australia, accepting an offer from the Highlands and Islands Emigration Society. It was a disaster in more ways than one. The eight families who braved the voyage were the strongest and best the island had to offer. They were the vanguard. Others waved them goodbye and hoped to join them some day. But their departure tore apart and demoralised the close-knit community.

Sometimes even the bravest are no match for disease. More than half of my people, parents and children, died on the ship. The survivors were held at a quarantine station near the southern tip of Port Phillip Bay, before being transported to Brighton, south of Melbourne, a short distance from another settlement called St Kilda. No more of the Scottish islanders followed. I am a descendant of John MacQueen, who arrived in Australia as a thirteen-year-old boy, and I live just a few kilometres from where he settled. One hundred and two years after they stepped off the ship I was born at Brighton Hospital, overlooking the pioneer cemetery where John MacQueen's father Finlay was buried.

I've always wanted to believe that resilient young John and his islander forebears passed some of their characteristics on to me.

My mother's side are Irish Catholic, probably as far back as St Patrick. The first of these ancestors to step foot on Australian soil was Mary Lee, a seventeen-year-old, who sailed to Melbourne aboard a ship carrying female orphans, arriving on 26 May 1849. She and two hundred other teenage girls were sent with prearranged work assignments, but mainly to fill a shortage of women in the soon-to-be-gold-booming colony.

A government official ordered Mary to work as a house-maid west of Melbourne for ten pounds a year, with freedom to be her severance pay. In January 1851 she married James Knight at St Francis Catholic Church, in Melbourne, while it was still part of New South Wales. St Francis' foundation stone was laid just ten years earlier. The church, like most of the town, was young and impressive.

After much research I discovered Mary Lee, my great, great, great-grandmother, was laid to rest in an unmarked grave in the dry-baked red clay of a gold-mining town called Clunes. I wondered if she ever longed for the cool and green of her birthplace, Limerick. When she died, aged forty-seven, the remarkable Mary Lee had outlived two husbands and five of her eleven children.

These two histories came together when my parents met.

I was the third generation of Catholic women to marry a non-Catholic man. When my grandmother was a bride-to-be, her future husband was made to convert so they could wed. My father didn't have to cross himself but my parents could not wed before an altar. Almost ashamedly, they had to take their marriage vows in the sacristy, a small side room in the church, where the priest and altar boys dress and prepare for mass, away from friends and family, the altar and crucifix. Someone ordained that God did not want to see my mum and dad's happy union, just like someone ordained that my mother, as a young adult, could not attend her non-Catholic friends' weddings. She was not allowed to step foot in the 'other' churches. Such was the control of the Catholic Church over its faithful.

When I married in 1980, at St Patrick's Church in the bayside suburb of Mentone, my vows were taken in front of the altar with friends and family. Anthony did not have to convert. He remained an atheist.

All of the children born of these marriages were promised, through signing of agreements by the non-Catholic spouses, to be brought up as Catholics. Generation after generation, we had to be Catholic. There was no choice in the matter . . . unless you wanted to go to hell, or worse, condemn your children to hell. This is what we were taught. Such is the power of the Catholic Church.

I was about eight or nine years old when I first raised an eyebrow to Catholic rules. It was during Vatican II, a controversial period in the 1960s when some members of the hierarchy agreed to relax a number of rigid rules. Mysteriously and suddenly, selected sins were not sinful – women no longer had to wear veils in church, you no longer had to fast for eight hours before communion, it was okay to eat meat on Fridays (except the Fridays in Lent and Good Friday), and Saturday night mass became an acceptable replacement for the Sunday ritual. This last rule change was too much for me. How could we one day go to hell for doing something wrong and then the next day it would be okay? A nun had taught us in grade 2 that we could go to mass six days a week, but if we missed Sunday mass and died before we could confess this sin to a priest, then we would go to hell – a hard and fast rule. There was no getting out of mass on Sundays.

Now all of a sudden we could go on Saturday instead. Who said? Did God say we would go to hell for missing Sunday mass or not? If He didn't, then how could men condemn us to hell when it didn't bother God in the first place? I applied this argument to all the changes arising from Vatican II. When it comes to splitting hairs, children are pretty capable and I reasoned that if God made the rules we lived by, then mere men shouldn't be able to change them just like that. I took being thrown into hell for all eternity pretty seriously, so I really wanted to know how men could decide who goes to hell . . . men were not God. But I kept my doubts to myself.

I could sense it was inappropriate to argue the point with the adult world.

The portable moral fences set up around us weren't the only things worrying me about my religion. From the beginning, confession was a frightening experience. We had to unfurl our sins every week, even if we had not sinned. I was terrified most of the time because I hadn't done anything wrong and I had to make something up. My regular fake confession was: 'I have disobeyed my mother and told lies.' That was the real lie, because I hadn't disobeyed my mother. I loved my mother and wanted to do the right thing by her.

One day in a weak moment, I pinched sixpence from Mum and felt relieved because that was a sin. I actually had something to confess and I was relaxed about not telling lies to the priest.

'Oh my God I am very sorry that I have sinned against you because you are so good and with your help I will not sin again.'

. . . I will not sin again? Oops, another lie?

Our priest was the other reason for fear and distress at the dreaded confession time. The nun told us that the man listening to our misdemeanours was not interested in seeing us or knowing who was confessing their sins. Confession was meant to be anonymous, yet every time I spoke inside the box it was through a small sliding panel with my face at the opening. The Father, on the other side of the partition, would bend down and look right at my face for the purpose of identifying me. I assumed he did the same to every child who entered the confessional. I hated this but could do nothing about it. He was curious, I suppose, about who was doing what inside his parish. I, however, took it as an affront, knowing he should not be invading my privacy. According to the nun, this was not supposed to happen.

Once, I was so determined to avoid his unethical detection that I leaned my body away from the window so he could not see my face through the metal grating. Much to my alarm, this did not stop Father. He bent further and further down, trying to see who was there. I contorted my body and managed to keep away from the peephole, despite the cramped space. The priest, from what I could tell, was doubled over and must have strained his neck trying to catch a glimpse of the sinful child whispering to him. By this stage my face was flat against the wall and I was almost standing, still trying to avoid his gaze. Each time I saw the corner of his face I moved further away. His head was almost at his knees in order to look up. My heart was pounding with fear, knowing that if I was identified after all of this I would be in trouble.

He wasn't listening and made straining noises. I sensed his frustration. He was still muttering: 'For your penance . . . um . . . three Hail Marys . . . an act of contrition . . .'

'Oh my God I'm sorry that . . .'

The confession over, I stood completely upright and, with my face still against the wall, I slid past the window so that he could see only my torso. I snuck out to the pews that day with a cat burglar's stealth, hiding in the crowd of my schoolmates. If curious Father came out he would have seen only a sea of faces. It felt like a victory because just that one time I made him perform it correctly – the confession happened as it should have, without him identifying me.

When I was about twelve years old my agnostic father asked me, although I don't know why: 'Are you glad you're Catholic?'

'No,' I shot back with a force that surprised me. 'Everything I say and do is a sin.' That is how it felt living under the Catholic regime at school and at home.

When I was fifteen I took a summer job as a government clerk. A friend, who also took the school holiday job, encouraged me to stick with it after school resumed. I wanted to return to school but didn't want to lose my friend so I ended up staying at work. My academic education was over after grade nine, something I have regretted ever since. At the time, however, I liked the work very much and continued to be employed as a public servant in two different departments for a total of nine years, with a two-year gap, during which time I travelled overseas.

My first job was with the Department of Agriculture, housed in a grand old white Victorian building situated atop a green embankment looking down over Melbourne's Treasury Gardens. For the first year I worked in the Information Branch, posting out literature to farmers and helping print booklets for the department to distribute. The following year I brushed up on my typing skills, and to my delight was given a typist position in the Department of Agriculture's library. I helped make catalogue cards for the librarian and was further immersed in the earthy sciences of animal husbandry, high-protein milk biscuits (which would feed a hungry world), chicken sexing, horticulture, beekeeping and fruit growing. After a couple of years I began a library technician course at a technical college, winning a departmental scholarship which paid for my education. I completed two years of the three-year course at the age of twenty and then decided to travel.

I spent nine months in Europe and then arrived in London, where I lived and worked for a year. My work there in 1977 was in a typing pool that had progressed from using electric typewriters to a new technology called 'computer word processing'. It was cutting-edge stuff, only the second such system in England. The company that employed me created and installed these computer systems for businesses and we provided them with specific operating manuals. The word processing centre I worked at had about eight typists and only two of them were English. The rest of us were from around the world.

One of my colleagues was Pinky, an Indian girl a little younger than my twenty years. The day after I had met her, as we were leaving the office, she asked me where I was heading. I said the underground train station. She was going my way so we began our walk together. Suddenly she put her arm through mine, which I found alarming. I wasn't sure what to do. The last time I walked like this or held hands with another female was in primary school. I felt eyes would be upon me and people might think us a gay couple. But as we strolled I saw other women doing the same thing. It was the English way. I grew to love our arm-in-arm walks to the station and when cold winter months arrived I felt I was protecting my skinny and small friend Pinky as she snuggled closer and we talked and laughed.

I commuted each day to the heart of London by train. The trains were different to the ones I knew back home. Each carriage was divided into compartments, with a row of seating on either side of a centre aisle and a door at each end. Most days the seats were full of men reading tabloid newspapers.

One morning, on the way to work, I stretched the budget and bought myself a paper. A big story had everyone's attention. The British Government had inadvertently given a grant of a thousand pounds to a paedophile organisation. Public outrage was coming from many quarters. The seventy-something-year-old group spokesman (with a thirteen-year-old 'girlfriend') was happy with both the attention and the money. The debate raged in the papers and on television for days.

'Bloody paedophiles,' a commuter swore, his nose in his paper as he read.

Other passengers nodded to themselves and each other. Some muttered in agreement. I looked at the crowd from my corner seat. We were all strangers but for that rare moment, united by opinion.

It was the first time I had seen or heard the word 'paedophile'. (Even as late as 1981 the *Macquarie Dictionary* did not contain this word. It appeared for the first time in the second edition of 1991.) Up until then I had only ever heard the warnings of the 'man in the bushes', the 'bad man', or the 'man who would take me away'. Later these titles all fell under the banner of 'stranger danger'. But here was something new, unheard of, an organisation of paedophiles was basically doing the same thing as the man in the bushes. But they were flaunting their behaviour and their victims were not running away. After that scandal died down I heard nothing more and my knowledge of paedophiles remained as it was.

I left the job I loved in England to travel through North America and Mexico for three months before returning home. I had been away for two years. The public sector welcomed me back and I was offered positions at the Parliamentary Library and a police department called D24. I saw the job at police headquarters in Melbourne as an exciting opportunity that I could not refuse. I stayed there for two years, until the 5 am wake-up times wore down my enthusiasm. I was transferred to a crime car squad, stationed just a kilometre from my parents' house. While in this job I met Anthony.

I had been going out with another man, a flight instructor. Anthony was his acquaintance and a recently qualified commercial pilot. I dropped in one night to see my boyfriend and Anthony was at his house. The man I had come to see was not home – the man with whom I'd share my life was standing behind the fly-wire screen.

'He's not here,' the tall, slim stranger said. 'But you're welcome to come in.'

'No. I couldn't,' I replied.

'You could, it's alright,' Anthony insisted. 'If you want to.'

He was very polite. I knew he liked me and I immediately liked him. But I felt it would be wrong to go inside the house.

So I left, not knowing any more about the mysterious man with the warm smile.

Anthony and I next met months later at a leap year party – 29 February 1980. I was single again by then. Hardly anyone else turned up and we talked all night. At one point the penny dropped for Anthony.

'Oh, you're the girl I met at the front door that night,' he laughed.

'Yes. That was you I spoke to?'

We both laughed at having chatted for so long without realising we had already met.

Before this special time, Anthony and I had both been unlucky in love and independently developed strong ideas about the type of people we wanted to spend time with. On our first date the following week we talked about marriage and kids. (Talk about leaping ahead!) But I was relieved when those subjects came up because I was sick of being polite and holding back in relationships, only to find out later I was wasting my time. I put all my cards on the table. Luckily, we wanted the same things. There was a great outpouring of feelings and I was delighted that Anthony was so friendly. The more I listened to him, the more I was drawn to him. He was clever (I was to find out there was almost nothing he couldn't make or mend), kind and patient. He didn't smoke, drink much, gamble or read *Playboy* – all ticks in the 'yes column'. And he was handsome. It was as if I had only ever gone out with boys. Now I had met a man and this man was everything I wanted.

Six weeks later we went to the country for a picnic, choosing a spot at the top of a mountain range. The scenery was wonderful, the breeze gentle and we were in love, as comfortable a feeling as I had known. We were so happy, so grateful to have found each other.

Anthony did not bend down on one knee when he said simply: 'Will you marry me?'

Our life together was just beginning and we could both see the bright future that lay ahead. We dived headlong into it.

I recall a moment of euphoria at our wedding reception, held at Anthony's parents' house. What stood out was the bliss with which the wedding party ate dinner in a small room removed from the other guests. We chatted and laughed the way young people do when they have reached a point in their lives that boasts freedom without the burden of responsibility. Champagne had never tasted so sweet. I look at those old wedding photos now of cheeky Anthony, in his red bow tie, with a red rose on his jacket, and me, in my magnolia fitted dress (passed on from my mother), with a waxed orange blossom tiara holding the long veil, and I feel the warmth of memories that will never leave me.

We had met and married in less than five months. It wasn't long after that I fell pregnant. The crime-squad lifestyle was a bit rough-and-tumble for my condition so I was again transferred, this time to another section where I accepted police clearance requests and took applicants' fingerprints in the old ink-and-press way. My work life was winding down, even though I was still young. I had much busier days ahead as a parent.

On 6 November 1981 Emma arrived.

It was a quick labour. I woke up one night after being asleep for only half an hour, sensing what was going on but without certainty. It was happening ten days early.

'We should ring the hospital,' Anthony suggested, but I was already picking up the phone.

The nurse who took my call and listened to my symptoms wasn't sure whether I was in labour yet, so I went back to bed. Then my waters broke properly and I no longer doubted myself. We went straight into hospital. We had been to classes and learned about the delivery, the procedures and stages, so I felt I knew what to expect.

'This part takes a couple of hours,' the nurse had told us. 'And then the next phase takes another couple of hours.'

But my body seemed to be skipping phases. The pain escalated quickly and I grimaced and struggled.

A nurse's voice rose and said something I will never forget: 'C'mon, darling, don't waste your pain!'

It made perfect sense to me. Emma was born at 2.22 am. Two was my lucky number and Emma's birth time struck me as a good sign. The doctor did not smack her bottom as I had seen on television. I was elated when he didn't. To me, it was such a cruel thing for a baby to enter the world with an act of violence – I didn't want that to happen to my peaceful and beautiful little girl.

When he handed her to me, the first things I looked at, after seeing she was healthy, were her ears. I don't like my ears and was so hoping my children would be born with Anthony's ears. Little Emma's were perfect.

Like all new parents, we felt very proud and honoured. We were in awe of her. She opened her eyes and looked around the room; an adventurous little girl from the beginning.

I remember when Emma was only a few weeks old, holding her in my arms and looking at this most precious, delicate person, understanding her utter dependence on someone to look after her for everything – food, warmth, shelter, protection. I thought of her vulnerability and imagined that anybody could just pick her up and take her away, even harm her, and she could do nothing to stop it.

'No-one will hurt my child,' I silently declared.

This loving force I felt, this purity in the defence of total innocence, was humbling. It would be an honour to carry out this job I was blessed with. I believe this degree of integrity exists in every mother and father in relation to their children, and every child, without exception, is worthy of this degree of protection. I would protect my children to the end.

Twenty months later our second daughter Katie was born. I had Emma's quick birth in mind throughout my second pregnancy and wanted to be prepared for another speedy delivery. I visited my doctor nearing the end of nine months. I still had a week to go but felt a larger than normal Braxton Hicks contraction (which is a false contraction that occurs before the onset of labour); they had been happening for months now, just as with Emma. I was not sure if that one contraction was signalling I was ready to go into labour or not.

As the doctor checked me he suddenly became very serious.

'I want you to go straight to the hospital,' he ordered with an urgency that should have alarmed me. 'I'll meet you over there.'

Luckily the hospital was next door. Anthony drove us the short distance and I waddled into the maternity ward, feeling the contractions increasing in intensity.

'I think something's happening,' I muttered.

'Where's the doctor?' asked my helpful husband.

A nurse replied, with the hint of a mischievous smirk: 'He was last seen sprinting from his surgery across the front lawn. He's here somewhere. Looked to be in a hurry.'

A few minutes later he arrived – and so did Katie. It had been thirty-six minutes since I had seen him in the surgery. He later said his serious demeanour was because he knew Katie was about to be born and one false move from him would have caused her birth in the clinic.

Again we experienced great joy at the safe arrival of another healthy little girl (with perfect ears).

A couple of months before Katie's birth we took over Anthony's parents' business, which we managed from home. The company supplied, installed and serviced hydronic central heating systems that Anthony, and previously his dad, Ken, designed. Working as a family from the house meant that I could look after our babies without placing them into care.

In March 1985, twenty months later, our third daughter was born.

This time Anthony had been instructed on a home birth, my doctor believing that I wouldn't even make it to hospital. It was stressful monitoring every twinge, trying to identify an unusual pain as the first signs of labour. I wanted to be as prepared as I could because I had images of walking up the street and suddenly giving birth.

A week before the expected birth I had a very minor symptom, different from the previous pregnancies and so, taking no chances, off to hospital we went. I was admitted. Once there I felt we had overreacted. Nothing was happening. The plan was to stay a while and if it wasn't labour I would go home again. I rang my mother from my bed and gave her an update.

'I think it's a false alarm,' I explained. 'We'll wait a little while longer and if we're convinced it's not happening we'll go home . . .'

As I was speaking my abdomen felt as if it was turning to concrete. Then the feeling abated.

I kept chatting, wondering at the sensation I had just experienced.

Still talking, I looked at my watch as again I felt the concrete belly. The next time it happened I glanced back at the time and what had seemed like a five- or ten-minute interval between contractions was actually one or two. Understanding the significance I said, 'Mum, I have to go now.'

'Okay, love,' she said, not suspecting anything. 'Let me know what you decide.'

'Okay, Mum. Bye.'

After hanging up, I started to get out of the bed. 'You'd better get a nurse,' I suggested and my husband dashed off along the corridor, searching for help.

Sixteen minutes later I was holding our newest little girl in my arms. Yet again we shared great delight at the safe birth of another healthy child, again with Anthony's ears – three out of three!

A couple of days later I walked past the nurses' tea room and overheard one nurse telling the others an anecdote: 'The other day there was this woman who hugged her husband and the baby just fell out. It was quite a hug.' They all laughed and made comments. I realised that she was talking about us. I was pleased we had left such an impression on the ward staff. My little girl was already a legend.

We had assumed that after having two daughters we would have a son (I even had a dream it was a boy) so we hadn't chosen a girl's name. After five days of searching I saw a French name and knew that this beautiful word was the one.

Emma and Katie were introduced to their sister Aimee.

We lived in a big old house in Oakleigh, in a street lined with large, leafy oak trees. It was a quiet place and you wouldn't think it was within fifteen kilometres of the city. Without the pressing needs of crying babies it would have been a serene home, but I had given birth to three babies in forty months and being a mother of three girls – two toddlers and an infant – wasn't easy. We had happy hours and moments of distress, sunshine and rain, like all families. Emma was a handful, always busily exploring things she shouldn't.

A few days after Aimee's birth I felt anaesthetised, even though I hadn't been. I felt nothing but flatness. It was the onset of postnatal depression, a dark period that would prove to be intense and long lasting. Life was so busy. It was non-stop. Many nights I couldn't sleep, dog tired and exhausted both physically and mentally, but unable to even nap. My thoughts became exaggerated and distorted and I grew over-sensitive. Fears were magnified way out of proportion. I thought about death and its inevitability as though the concept of dying was new to me. Its intensity was both frightening and confusing. Events that I had no control over presented themselves to me as unbeatable battles, making them all the more alarming.

On one such occasion I felt ice-cold fear of the possibility of a stranger taking away one of my little girls. I struggled with these paralysing thoughts and scenarios.

I kept thinking to myself: I have only two hands but three children. I don't have enough hands to hold them safely.

The growing fear of someone harming my children invaded my mind. It was another impossible-to-beat dilemma, another mental and emotional fight I could not win. I could not be with them all day, every day. At some stage they would have to go to kindergarten and then school. The inevitability of them being away from my protection was distressing. So I prayed with passion and my whole heart that while I was not with them, God would protect them. And I felt a peace come over me.

But the weight of the depression remained.

I attended mass every weekend at our parish church, Sacred Heart, a short distance from home. The church was tall, commanding and presided over by Father Kevin O'Donnell. He was the man I sought help from during one state of distress. Anthony had had a vasectomy, which was against Church rules, and my exaggerated thoughts were damning me.

Seeking absolution, I went to the presbytery, a brick house without distinction. Father O'Donnell was on his way out of the front door when I arrived.

It was my first interaction with the person who would rape my children.

I politely asked for a moment of his time.

'Father, I wonder if I could ask you for some advice?'

He did not even look sideways at me before he raised his hand in protest and waved me away, like he would a pest, a nuisance dog. But I did not disappear.

'Oh, what is it?' he snorted quietly, as if to himself.

'I am depressed and can't sleep . . .' I was feeling sinful, I added, mentioning the vasectomy.

'I can't talk about that,' he said, before glaring at me, expecting me to leave.

Shooing me away again, he told me: 'Go home and get some sleep.'

'I can't sleep.'

I am a respectful woman and softly spoken but I do not like being treated unfairly. By not stopping, he had walked us all the way to the footpath. He looked as if he thought that I might depart, as he wanted me to. However, to protest against his rude dismissals, I sat on the front fence and folded my arms in defiance, refusing to leave without a better response from a leader of our community. My eyes stared straight into his – I would not be shoved aside.

'Oh, alright,' he buckled. 'I'll send a nun around.' He marched back into the presbytery.

A cross-looking nun knocked on my door some time later. In icy tones, she gave me the 'pardon' I was seeking. I gladly took the message and pardoned the messenger's seemingly resentful attitude.

It was almost nine months after Aimee's birth when I started to recover from my depression. I had been to my doctor on this particular day, desperately lost, only to come away feeling no better. Nothing helped. I had taken useless medication for one month before throwing it away. I had driven home and pulled up in the lane beside our house. As I walked to the gate, I was still wondering tortuously what I was going to do. Who could help me? I felt so lost and weakened. It was as though the weight of the world had been on my shoulders for months; my combined stress and fears had turned into panic attacks, a terror within themselves. If you have suffered a panic attack, you know the desperate desire to never suffer it again and avoid the terror at all costs. And so it feeds itself.

The cure in the end is to stop running from it, turn around and face the fear.

That cure was two years away but my depression rescuer – my determined self – appeared to me at the moment I unlocked the gate. I had no sooner finished my desperate thoughts than out of the blue a strength rose from within me. I said to myself: 'I will get better. I'll do it myself.'

It was so sudden. It just emerged and made me feel happy, a feeling that had been lost to me for months. From then on, when life was dark, I thought back to that positive moment and held it, knowing that one day feeling happy would not be just a memory. The clarity in the laneway was a turning point. Previously, it was as though I had lost myself and had relied upon other people to help me. But they couldn't. Now I would do it for myself. I was back in charge of my life and I wasn't going to give that power away or lose it again.

Life stayed hectic as the girls developed, every moment – a roll, some crawling, a couple of steps, milk, soft food, solids, laughing, one word, two words, sentences, questions, answering back – was a big event laced with pride. It was as if the girls' achievements also belonged to Anthony and me. Christmases were particularly fun. The promise of Santa brought stockings and presents and possibilities that made eyes widen with delight. Our daughters enjoyed the attentions of four loving and doting grandparents and several aunts, uncles and cousins, all of whom we saw regularly on weekends, birthdays or other times of celebration.

Catholicism remained a part of our lives. After church on Sunday, I would chat with other parents from the parish. Sometimes we would talk for a long time while the children played in the neat church gardens or the neighbouring school-yard.

Back when Emma turned one in 1982, we joined a play-group held in a church-owned vacant 1930s house dubbed 'the cottage'. It stood directly opposite the Sacred Heart Presbytery. Beside the cottage was a lawn and garden that stretched across to the church itself. Behind and to the side of the church was Sacred Heart Primary School. The Catholic Church owned the whole doglegged block. It was a little realm in the middle of suburbia and Father O'Donnell was its wandering king. Then sixty-five years old, the Father lived with an assistant priest, who helped him in the parish and who had baptised Emma.

No-one lived in the cottage but it was furnished with a mishmash of old stuff, including a large billiards table, which took up most of the lounge room floor space. This left the playgroup confined to the kitchen area and the cramped remains of the lounge room. Not an ideal meeting place. I was at the playgroup in the cottage one day when our group's organiser said: 'Come and look at this.'

She led several mothers to a nearby room.

'Check this out,' she said.

She pushed the door open and I immediately noticed how dark the room was, with very little natural light coming through an unusually high and small window.

Our tour guide fumbled for a light switch.

The dim light bulb barely illuminated the floor and the darkness seemed menacing. We crept forward, now curious about the room's purpose. Venturing in a little we could see the window had been boarded over from the inside. Squinting harder I could see what looked like fence palings nailed into the timber window frame. The only piece of furniture I remember seeing was a narrow single bed, unmade and covered with dirty crumpled bed linen that looked as though it hadn't been washed for years – used but not washed. It was all very odd. We stood there absorbing the peculiar scene.

The room needed an explanation but there wasn't one forthcoming. I thought there must be some simple reason for the boarded-up window, perhaps the glass being broken, so I went outside with another mum and had a look. Standing underneath and craning my neck up at the window, I searched for a fault but the glass and frame were completely intact. I strained my eyes to examine the panes as well as I could. They were old. The nailed-up boards were barely noticeable from the outside.

'That window has never been broken,' I said to the other mum.

'It's so strange,' she replied and I was glad I wasn't the only one thinking that.

We looked at each other and shrugged. It made no sense; why was the window boarded up on the inside? Why was it boarded up at all? The dark room needed a more powerful light bulb, not the dim one it had. Why was the bed so dirty?

Our time at the cottage was short-lived. Not long after I joined the playgroup it moved to a local Uniting Church hall, better equipped and with space for our children to play.

I believe both Anthony and I looked after our children well. We worked very hard to keep our daughters safe. We never left them at home alone, and made sure we had the safest pram, pusher, highchair, bassinette, cot, bed, car capsule, car seat or high-rider seat. We bought the right foods, soaps, toys, shampoo and toothbrushes. Car seatbelts were worn rain, hail or shine; they were never alone in the bath, pool or at the beach. After use, a knot was tied in every plastic bag that entered the house. Medicines, cleaning fluids and knives were all kept out of reach. And only the back burners of the stove were used, to avoid a little one pulling a boiling pot over the edge.

Everything I could think of I made safe. I was their guardian, the protector of their innocence, helplessness and vulnerability. I was their mum, nurse, counsellor, educator, referee, book and nursery rhyme reader, cleaner, cook and driver. I didn't allow them to play in the street because of the worry of strangers. I always crossed roads with them at the pedestrian lights or zebra crossings so that they would learn not to be reckless when I wasn't around. I warned them against being tricked by the words of a stranger hoping to lure them away. I was forever on alert to any sort of danger. It was my job to look after them and that is what I did – happily.

Not surprisingly, I also took them to mass with me.

In 1988 I took three-and-a-half-year-old Aimee to a Saturday night mass. At communion, we, the churchgoers, stood in two long rows to receive the communion bread from Father O'Donnell. He held the bread host up and said: 'Body of Christ.'

We held up our hands and responded.

'Amen.'

The priest placed the bread in my hand, I stepped a few paces to one side, paused in front of the altar area and put the bread in my mouth. As I was finishing I heard Father O'Donnell's guttural objection, his voice rising.

Looking back to see what he was angry about, I saw Aimee at the head of the communion queue. I had let go of her hand to receive the bread and assumed that she had followed me to the side, as she always did. But there she was, my beautiful toddler, with her hands up like all the other people waiting for the bread.

'Who does *this* belong to?' Father demanded to know, reducing my child to an object. 'Children aren't . . . Off you go . . .' he said, shooing her away. 'Where . . .' he muttered and grumbled, only part of his rant reaching my ears.

Father O'Donnell was looking down the row of people, demanding an explanation and for someone to remove Aimee, gesticulating his annoyance with one hand, while holding the chalice full of communion bread with the other. Initially I felt embarrassed and guilty that I had done the wrong thing, causing this disruption. But as he carried on with his tirade I began to feel angry at him for his overreaction. When he saw me coming for Aimee he toned down his annoyance, attempted to smile and murmured something about it being hard to tell if she was old enough to receive communion or not. Obviously he already knew she wasn't, hence all the fuss and his refusal to give her the bread. Children make their first communion when they are seven or eight years old. He of all people knew that.

Ignoring him and making no apology, I took Aimee by the hand as we walked back to our seat. I was not impressed at all by this rude and impatient man.

I now wonder if this incident was what saved Aimee from his sexual assaults. On that evening, despite Father O'Donnell's ire, Aimee did not flinch. She did not back down from what she wanted. His intimidation had no effect. When I saw her she was still looking expectantly at him with her little hands up, waiting for the bread; no amount of his public bullying had dissuaded her. Instead, she was waiting patiently, unmoved. Did he recognise in her a strength of character, a dogged determination, which he would not easily dominate? Did he identify an individual persistence, which would not readily bow down to his whim or be silent about his sexual assaults?

The single most important thing to a paedophile, after the sexual pleasure derived from raping or molesting a child, is the silence they enforce upon their victim, for without this silence the criminal game is over. Prison, disrepute, hostilities and, worst of all, the cessation of their sex with children awaits the paedophile unable to maintain silence and secrecy.

Bullies and child molesters hunt for a victim, not a problem; they pursue someone they can easily manipulate into compliance. The more effectively the victim is intimidated or frightened, the better the control. Perhaps Father O'Donnell saw Aimee as a problem not a victim.

My other daughters he saw differently.

Chapter 2
When alarm bells should toll

Taking your children to school for the first time is confronting. You wander up, nervous but trying to appear calm. You queue for a name-tag, holding hands, wondering if the sweaty palm is yours or theirs. You worry about their reaction to being left in the care of strangers. But you tell yourself not to fret. You've taught them manners and values. Most importantly, you've loved them and made sure they're happy.

They are as prepared as they can be.

'You'll love it, darling,' I told Emma. 'You'll learn to read and write and you'll make friends.'

None of my girls kicked up a fuss. They were all brave. I was the most likely to cry. Just the thought of any pain or distress for my children was heartbreaking. When I took them for immunisation as infants, out came the needle and out poured the tears – mine. The look on my daughters' crumpled little faces, anticipating and then feeling the pain of an injection, was too much for me. I cried, despite trying to hide my adult tears.

Emma wasn't the least bit concerned about starting her education. When we bought her uniform from the local shopping centre we talked about what she could expect. I loved those mother and daughter discussions. She was quiet and thoughtful, her confidence reassuring.

At first, Anthony and I didn't agree on the best school for Emma. My husband thought the girls should be educated in the public system, without religious interference. 'These will be their formative years,' he pointed out, feeling the Catholic system would be too heavy a burden for children to bear. 'They can then choose which high school they want to go to when they're older,' he said. He didn't share my devotion to prayer or my fears of disobeying the rules of the Church.

It would have been easier practically to do it Anthony's way. The local state primary school was a brief stroll from our house. I could have walked with Emma and Katie and pushed Aimee in the pram. It was less than two blocks away. Sacred Heart Primary School on the other hand, which was my preference, was a drive to the other side of the shopping centre and train station. But it was a daily trip I urged we should take, despite the difficulties of travelling with three children under six. It was a matter of securing, through a down payment of faith, life after death.

One of the responsibilities of being a Catholic is to raise your children as Catholics. And one of the easiest ways to achieve this is to send them to a Catholic primary school, with the hope of them being guided and shaped by an environment of faith, giving them a better chance of going to heaven. It is not said to you so plainly but that is what it boils down to. It's pretty simple. Don't go to mass on Sundays – go to hell. Don't send your child to Catholic school – face the consequences. These rules swayed those of us who stuck with the Catholic faith. We were safe while we stayed on the Church's neat and narrow path; did as we were told. I was the product of many, many generations of doing exactly this. I did not want to be responsible for their lack of faith so Anthony and I compromised; the girls would go to Catholic primary school and a state secondary college. Years later, however, I still hadn't overcome my fears of disobeying Church expectations and Emma, Katie and Aimee were all enrolled at Sacred Heart Secondary Girls College.

How I wish with all my heart they had gone through the state system.

From the beginning, Emma was driven to school every day. My Catholic neighbour and I took turns dropping our kids off and picking them up.

When I dropped Emma off the first couple of times, I sensed a healthy environment, or a controlled one at least. Father O'Donnell had been the parish boss for eleven years and although he was nearly seventy years old by this stage, he maintained order. In charge of all the church and school properties and school employees (he could single-handedly hire and fire teachers, even principals), his power was never questioned. As one teacher later said: 'What Father O'Donnell wanted, Father O'Donnell got.' He was also the school's chaplain, in charge of the children's wellbeing, so it wasn't unusual to see him roaming around the school or playgrounds.

His personality was unpredictable but his record, as far as the archdiocese and his colleagues were concerned, was grand. Father O'Donnell was ordained in 1942. He had been presiding over churches within the State of Victoria for decades. For many reasons, he seemed to be a man of influence within the Catholic hierarchy and was certainly revered by his congregation and employees. In our little school and parish, he was the closest thing to God – a notion instilled in us since childhood by Church authorities. This distortion caused a blindness in which we could not see Father O'Donnell as an ordinary man. We suffered a multilayered and multifaceted dulling of both eyes and mind. Maybe, too, the cause was the infallibility that the popes bestowed upon themselves. Then, by association, it was passed down through cardinals and bishops to our very own parish priests. Or maybe it was the copyright they seemed to possess on God and heaven, born of rules they wrote. According to these rules, who was the only person entitled to say mass? The priest. Then if we did commit the grave mortal sin of missing mass, who was the only person who could forgive us this and other sins? The priest. So the only way we could get to heaven, according to them, was through them – the priests.

They have placed themselves between God and us. As somebody once said: 'He who holds the keys to the kingdom of heaven, rules the world.'

So, with all of this ingrained in our minds from childhood, we didn't complain or think suspiciously about any of the things our priest did within the boundaries of the presbytery, cottage, school and church. As I prepare to write about them now, hindsight is taunting me. Old memories, oddities, questions marks, little mysteries that lay dormant in my mind for years have been transformed into comprehension and understanding. It is a pain that will never cease.

As a newcomer to Sacred Heart Primary School, it was obvious to me that Father O'Donnell preferred boys. He favoured and doted on many of them – they were known generally as 'O'Donnell's boys', 'O'Donnell's favourites', 'the anointed ones' or 'O'Donnell's golden-haired boys'. The priest sauntered into the school and took mainly boys out of class to do his jobs or altar service. They would go off with him and return sometimes hours later. There were pupils that became guests at his holiday house on weekends. Clear-minded friends of ours repeatedly said 'no' to the invitation issued by Father for their very young son to visit his retreat although they were pressured for years.

Father O'Donnell was an eager and insistent host.

We all knew he had a generous side because the priest had a seemingly endless supply of gifts for the children. He particularly liked giving away cans of Coca-Cola. He had a little fridge in the back of the church, near the meeting rooms, for this very purpose. One day a senior church parishioner complained to me about the priest's Coke supply, bemoaning the leaking fridge, which had stained the carpet brown. The man was a parish council member but even in his position he felt powerless to say or do anything about it.

I never saw Father O'Donnell drink a can of Coke. Instead, he gave them to his favourite boys. I once saw him with a crowd of children, his arms full of soft drinks. He handed the cans out to all the boys then reluctantly gave the last one to a girl, disappointing one of her late-arriving male classmates. The girl beamed surprise, as she knew from experience it was only the boys who received the drinks. She wasn't even trying to get one. The lad who missed out was unhappy and pouted a bit. The Father saw his disappointment and without hesitation snatched back the can and gave it to the boy, along with a smile. The girl was given no apology, just an impatient grunt and a shooing away by the priest's dismissive hand.

I saw Father O'Donnell another day outside the school-yard gates while I was waiting for my daughters to finish their classes. The priest was just standing around but, as the exiting children began to pass him, he reached into his pocket and pulled out a fistful of coins. He threw them into the air and they fanned out around him, making a great noise as the coins rained down, bouncing and rolling all over the place. Frenzied celebration followed the clinking on bitumen and the children went wild in search of the runaway coins. Some bent down; others crawled on their hands and knees trying to pick them up. Father O'Donnell was pleased with the reaction and took another handful of money from his pocket and repeated his game, this time lobbing them not so far afield. Some bounced off his shiny black shoes. The priest had the giggles watching the children crawl around his feet, grabbing, bumping into each other and him. It was a strange sight to see and a strange thing for someone to do. But Father O'Donnell appeared almost giddy with pleasure. I later learned this trick was repeated at a school excursion in a public park, much to the dismay of the teacher witnessing the children crawling in the dirt. Again, no complaint was levelled against the 'holy' man in charge. Another of his practices disturbed me more. Almost every weekday morning, two selected and unsupervised children would walk from their primary school classroom to the presbytery to receive money from Father O'Donnell, head across a quiet street, through the picturesque church garden to a main road (one of the city's busiest thoroughfares), push the pedestrian crossing button and wait for the beeps and the green walk light. The pair would then hustle across the arterial road and along the footpath on the other side to a corner, traverse another busy street and enter a shop where they bought the old man his daily milk.

When I learned of this ritual I was horrified. I was fearful Emma, who was in prep, might one day be called upon to do the milk run. I was petrified a car would hit her. Also, in my mind, there was a possibility that someone at the store or in its car park could just take a child. There were so many things that could go wrong on such a journey.

I wanted to say something about it or make a complaint. But did I march into the primary school office and demand an end to the dangerous errand? No. I just hoped and prayed, as a lot of parents did, that my daughter would not be selected.

It wasn't until a couple of years later that I heard from one of the other mums that Emma *had* done the milk run. I pictured my little girl scurrying across the main road in her uniform, determined to complete her job in good time. I felt stressed and wanted to complain. But did I then go to the office and demand that she be banned from doing it again? No. I just hoped and prayed the priest didn't choose her a second time. Such was the power held over us by the system of the Catholic Church. We were never encouraged to speak up, nor were we asked for our opinion. We parents felt powerless to demand anything. We were encouraged to pray but not to ask. That's all I was left to contemplate – unspoken rules within the rules.

We could not know the danger wasn't in the speed of the traffic along the congested road, or in the eyes of criminal strangers, as much as it was within the presbytery, where Father O'Donnell handed over the money and waited for the children to return.

Older parishioners complained to each other about Father O'Donnell allowing boys to drive the new car the parish had given the priest. He said he was giving the children lessons. It wasn't very priestly but no-one confronted him.

Word also came from a number of children that Father had guns in the boot of his car. Parents asked themselves whether the kids were inventing stories. He also allowed a gun club to hold its meetings in the rooms at the rear of the church. A church and guns? They hardly went together. After Father O'Donnell retired we learned that a fellow priest took a number of guns from the cleric, validating the whispered words of the children.

To his chosen ones, the old priest would smile as he tickled or rubbed their hands while giving them the communion bread. When some of those children grew into teenagers, they would hang around the presbytery – Father O'Donnell's combined home and office – after school or on weekends, we assumed, to earn money for odd jobs. We should have been suspicious but he was beyond suspicion because of his collar. To look further into his relationships with students would have been a sin. Our collective blindness sprang from our Catholic upbringing, from our own days at primary school, and old teachings that were neither developed nor discussed because you don't talk about priests and sex. These old teachings led us to explain away anything that may have stirred our curiosity.

I was attending a weekday mass once when I saw Father O'Donnell slap a boy so hard across the face that he shocked even himself. The silence immediately afterwards seemed to echo; then came painful and embarrassing tension. The priest froze and didn't know what to do. Aware of his own violence and guilt, his eyes darted along the front pews to gauge our reaction. I wondered what he would do next. The victim was an older student, from grade 5 or 6. He was one of six altar boys sitting on the floor behind the lectern and his crime was to whisper and stifle a laugh during a quiet part of the service. Other boys were doing the same but were not hit. The struck child's cheeks went red, one redder than the other, and he looked stunned, then distraught and ready to cry.

I regret to this day not defending the boy, but it would have been a brave or crazy Catholic to get up and argue with a priest at the altar. Without a word from anyone the service then resumed. Father O'Donnell went on with what he was doing before the assault but the effect of that slap seemed, like a threat or a promise, to last an age.

The strange things within our family life that I recall from those years had no apparent relationship to Father O'Donnell, the church or the school. They came and went unquestioned.

As a dancing, smiling five-year-old, I overheard Emma one day say to some other children: 'Coke makes me drunk.'

We didn't give Emma Coke, nor was it available from family or friends and I had never seen her drink it. I probably shrugged. Children say things you can't explain. I assumed the 'drunk' she was talking about was the sensation and tingles of the bubbles. But where had she tasted Coke? Was it Coke? I didn't know . . .

About halfway through prep, she started wetting the bed, something she hadn't done for almost three years.

Early the following year, February 1988, while in grade one, Emma's body was changing in ways that concerned me.

With growing alarm at her six-year-old body showing signs of teenage development, I took her to our doctor. After a short examination, he declared the changes were due to a hormonal influx and were nothing to worry about.

Life did not slow down for these seemingly small moments of worry.

At a birthday party at home, when the girls and their cousins were playing and laughing, making noise and brimming with youthfulness, Emma, six or seven years old, again mentioned that Coke made her drunk.

The parents were drinking wine or mixed drinks. There was Coke on the table for the adults but it was not for the children.

'Yeah, it makes me drunk.' She smiled in a way that, to remember, takes my breath away.

The words jumped out at me and I listened, trying to figure out why she was saying this.

It was Emma's younger cousin who said: 'No, it doesn't.'

'Yes it does,' Emma shot back, assuredly.

The exchange between them became entertainment for the other children.

Emma's cousin grabbed a glass, poured some Coke and then gave it to my daughter. Emma took a sip and put the glass down then reeled around in circles across the room, with her little cousins and sisters following her, laughing. Then Emma fell down in a heap under the coat rack, her eyes closed as if asleep. All the children gathered around quietly. Her antagonistic cousin went nearer and poked her with his finger. Emma jumped up with a roar and they all took off up the hall laughing. It left me smiling – she was only kidding.

Emma developed what I called 'anger headaches' that happened fitfully after innocuous incidents. She would yell and scream in anger and it would end in tears, with Emma holding her head, saying she had a headache. I took her to the doctor but with no resolution. After some time I decided she might be suffering from eye strain and at seven years of age took her to the optometrist, who tested her and found a slight vision defect but no need for glasses. Those anger headaches never disappeared. Convinced she must need glasses, the only explanation I could conceive of, we returned to the optometrist a year and a half later in November 1990, when I insisted Emma be given glasses. They made no difference to her anger or the headaches.

The oddities, the question marks, were piling up like dirty dishes I could not keep up with.

A mysterious pair of underpants – white and old-fashioned – appeared in our washing basket. We regularly had other girls, cousins or friends, staying the night at our house but at the time, hadn't for weeks. Most of our guests, like my girls, wore bright-coloured undies with wide elastic bands, the newest and latest thing. I was surprised to see this pair because they were underpants like I wore as a child. Who would buy old-fashioned undies like that? It made me think they came from school. They were a cheap choice, the choice of an old person. That was my impression.

When I was a child the teacher at my primary school had similar white underpants for young pupils who accidentally wet their pants. Maybe one of my girls had had an accident, causing a teacher to give her a dry pair and that's where they had come from. But at the same time I wondered, if an accident had occurred, surely a note would have been sent home. And if this was the case . . . where were our underpants? Also, I hadn't put them in the washing basket, which I usually did each day, meaning one of the girls had done so. It was out of the ordinary. Was one of them hiding something, suffering embarrassment? I asked my daughters about the undies but received only shrugs. I thought I would find out what had happened the following week but I never did. I heard no word from a teacher and the incident was lost in a busy life.

Not long after that, Emma started compulsively pressing and rubbing one corner of her mouth. She did this so often that the area was always red and chafed, often turning into a sore. It remained a habit for many months, possibly a year, with me constantly encouraging her to stop.

At the end of grade 2, in November 1989, I bought Emma a new uniform. She had broad shoulders so the dress that fitted her was too long for her body. The sales assistant assured me that this was the correct size but I would have to take the hem up a long way. Even though Emma was tall the dress ended halfway between her knees and feet. It looked comically old-fashioned. When we got home Emma refused to allow me to take the hem up; she wanted it left long and I could not talk her out of it. She wore it to school and was the centre of attention, receiving a great deal of teasing and laughter, which hurt my feelings. I tried to minimise the damage, hide my discomfort, by joking to the other mums that she was starting a new fashion.

It was contrary to all logic that she wore the dress like that. I couldn't understand why she would endure such a ribbing to keep it so long. What could be worse than so much peer ridicule for a child? Some weeks later I just took the hem up, without another protest from Emma.

I now see this incident as an attempt by Emma to protect herself by hiding her body.

Father O'Donnell had no more contact with Emma, to my mind, than with any other female pupil at primary school. It seemed he barely tolerated girls and women anyway. But one evening, during a twilight school session, which was held every now and then so working parents could watch their children learn, I witnessed a rare interaction between my daughter and our priest. Emma was happily playing by herself on the school hall porch, swinging around and around on a verandah post a few metres from me. I was chatting to another parent and people were coming and going. Suddenly my attention was drawn to the porch. Father O'Donnell had entered the playground and walked up the two stairs towards the hall doors, speaking to Emma as he went. When he got close enough he patted Emma's head. Emma, in an instant rage, swung around with a clenched fist aimed at his fat stomach. Seeing it coming, Father immediately pushed her head back with his hand, moving his girth out of the way just in time to miss the otherwise perfectly aimed punch. I stood there with my mouth open. My daughter had just tried to king hit the parish priest in the stomach. I called her over, asking quietly why she had tried to punch him. I could see by her face she was furious, but she wouldn't answer me.

I asked her again, gently: 'Emma, why did you do that?' The few people who had witnessed the incident stood watching, waiting for Emma's response. So did Father.

Emma refused to speak. She simply stood there fuming. I persisted in asking her to explain her actions and she looked as if she was about to reply. While I had no idea of what I was enticing out of my daughter, Father O'Donnell knew very well the incriminating words that could have flowed from her mouth in her angry state. He cleverly intervened and put a stop to the possibility.

Smiling pleasantly, acting completely out of character in reaction to such an offence, he whispered to us: 'It's okay.'

I was shocked and relieved not to be subjected to one of his famous tantrums.

'It doesn't matter,' he concluded, before smiling and walking away.

I let it drop, just as he was hoping I would. He defused the potentially revealing situation in a manner that negated the need for any further discussion.

All my thoughts and conclusions, all my answers and explanations of these events, were conceived from the information I had before me. There was so much more happening in Emma's life but I could not see it. It turns out there was a whole parallel secret world of deceit I knew nothing about.

With the knowledge I now have I realise I should have asked many more questions. But my growing up in a world where children were better off 'seen and not heard' didn't help. Neither did my Catholic Church straitjacket that kept me from questioning religious authorities or anything else. The social taboo of speaking about the sexual assault of children left me and every other parent in the dark. I knew by then what paedophiles were and I detested them and their crimes, but I did not know how close they could be; nor could I recognise their behaviour or identify behaviours of their victims.

The memories I have of my early parenthood I now call evidence, as clear as the burning blue sky the day Emma died.

Chapter 3
The priest

Father O'Donnell retired in 1992 after serving the Catholic Church for exactly fifty years. He was seventy-five years old.

The timing of his departure from the Oakleigh parish was curious. Soon after he reached his half-century milestone, he was gone. The Code of Canon Law (the body of law the Church makes up for itself) states that priests aged seventy-five must offer their resignation to their superior. But it is not mandatory for bishops or archbishops to accept these resignations – many priests continue working into their eighties or until they are no longer capable. Father O'Donnell's energy and enthusiasm to manage his parish appeared undiminished, even if he seemed perpetually grumpy. But someone of high standing at the headquarters of the Archdiocese of Melbourne decided that the old man should finish up. So he did. I presumed that meant he would no longer perform religious duties anywhere. Later, I found out that he continued acting as a priest at other parishes, albeit on a casual and unofficial basis. Thanks to his connections within the priesthood, he was able to continue having access to children.

Our family attended Father O'Donnell's Golden Jubilee of Priesthood Celebration, a special mass to commemorate his priestly longevity. It was his send-off. We dressed up, prayed and paid our respects. His Grace, The Most Reverend Sir Frank Little, Archbishop of Melbourne, was there to preside over the significant occasion and congratulate his charge on a fine career.

The Church decorated the retiring Father O'Donnell with the title 'Pastor Emeritus'. I didn't know what this meant but years later read the words of Monsignor Christopher Prowse, then Vicar General of Melbourne Archdiocese: 'Pastor Emeritus . . . means Distinguished Pastor. It's honorific. It's like an OBE of the Catholic world.'

A packed church of laity and clergy honoured Father through hymn. Father O'Donnell called out: 'May almighty God have mercy on us, forgive us our sins and bring us to ever-lasting life.'

'Amen,' we said.

Other parish leaders were involved in the golden jubilee service, perhaps out of a sense of priestly solidarity, but it didn't look like any of them wanted to be there. I recall nothing jovial or joyous about the occasion. Father O'Donnell was grim-faced. Perhaps he was contemplating his departure – the stripping of his ability to move freely among us, his parishioners and, of course, our school-aged children.

There was a long period when Father O'Donnell was respected in the halls of the Catholic Church, not just as a senior priest but also as an acquirer of valuable real estate. Throughout his many decades of service, he identified pieces of land all over the state and advised the cathedral administrators to buy them. He boasted that he had a keen eye for a bargain and the Church took ownership of property on his say so, which added greatly to its riches. For his entrepreneurial skills alone, he was a man of influence within the archdiocese.

By the time he reached retirement, however, Father O'Donnell was no longer valuable to his employer. In fact, he had become a liability. His temper made him repugnant, even to some fellow priests, who were complaining about his dysfunctional behaviour. There was nothing 'supreme' about him any longer.

Perhaps he was frustrated by losing the fight with something he was unable to manipulate – time.

Other than what I saw as a parishioner in his congregation and during a few interactions with him, Father O'Donnell was a virtual stranger to me. He donned an arms-length persona, which I adhered to. He was like that to a lot of people and few were upset when he packed up and relocated. I think most of us hoped a better priest would be sent to take his place.

After the golden jubilee celebration and his final farewell mass two weeks later, Father O'Donnell was not seen again at Oakleigh. At the time, I was uncertain where he went after he left our parish and suburb. Someone told me that he refused to go into a retired priests' home, declaring he 'didn't want to live with a bunch of old priests'. I then heard he was housed for a while in a church-owned unit, in the outer suburb of Dandenong, where he'd lived and worked in the 1950s and 1960s. That accommodation wasn't suitable for him after several months, I was told. Some of the locals there remembered him too well. The children of his time as a parish priest in Dandenong had grown into middle age and a few warned him to find somewhere else to live.

He moved once more and eventually settled into a one-bedroom weatherboard flat just a hundred metres from Port Phillip Bay, with the smells of the beach and his sinful thoughts for company. He probably thanked God he could spend the rest of his years comfortable in the knowledge no-one would ever find out who or what he really was. There was no reason to think that he was going to be held accountable for his actions now. Apparently he didn't change his ways. He still attracted visitors at the beachside unit; loyal families with children (he offered to act as a babysitter), or sometimes children without parental supervision. One of

O'Donnell's neighbours, a relative of an Oakleigh parishioner, complained about all the children who hung around the old priest's unit.

All visitors were welcomed. Well, almost all.

In February 1994, two police detectives knocked on Father O'Donnell's door.

The pair stood with their hands on their hips and turned to take in their surroundings. The laughter of beachgoers just over the back fence of the property made them feel like they could be on holidays. The sea breeze was refreshing, making the police forget that they were wearing suits and leather holsters on a hot summer's day.

'Nice spot to retire,' said Ken MacKenzie, the younger officer, to his senior partner Barry Flentjar.

Before Detective Flentjar had time to reply, the front door opened and Father O'Donnell appeared to the officers, a grandfather figure with a grimace.

'Yes?' the old man said.

'Kevin O'Donnell?' asked Detective MacKenzie.

'*Father* Kevin O'Donnell,' the old man corrected. 'That's me. How can I help you?'

'We're detectives from the Hastings Police Criminal Investigation Branch,' Detective MacKenzie continued. 'Father, we'd like to ask you some questions about a complaint we've received.'

'What is it about?' Father O'Donnell enquired.

The detectives explained that they would go through the details of the accusations made against him back at the police station. In accordance with procedures, O'Donnell was arrested and both officers were surprised he didn't ask more questions before agreeing to go with them.

'I'll just need a few minutes to get ready,' he instructed, with a forced smile. The old man visited the toilet, and then the officers watched him grab personal items: keys, medication for his high blood pressure and two inhalers.

'I've got some emphysema,' he explained, as the trio climbed into the unmarked police sedan.

On arriving at the police station, Father O'Donnell was handed a two-page written statement from a man who claimed that the priest had sexually assaulted him in the 1970s. The accuser – Bill Nelson (not his real name) – had been an altar boy. The police statement detailed how the child was groomed and repeatedly molested by Father O'Donnell in many different locations, weekly or fortnightly, over many years.

Father O'Donnell read the complaint the police placed in front of him without emotion.

The statement recalled a night when Father O'Donnell placed his finger on the boy's anus and whispered to him: 'I should get my knife [a Swiss army knife] and put it in your tail.' The statement said the boy became 'very frightened when he said that' and 'thought he really should wash his hands very well . . . because he was right-handed and gave out the communion bread with his right hand'.

The altar boy was forced to have his first ejaculation at the masturbating hands of Father O'Donnell, which caused the victim trauma at the time and for decades after. The assaults against this child happened at the parish property, in the man's car, on trips away and various other places. Father O'Donnell was relentless in his assaults. 'I can never remember him (Father O'Donnell) without an erection,' the former altar boy wrote in his statement.

When O'Donnell finished reading the complaint the two detectives instructed him that they would begin a formal interview. Detective MacKenzie reached across the cassette player to press 'record' and the interview began.

'Now, as I've already informed you,' the policeman began, 'I intend to interview you in relation to some allegations of indecent assault. Before continuing I must inform you that you are not obliged to say or do anything, but anything you say or do may be given in evidence. Do you understand that?'

The policemen watched closely for a reaction. Father O'Donnell did not appear fazed and replied: 'Yes.'

'I must inform you of the following rights,' Detective MacKenzie added. 'You may communicate with, or attempt to communicate with, a friend or relative to inform that person of your whereabouts. And you may communicate with, or attempt to communicate with, a legal practitioner. Do you understand these legal rights?'

Father O'Donnell said he did.

Detective MacKenzie started the next question. He and his partner were aware that the priest's answer was critical to their investigation progressing much further. 'Do you wish to exercise any of these rights before the interview proceeds?'

They paused and looked at him.

'Not at this time,' Father O'Donnell said. 'No.' None of the three men in the room could know that the answer the priest gave to that question was a critical moment in the lives of so many people, including my family. If he had contacted a lawyer he may never have been brought to justice. A Church-appointed solicitor probably would have advised him to say 'no comment'. Indecent assault against a child is a difficult charge to prove because there are usually no witnesses. Detectives MacKenzie and Flentjar pressed on without delay.

Detective MacKenzie: 'Alright. Now, Father, as I've informed you prior to the start of the interview, there's been a number of allegations made by a person. Do you know this person?'

'Yes.'

'Now, what I intend to do is go through his statement with you and inform you of the allegations that are contained and you may wish to comment on these allegations. Do you understand that?'

'Mmm.' The priest seemed to be thinking deeply.

The policeman conceded: 'Alright, I won't read the whole statement verbatim, but I'll . . .'

The priest shook his head slightly. 'I'd prefer not at this stage, of course . . .'

'I'll pick out . . . where allegations are contained and give you a chance to comment,' the detective offered.

Father O'Donnell agreed.

It's hard to imagine what he was thinking at this moment. Was he trying to come up with excuses or alibis? Was he totally unafraid and arrogantly underestimating the policemen? Perhaps he was picturing the altar boy who made the complaint, remembering the things he did to that poor child . . .

It was 1972. Father O'Donnell had been a priest for thirty years and was at the peak of his powers: a strong, bold, irrepressible figure. He'd served in many parishes since his ordination in 1942 and the cathedral had just relocated him yet again, this time to a small country church in a town called Hastings, in the middle of a farming community. The town rested on a peninsula of long green hills and beautiful beaches.

He seemed a happy priest.

Father O'Donnell made his presence known to the community from day one of his new assignment. His predecessor had been softly spoken and needed to use a microphone to address his congregation. Father O'Donnell was short but had a big voice. He boomed prayers and religious instruction without an amplifier and his parishioners sat straight-backed to attention.

Locals noticed Father wherever he went, driving his car, a cream Valiant, with his overweight dog always peering out the back seat windows. When the clergyman walked into the classrooms, all the children stood up and said in unison: 'Good morning, Father. God bless you, Father.'

'Sister,' he would say to the nun teacher, 'can you spare some lads to do some work around the convent?' All of the children would raise their hands and hope to be chosen. It was considered a great honour to be hand-picked by a man of such high standing but also, perhaps more significantly, it was fun to be allowed out of the classroom. The chosen ones were asked to stack firewood, trim hedges or complete any number of other chores. If Father O'Donnell needed a tool – a spanner or wrench – he would send one of the children to the boot of his car to fetch it. This is where the priest kept his rifle and ammunition. The students were in awe of the weapon and wondered why the Father kept it.

One of Father O'Donnell's favourite students was Bill Nelson, a quiet boy whose parents were devout followers of God and His representative in Hastings. The priest paid particular attention to Bill and told him he was 'the special one'. It was all part of the fifty-six-year-old clergyman's mental conditioning of the primary school student.

When Bill was in grade 6, Father O'Donnell took him and a group of other schoolchildren to the beach. Bill got sunburned. Days later, the child was mowing the lawn outside the presbytery when Father O'Donnell called him inside. The priest had a ritual of giving boys rewards for their work: soft drinks, cake, cash.

He gave Bill some money and embraced him.

'You've done a great job,' Father O'Donnell praised. 'I'm very pleased with you.'

Father O'Donnell then placed his hands under Bill's shirt and rubbed his stomach and back. The boy was silent, trapped and frightened – he froze because of the discomfort of this unusual contact with the priest. Also, he was in pain because of his blistering red skin, which the priest was stroking. It was stinging. Father O'Donnell did not sexually assault the boy on this occasion, but he had clearly made his mind up to target Bill in the near future.

Bill wrote in his statement to the police: 'I dared not to complain because he was the Father. It felt very strange that a Father would act like this.'

Ten minutes after the incident, Father O'Donnell drove the boy home.

As his complaint to the detectives would much later detail, Bill was assaulted from that day on. Often it was when Father O'Donnell was driving him back to his family's house after a church-organised event. The priest became close to his victim's parents, thereby earning their trust, and always arranged it so he could give the child a lift home. 'I'll drop Bill off a little later,' he told the parents, who were pleased that such an esteemed community leader was taking a keen interest in their son. When Father O'Donnell organised to give several altar boys a ride home in his Valiant, which happened often, Bill sat and hoped he would not be the last one to be dropped off. If he were, he would definitely be assaulted. He had no idea the other boys feared the same outcome.

Father O'Donnell gave Bill, who was way too young to have a licence, special permission to drive his car. 'I'll teach you,' the clergyman said. Father would park on the side of the road and urge Bill to climb across or up onto his lap. This was one of his preferred ways to begin his molestations. 'My chauffeur will drive me now,' the priest boasted, before reaching into the child's pants. Sometimes, while they drove along lonely country roads, before or after an assault, Father O'Donnell would reach out and grab Bill's hand. It was yet another controlling action, as if to say 'you're mine, lad'. The boy felt uncomfortable and was horrified by the man's firm grip.

After each sexual assault, during which the priest masturbated and ejaculated after molesting his victim, Father O'Donnell followed the same clean-up routine. He retrieved a pristine white handkerchief from his pocket and quietly, carefully wiped himself down. Bill noticed the handkerchief was always perfectly pressed and folded; the priest's housekeepers kept them this way. Those mostly older women lived with Father at the presbytery, cooked his meals, washed his clothes, did his ironing and treated him like a higher being. Did they never question why he routinely needed so many handkerchiefs?

'Make sure you've tucked yourself in,' Father O'Donnell would say to Bill after an assault. The priest was covering his tracks. He didn't want the altar boy's parents asking why his clothes were continually dishevelled after spending time with Father.

In Hastings, the priest presided over every Catholic community event, parish discussion, regional school meeting and working bee. He threw parties for other priests, inviting clergy from all over the archdiocese. He played football and cricket games, bought small motorbikes for the altar boys to ride, and fixed up an old boat so he could take the children fishing.

Father O'Donnell owned a holiday house near another rural town, further south along the peninsula. This is where he took groups of boys for weekends away.

In September 1972, the priest took Bill Nelson and a few others to his weatherboard retreat. The first evening of their sleepover was a cold one and the boys huddled close to the heater in the lounge, watching a scary movie on television. Father O'Donnell came into the room.

'I think it's time for you younger lads to go to bed,' he announced. 'Make sure you come into my room and say good night first.'

Bill pressed his back teeth together and held his breath. He and another boy, Robert Land, were the 'younger lads'. Slowly the pair did as they were told. After they went to the toilet, brushed their teeth and dressed in their flannelette pyjamas, Bill and Robert went into Father O'Donnell's room to say good night.

The priest was propped up in bed, reading a magazine. His new dog, a border collie called Laddie (the older dog had died) was on the floor, under the bed. The priest started chatting to the boys, about nothing in particular, then said: 'C'mon, it's cold . . . you'd better jump in here with me.' Father O'Donnell folded down the sheet and blankets he was lying under. He was wearing pyjamas but the top of his pants was undone. Bill clearly saw Father's erect penis and became frightened.

It was a double bed. Bill hopped in first, climbing over Father O'Donnell, and then Robert got in, leaving the priest in the middle. Bill wondered if Robert, who was his best friend, had seen Father's penis. The boys then lay identically, on their backs, staring at the ceiling and feeling very scared. Bill felt Father O'Donnell's hand moving over his stomach. It reminded him of the first time. After a few moments, Father's hand moved down to Bill's penis. His fingers played with the boy's testicles. Bill's greatest fears at this moment were that his friend Robert was being assaulted in the same way, and that the priest would painfully squeeze his testicles.

Robert did not make a sound. Of course, he was thinking the same as Bill.

BOOM. YELP.

A small electrical explosion interrupted the horror. The dog under the bed had chewed through the bedside lamp cord. The older boys, hearing the commotion, stopped watching television in the lounge and ran to the bedroom to find out what had caused the loud noise.

Instantly stopping the fondling, Father O'Donnell sprang up into a sitting position.

'What's going on?' one of the older boys asked as he came barrelling into the room.

'We were sitting on the bed and Laddie chewed through the cord,' said the priest.

Bill, Robert, the older children and Father O'Donnell then laughed at the absurdity of the situation. None of the boys questioned what Father was doing in the bed with the two younger lads. Not then, not for the rest of the weekend, not for a long time – another two decades.

With guilt, shame and fear as his weapons, Father O'Donnell was able to keep the two boys from talking even to each other about what had happened that evening and, under that heavy blanket of secrecy, Bill continued to be defiled for years. The night the priest mentioned he should use his Swiss army knife in an assault, while pressing his finger on Bill's anus, was just one example of the terrible things the man said to the altar boy. The victim could not imagine telling anyone what was happening to him. How could he utter the words? Who would believe it? Who would accept his word against the voice of God's representative?

In return for Bill's silence, Father treated his victim to gifts and special jobs around the parish, such as printing the newsletter, counting the church money and driving the tractor around the church grounds. It was all part of Father O'Donnell's thorough con.

The priest staked a claim in Bill's life for as long as he could; even for a few years after the child sexual assaults stopped and the boy grew through adolescence – such was the man's control over his victim. When Bill was married, he felt pressured to ask Father O'Donnell to perform the ceremony. If he did not, his family would have thought something was amiss and asked questions. Bill still hadn't told anyone about his assaults and his subsequent secret trauma. The boy – now a young man – was falling apart inside. Horrible memories of the abuse never ceased or diminished. Men dressed in black chased him in his dreams. He woke frightened and wide-eyed. Always. The stress from being pursued by a paedophile, the hypersensitive state of fearful alertness, was made a part of his brain's everyday function. Peaceful sleep became an unachievable wish – like childish happiness or innocence, it never, ever returned.

Eventually, hatred overcame Bill so completely that he severed all ties with his tormentor, writing him a letter to express his disgust at how he had been treated. Father O'Donnell wrote back to him and humbly pleaded for Bill to stay in touch. It was a desperate attempt to keep his past a secret. He wanted to make sure Bill did not tell anyone.

The years passed without Bill disclosing the assaults. But when the deeds of another priest were mentioned on a radio news bulletin in 1993, it triggered in him an urge to speak out.

Bill courageously picked up the phone. He willed himself to make the call. 'I'd like to report a paedophile priest . . .'

Now that old paedophile priest sat in the police interview room.

'Was that correct that you would use the boys to do odd jobs around the place?' Detective MacKenzie asked.

'Occasionally, only occasionally,' Father O'Donnell offered as his first lie in the police interview being recorded at Hastings Police Station.

The detective asked him about Bill going into the presbytery after the chores and being paid for a job well done. 'Was that usual practice?'

'Yeah, I think it was, yeah. I don't remember the detail as well as he [Bill] does,' Father O'Donnell answered.

The policeman read through the part of the statement where the altar boy remembered being touched by the priest, rubbed and stroked, after being sunburned at the beach.

'I don't deny it, go on,' Father O'Donnell ordered, trying to wrestle back control of the interview.

Detective MacKenzie continued reading aloud Bill's complaint to Father O'Donnell. He went on to say: 'I dared not complain because he was the Father . . . it felt very strange that a Father would act like this.'

Detective MacKenzie looked up from the paper to the accused man. 'You have any comment to make about this?'

Father O'Donnell responded: 'No, I . . . I don't remember the detail of that.'

'Right . . .'

Detective MacKenzie then went quiet, leaving a silence in the room that the priest felt compelled to fill.

'I suppose I . . . had that happened . . . just embracing someone . . . with . . . without realising it would either physically or emotionally upset him.' Father O'Donnell stammered.

The clergyman was scrambling for answers. Detective MacKenzie's confidence grew. He read another part of the victim's statement, which included allegations of sexual assault. The priest at first said he did not remember details but then decided he would try to explain away his crimes.

Detective MacKenzie continued reading Bill's written statement: 'After a while he moved his hand down my pyjamas, down to my penis. He was just fiddling with his fingers and feeling my testicles.' The policeman stopped reading and addressed the old man. 'Would you care to make any comment on that?'

'No, it's possible. I . . . he was somewhat affectionate, and I . . . came towards . . . at occasions like that. I didn't really . . . I can't really agree that he was frightened in any sense, because . . . not only that but for years later he used to come of his own volition to me. I didn't go to . . . force him or pick him up or to . . . get him to come and do

anything. But he . . . I found it a bit hard to resist the . . ..
his advances . . .'

Detective MacKenzie: 'Well are you saying that he . . . that
he's made . . . or done things that have given you the impression that . . .'

'That he didn't object,' the priest said.

'That he didn't object, or was looking for this sort of thing
to happen, or . . .?' Detective MacKenzie was being patient.

'That he didn't object,' Father O'Donnell said.

Detective Flentjar was watching and listening to the
conversation but had not said anything. But now he wanted
to get some things straight and interjected, directing the priest
to a different allegation in the statement.

'Do you actually recall fondling him on that occasion?'

'Yes.'

'You do?'

'Well, I . . . I, yeah.'

'Do you recall . . .?'

Father O'Donnell knew he was starting to fall deep into
trouble but still thought he could talk himself out. 'But
not . . .'

The police were starting to take firm control of the
interview.

' . . . where you fondled him?'

'Not exactly.'

'Well, he says in his statement that you fondled his penis
and testicles,' Detective Flentjar said.

'Yes, I will . . . I'll pass that . . . I . . .' Father O'Donnell
said.

But he wasn't being let off that easily.

'How do you mean, you'll "pass that"?' Detective Flentjar
asked.

'Well, I won't . . .'

'Do you actually recall doing that?' the detective pressed.

'I . . . you see, I have only a hazy recollection of the whole thing . . . it's been a shock to me today.'

'Yes? Go on.'

'But I . . . I can't deny it. Put it that way and what I mostly remember about the incident is going on from there as the . . . it . . . it . . . I . . . it could've happened.'

The interview continued and Detective MacKenzie resumed asking questions. Father O'Donnell denied other accusations of sexual assault. Later, Detective Flentjar asked: 'Do you recall having an erection while you were . . . touching his penis?'

'Yes, yes, yes.'

'On occasions . . . all that was occurring . . . did he ever . . . what was he [the victim] actually doing himself?'

The priest said: 'Well, that's the point . . . that he didn't show any reluctance, he . . . he was . . . a good healthy lad . . . who could've refused . . . who could've gone away . . . could've . . . I mean . . .'

But the victim was frozen, paralysed by fear, controlled completely by the power of the priest.

'Alright.' The officer had heard enough of that line but Father O'Donnell was starting to second-guess his defence.

'Does that make sense?' the priest asked his interviewers.

'Yeah, I think I know what you mean,' said Detective Flentjar, knowing that Father O'Donnell had just made a confession.

The interview was starting to become draining for the old man. 'It seems to me that with time and with the publicity these things are getting that perhaps it's played on his mind a bit to the extent that he's exaggerated some of these things a bit,' Father O'Donnell summed up.

Soon, the interview was over. The detectives knew that the paedophile was caught.

'So at this stage, Father, do you agree that the time is 12.13 pm by my watch?'

'Yes, that's right,' Father O'Donnell confirmed.

Detective MacKenzie reached over and stopped the tape.

The arresting police officers did not yet know that Father O'Donnell had more victims – hundreds of them. Early local newspaper reports of the arrest encouraged others to come forward. Some of the victims started contacting people they went to school with, to finally talk about the priest's actions, and the list grew and grew and grew . . .

Bill phoned his friend Robert Land, who was in the bed with him and Father O'Donnell the night Laddie interrupted the assaults. 'It's Bill Nelson, mate,' he said.

They hadn't seen each other for a long time.

'Do you remember that night with O'Donnell, when the dog chewed through the lamp cord?' Bill asked.

There was a brief silence between the men, before Robert responded. 'Thank God you're finally going to do something about that.' Father O'Donnell, of course, had also repeatedly assaulted Robert for years, leaving him similarly traumatised and suffering in grim silence.

Robert Land then bravely made a statement to the police. He wrote that the priest identified him as an introverted eleven-year-old, and molested, controlled and threatened him. 'He was an intelligent man, very astute,' Robert described. 'And had a violent temper.'

Father O'Donnell used to take Robert shooting. They went to a farm property just outside town and lined up tins and bottles on fences for target practice. Father O'Donnell would gleefully grab his rifle from the boot of his car. 'He called it his elephant gun,' Robert remembered. 'Because it was so big.'

One day, Robert made a remark about the priest's behaviour towards him, which Father didn't like. The priest pointed the barrel of the gun at the boy's face and told him to be quiet.

Father O'Donnell often assaulted Robert in his Valiant, just as he did to Bill and so many other children. The priest sometimes played with Robert's penis with one hand, while he was controlling the steering wheel with the other hand. He did not even bother to stop the car. One night Robert was so frightened and sickened by the assaults against him, he tried to jump out of the speeding sedan. He was prepared at that moment to die for an escape. But Father O'Donnell grabbed him so tightly he could not go anywhere.

Father O'Donnell anally raped Robert at least three times in his presbytery. With the intimidation of his victim complete, he was making use of his strength and omnipotence. Robert said: 'I just went into my shell and didn't tell anyone. I was scared shitless. He was the closest thing there was to God.'

Detectives MacKenzie and Flentjar took statements from people Father O'Donnell assaulted in the 1940s, 1950s, 1960s and 1970s. The officers began to understand that he was one of the most prolific and worst paedophile priests in Australia. His earliest crime was traced back to 1946, when Father O'Donnell was an assistant priest who liked to take altar boys to the beach and also into the sacristy. One of these boys was eight-year-old Peter Taylor.

Peter lived just behind the scrubby foreshore and spent his childhood playing and swimming near a pier that stretched out into Port Phillip Bay. The boy was standing in the shallows one day, when Father O'Donnell arrived at the beach wearing only his bathers.

The priest was in his early thirties and physically at his peak. He had a thick mat of body hair and was stout. Father O'Donnell approached Peter, picked him up and started to walk into deeper water. When the sea level was up to the priest's neck, Father began fiddling with Peter's shorts. In those days, swimming trunks were made of flannel; they also had a sort of skirt on the front and a belt to hold them up. As Father O'Donnell tried to take the boy's bathers off, Peter became very angry and started yelling. 'I'm going to tell my mum and dad on you,' he screamed.

'What are you going to tell them?' the priest shot back.

'What you've been doing.'

The Father started laughing loudly and at the same time pushed Peter's head under the water and held him there. Peter, suddenly panicking, grabbed handfuls of the man's chest hair and twisted them furiously, until his attacker let go. The boy dived to the sandy seabed and swam a long way under water like a fish. After he resurfaced, he made quickly for the shore. Father O'Donnell didn't follow him.

Peter told his parents that the priest tried to drown him. They said: 'Oh, don't be such a sook, he was only playing with you.'

He didn't tell them anything again.

Peter Taylor will never forget that day, just like he will never forget the day Father O'Donnell took him into the sacristy of the local parish, sat him on his knee and assaulted him. After the molestation, the boy left the room and passed the altar, pausing to genuflect. What power the Catholic Church had over the child compelling him to do that, even though he was surely terrified and confused. Peter, kneeling on one knee, lifted his eyes and noticed the red glass-encased candle flickering on the wall. The presence of this red light indicates God's presence in the church. 'If He is here,' the trembling child thought to himself, 'why doesn't He stop Father O'Donnell? Why?'

When Peter made his complaint to the police almost fifty years later, he said he had never been able to forgive the Catholic Church. He was a grandfather by then, but unable to sit his grandchildren on his lap, which is so sad. The effects of child sexual assault spread like ripples in an infinite ocean.

Detectives MacKenzie and Flentjar took statements from childhood victims in multiple parishes, from beachside Chelsea and rural Seymour to suburban Dandenong, where Father O'Donnell was appointed as a senior priest in 1956. It was there, at St Mary's Parish, that he became a parish boss for the first time, with unfettered access to children. He did what he liked to them, ruining many, many lives.

I guess he was supremely confident that the victims would not tell. He was wrong about that. Some of them did tell. The problem was, the Church didn't do anything to stop him.

When the police finally learned about these arrogant and reckless instances of abuse in 1993, the serious charges mounted.

Another victim from St Mary's in Dandenong who made a statement to the detectives was Alan Timmons. Like the others, he was groomed and assaulted by Father O'Donnell for a long time. Once, the priest called for him to visit his presbytery. The child was told Father was sick. The supposedly ailing priest lured Alan into his bedroom and lay on top of him, beginning another one of his horrible molestations.

Just then, Father O'Donnell's assistant priest walked in and stood at the head of the bed. Alan looked up at the young clergyman standing still and taking in the scene before him. The child thought it was a breakthrough. Something is going to happen about this, Alan thought. Now it will stop . . . But the curate said nothing. He simply spun on his heels and walked out, ignoring the crimes of his senior colleague. Why didn't he do something to protect the petrified child? Why did that coward leave the room?

When Alan Timmons summoned the courage to report his assaults to the leaders of the archdiocese, he was met by a lack of compassion. Only when he made his complaint to the police, decades after the attacks, did he see action. The detectives' list of charges was extended by a few more.

Finally, the detectives took complaints from victims at Father O'Donnell's most recent parish, Oakleigh. The sexual predator had taken over the Sacred Heart Parish in 1976. One of the altar boy victims made a statement to police, detailing how Father O'Donnell once drove him home to an empty house and followed him into his bedroom. The sixty-year-old priest straddled the child, almost suffocating him with his weight.

The overweight paedophile whispered to his victim a well-worn line. 'I love you – you are the special one.'

Father O'Donnell was charged with committing dozens of offences, including indecent assault and buggery (rape), against twelve children. The detectives could have kept going, compiling charges, taking statements from potentially hundreds more victims, but they did not want their investigation to drag on too much longer. They chose the strongest representative cases. With the confession from the first interview about the crimes against Bill Nelson, they had enough evidence to go to the Director of Public Prosecutions with the case. They wanted the priest jailed as soon as possible.

I did not know any of this was happening until it reached the newspapers. After that, most people stopped calling Father Kevin O'Donnell 'Father' or 'Pastor Emeritus' (although the Church still insisted that he keep his titles). To us he became O'Donnell; one of those accused paedophile priests. But, of course, by the time I learned his true identity it was too late for my daughters.

Chapter 4
The past becomes the present

It was 1 March 1995. Emma had just started year 8 at Sacred Heart Girls College when she read a small newspaper story about O'Donnell. She was thirteen years and three months of age. Her eyes widened in fright. I read the story too, as did Anthony.

We were all stunned by those few brief paragraphs in our local paper, which stated O'Donnell was facing forty-nine charges. I read the article over and over to be sure I wasn't seeing things.

'Indecently assaulting boys . . . offences committed over a thirty-year period prior to 1977.'

Yes. It was real. Someone must have checked the facts before writing the story and the newspaper's editors and lawyers wouldn't let such an article go to print without assuring its accuracy. The crimes O'Donnell was accused of committing were from a long time ago. I concentrated on the date mentioned '. . . *prior to 1977*' to stop my imagination charging ahead of me. O'Donnell arrived at our Oakleigh parish in 1976, well before my daughters were even born. He was not accused of sexually assaulting children in the 1980s or 1990s.

But although an entire parish of parents told themselves O'Donnell's alleged deeds were ancient history, the police action against him brought a chilling air of understanding to behaviour we had all witnessed. It was unsettling and opened up the minds of many local mums and dads to the possibility of O'Donnell having touched their children.

Peace of mind left me instantly and I have not known it since.

The article mentioned the victims were boys. No girls? It happened so long ago. Does that mean the priest changed his ways when he came to Oakleigh? Was he guilty? Perhaps he was innocent and he only appeared strange with all those boys hanging around the presbytery. Was O'Donnell the victim of a misunderstanding? I tried to use the unanswered questions to allay my fears.

Regardless, I had to ask Emma if O'Donnell had ever abused her.

'Emma, did Father O'Donnell ever touch you?'

Her response was strange. She did not reply with words but merely looked up at the ceiling for a few seconds. I asked a second time but she only looked at the ceiling again. I wanted an answer to make sure she was unharmed, so I asked a third time.

'Emma?' I raised my voice ever so slightly to get her attention. 'Did Father O'Donnell ever do anything to you that he shouldn't have?'

She replied with a blunt 'no' and walked away.

Anthony and I both looked at each other with concern in our eyes but didn't push it. Maybe the curtness meant 'stop asking me such a ridiculous question, Mother'. So I went no further. She had said 'no' and I was pleased to hear it.

Two months later, another story appeared in *The Examiner*, a local newspaper delivered to homes in the Dandenong area, about a twenty-minute drive from Oakleigh. The headline read: 'Priest pleads guilty to 12 sex charges'. (The number of charges had been reduced due to his guilty plea.) The plea and sentencing were set for August. We did not know about this article at the time.

In June 1995, three months after we saw the first hint of O'Donnell's past made public in our local paper, we received a phone call from Emma's secondary school.

A teacher said: 'Emma's not eating her lunch and some of her friends are worried about her.'

My concern was immediate, for I knew Emma no longer had breakfast at home and ate only a small evening meal. Previously, if we had a pizza for dinner, the girls raced to see who could eat the most pieces, with Emma usually winning. I had noticed a difference and wondered why, and now this. But again I looked for reasons to think everything was normal. Maybe she was just being a typical teenager and wanted to stay slim but was getting carried away. The suggestion from the school was that it was something more. It was disquieting. In spite of my uneasiness, I made lunches for Emma every day and had assumed she at least ate those.

I thanked the teacher for alerting me to the problem and waited anxiously for Emma to arrive home from school. Then I cautiously broached the subject.

'It's very important to eat all your meals,' I explained. 'It'll help you with everything you do. It's good for your mind and body.'

I didn't want to make too big a deal out of it because I believed it would make matters worse. Experience told me if I forbade her from something she would want to do it more. So I talked with calmness and commonsense.

'Eating well doesn't just help you stay fit and alert,' I continued. 'It keeps your hair shiny, skin clear and fingernails strong.'

I was mounting an effective argument and to my initial satisfaction she nodded and agreed with everything I said. But

Emma was being passive-resistant – she would say yes and agree with me to stop further conversation or conflict and would later do anything she wanted regardless of my advice.

So I persisted: 'I'd like to see you stay the weight you are and not losing any more. You look good just the way you are, darling.'

'Okay, Mum,' was all she said.

I had no experience with eating disorders so I visited my doctor to find out more about anorexia and its symptoms and causes. At the end of our conversation I felt exhausted by the whole situation. Rubbing my forehead, I told the doctor that I didn't even know how to spell anorexia. She picked up her pen and patiently sounded out the word as she wrote, then ripped off the piece of paper and gave it to me. From then on I could spell it.

Emma and I spoke at length about nutrition. Mainly, I talked and she listened. I didn't let up easily and during our conversations looked for signs that she was annoyed that I was making too much out of a problem that didn't really exist. She didn't give much away.

From then, she left home each day eating toast for breakfast. I believed I had sorted the matter out but three weeks later the school rang again with the same concern. I found out that she had been throwing her toast away once out of my sight. At the end of that month, I took her to our doctor, who could only give her the same cautions I had outlined. It wasn't long before things worsened.

Emma was at a school camp in Mt Eliza, an hour's drive south of Melbourne, when she started shaking for no reason. Her skin turned purplish. The teachers took her to see another doctor, who suggested she was displaying symptoms of anorexia.

No amount of lecturing or advising seemed to make any difference to her starving herself and in July she was officially diagnosed with the difficult-to-spell condition.

Anthony and I scrambled to understand why she was anorexic.

'It's a body-image problem,' he said one night when we were sitting at the dining room table, the girls having gone to bed. 'It's driven by the media's perception of beautiful.'

'I know, but Emma is already tall and thin,' I added. 'She doesn't need to be thinner.'

We agreed it made no sense. Emma had never been the least bit interested in fashion, dieting or self-image. She had always had a slender build and a healthy appetite.

We were referred to a specialist but, frustratingly, had to wait over six weeks for the appointment date. It was such a long way off – forty-five days – and it seemed every one of those days Emma became thinner. I cooked all her favourite meals in the desperate hope she would take a few mouthfuls. But she was steadfast.

Meanwhile, confirmation of O'Donnell's guilty plea made its way around the parish like a filthy secret and, with it, the supposed reason for him doing so. A friend, another young mum, confirmed the explanation being whispered to the faithful.

'Father O'Donnell is pleading guilty but he is not guilty,' she said. Then she repeated the sentence.

'What's that supposed to mean?' I asked, confused by the concept of a priest not telling the truth to a court of law and the parish people's acceptance of such an unbelievable contradiction.

She shrugged and could apparently add nothing more. They were the only words being passed around, like gospel, giving me the impression one of the senior parishioners had started the rumour. O'Donnell had retired from Oakleigh almost three years earlier but his overpowering aura remained, ghost-like, with mysterious powers to confuse and manipulate people.

The older parishioners would speak to me because I was active, as they were, in church attendance and wider duties.

Not a lot of youngish parents participated in these volunteer services. A lot of it was left up to the oldies. Others my age were either too busy with other things or not interested. I only did my part out of a sense of duty and more so because the new parish priest had specifically asked me to do them. I never volunteered my services.

Then, one day, I believed I was talking to the source of the not-guilty rumour. An older parishioner, who regularly visited O'Donnell in his retirement, confided in me as I stood outside the church garden, opposite the presbytery. I was waiting to collect my children after school.

'You know Father O'Donnell only pleaded guilty to spare the victims any trauma,' he explained, lowering his bushy grey eyebrows in reverence. Then he shook his head solemnly, apparently at O'Donnell's self-sacrifice and naivety.

I didn't argue with this senior parishioner but I found his version hard to swallow. A man of priestly status would not plead guilty to such vile and scandalous charges if he were innocent. He would not bow to false accusations. How would becoming a liar before a court of law, to protect those who were lying about you, amount to the right thing? It made no sense at all. Plus, I never saw O'Donnell as the selfless, caring person he had suddenly become in the minds of others.

So I walked away from discussions with other parishioners, forcing myself not to dispute the version presented to me that O'Donnell had made a noble, misguided sacrifice for the victims. Somehow O'Donnell always made some people believe he was a hero and martyr until his end. Initially, many people in my church needed another reality to cope with the awful truth of their paedophile priest and the fact he had made fools of us all.

There was ignorance among us but kindness too. Our struggles with Emma's health continued and one of the senior women parishioners suggested our daughter's name be placed on the sick list, to be read out at mass, to be prayed for. It was a lovely gesture.

'Thank you,' I replied, fighting back tears.

A week later another senior parishioner approached me with a sterner expression.

'We won't be putting Emma's name on the sick list because she is anorexic, which is a self-inflicted ailment, so she's not going on the list.'

I was taken aback but didn't argue because he was an elite member of the parish and I assumed he had discussed it with those who compiled the list, and together they had reached their decision. To my obvious but quiet dismay, he added: 'Well, it's not an illness. Anorexia is a choice.'

No mercy. No sympathy. No Christianity.

Outrage didn't overcome me then as it does now to recall that moment. At the time, I felt ashamed, as if Emma and I were to blame. I didn't even request that people pray for my daughter. I wished it had never been suggested. I thought they cared, but they didn't. I thought they knew us, but that didn't matter. I was involved in church duties as they were, but that didn't matter either. This incident only added to my distress, confusion and hopelessness. The implication was that Emma's anorexia was somehow our fault and my 'Catholic guilt' accepted it because somebody in authority connected to the Church suggested it. But the shame I felt was double-barrelled. I wondered how I would explain it to Anthony. I had happily told him Emma was going on the sick list, to be prayed for, a bright spot on our troubles. It was a message from my church that it cared. And now I had to go back and tell him about a harsh and un-Christian act from my fellow Catholics. I didn't want to tell him. I didn't tell him.

A second rumour started circulating. It stated that O'Donnell had given the archdiocese a list of his victims. I was told it contained ninety names (and they were just the names he could remember). It contradicted the first rumour – of his innocence – and was far more menacing. The existence of the list would remain a mystery, but the truth about O'Donnell soon became evident.

I walked to my front gate on a wintry Saturday morning, 5 August 1995, to retrieve the daily newspaper from my letterbox; unaware that a front page could be so earth-shattering. I unfurled the *Herald Sun* to be confronted by an almost life-sized photograph of O'Donnell's face staring back at me. I couldn't believe it.

The headline screamed 'PEDOPHILE PRIEST LOCKED UP'.

His face was rounded and purse-lipped, with eyebrows tilted sharply in, through grim annoyance, anger . . . defiance. He had finally pleaded guilty and was remanded in custody to be sentenced a week later. The details of his criminal career had been made public for the first time. The caption called him '. . . pedophile priest John O'Donnell (his first name was John but he went by his middle name, Kevin), 78, who is set to become the oldest person jailed in Victoria'. He did not look withered or timid. He was old only in his dress, a skivvy and knitted cardigan, and his loose neck skin. Otherwise he appeared quite formidable. The headline and prominence of the story, however, stripped him of his power.

Stunned, I slowly walked inside, reading as I went.

I struggled to process the words. There were more stories and photos inside the newspaper. One caption yelled at me: 'Predator priest: as king of the kids, Father Kevin O'Donnell lavished treats on children – but it was all repaid later'.

With horror, I read the full story, the details, the truth – it was all there, revealed in print. Awful stories of victims' accounts, revealing details and highlighting their pain and acute betrayal – an entire history of sexual assaults spanning thirty-one years.

There were many more victims than the charges suggested, the reports confirmed.

The newspaper reported three of the twelve victims said they complained to Church authorities.

'Facing insurmountable evidence, O'Donnell's defence lawyer had claimed "the priest was born a pedophile".'

Reality bit deeply. They were no longer accusations or rumours but admitted truths. He had actually committed these terrible crimes; admitted to sexually assaulting all those children. It was true. He WAS guilty. We'd had a child molester in our parish for sixteen years. Although his most recent charge was from 1977, his undeniable guilt broke a mental obstacle I had put in place, the barrier that said this could never have happened to my children. The news brought the assaults much closer to home. Up until now we hadn't seen the legal phases of his case and knew few details.

But here they were for everyone to read about. And in the article lay the abhorrent details of a sly paedophile.

I carefully reread the words on page one. '. . . O'Donnell was remanded in custody yesterday for the indecent assault of 10 boys and two girls between 1946 and 1977.'

GIRLS?

. . . one of those 10 boys, now in his 50s, said he and another man had found 165 more victims in 48 hours by phoning 300 former classmates at two Catholic schools from the 1950s. And several of the victims said outside court yesterday they believed the Catholic Church was just as guilty as O'Donnell.

I scoured the sentences and statistics again. O'Donnell had *female* victims . . . *little girls* . . . Another barrier crumbled before me. In Oakleigh, while we could all see he liked boys, there were only two girls I could see he was fond of. One of them was my Emma.

It opened up a possibility that she was a victim. Ice froze my veins.

Emma had said 'no'. His last offence was in 1977, which was almost four years before Emma was born. According to the court, he stopped sexual activities in 1977. He was such an old man – forty years my senior, sixty-six years Emma's senior. The betrayal was inexplicable. He baptised two of our children, heard first confession of all three, and gave them their first communion. He said mass in front of me every Sunday for eleven years . . .

The following week, O'Donnell was sentenced in the County Court. It was 11 August 1995. We did not attend but many victims were there. The courtroom was brimming with people and expectation. The former altar boys, each supported by their understanding families, sat behind men in white-rolled wigs, shuffling stacks of papers on a great wooden table.

O'Donnell was led into the room by a police officer. A hush fell over the courtroom. The pastor emeritus sat and stared at nothing in particular.

By this stage there was no doubt that O'Donnell had committed illegal acts against hundreds of children. But he stood guilty of assaulting only twelve because for the police to take more statements, put the accusations to O'Donnell, have more seemingly endless discussions with the Catholic Church lawyers and lurch through more court appearances with uncertainty, would have been too time-consuming. It had taken eighteen months for the case to go from arrest to sentencing, despite the priest's initial confession to detectives MacKenzie and Flentjar. It took more than a year for him to plead guilty, agreeing to do so only after some serious charges (buggery) were struck out. It was a deal done for expediency. Also, the police and the Director of Public Prosecutions wanted to avoid a trial, or several trials, in which the victims would be required to trawl their horrible memories and talk about them in an open court, perhaps being cross-examined at length during individual trials. No, the authorities desired a conviction and they wanted it now. They already had enough evidence to hopefully send the old man to jail, so they went ahead.

Once Judge Murray Kellam was seated behind his raised bench, O'Donnell's lawyer called several character witnesses, who claimed the priest was sorry for harming primary school students. It was not convincing. The defence barrister, in trying to paint O'Donnell as a harmless old man, insisted: 'The court could be confident that regardless of anything there would be no repetition of this sort of conduct and I suppose if ever one could be sure about it, one can be certain about it in relation to this.'

The legal team for the defence then called the respected former prison chaplain Father John Brosnan to give evidence. Father Brosnan had worked at Pentridge, the toughest jail in Melbourne, for thirty years. He knew O'Donnell well, as they attended a seminary together in the 1940s.

Speaking in defence of O'Donnell, trying to solicit sympathy for the child rapist, Father Brosnan said, 'The perpetrator is a victim as well as the victims themselves and even before it was made public these people [paedophiles] suffered greatly.'

For victims like Bill Nelson and other ex-altar boys, it was a hurtful thing to hear O'Donnell, the man who ruined their lives, called a victim. If he was a victim, did he seek help? No, he just threatened the real victims to stay quiet. And his Church superiors continued placing him in positions that were perfect for a paedophile. The priest's crimes had been reported to the cathedral several times. Did not one of those leaders of their faith attempt to address O'Donnell's 'affliction'? If they believed he was a victim why did they not intervene?

Judge Kellam had heard enough to determine his sentence. Casting a long stare across his courtroom, seeing O'Donnell perched on the edge of his seat, he said:

John Kevin O'Donnell . . . You have pleaded guilty before me to ten counts of indecent assault upon a male person under sixteen years of age and two counts of indecent assault upon a girl under sixteen years of age.

The guilty and devious conduct in which you intermittently participated during the long period between 1946 and 1977 brings you before this court in tragic circumstances, both for you in the shame that now attends you in the consequence of the manner in which you have been found to have behaved, and in the effects of your crimes upon several of your victims.

The judge went on to detail O'Donnell's crimes, to the groans and sighs of those listening.

A distressed elderly gentleman near the back of the court held his face in his hands. It was the paedophile's brother, hearing for the first time his priestly sibling reduced to a miserable coward.

The attacks against one of the female victims were harrowing to hear described. She was a fourteen-year-old girl, who felt so trapped by O'Donnell's predatory tactics that she became a nun two years later to avoid him. She wanted to be a nurse, but a convent was the only place the powerless and silenced girl felt she could successfully hide from O'Donnell.

Judge Kellam continued until it was time to conclude and issue a sentence.

Your outrageous behaviour remained concealed for many years. I do not detect any substantial remorse being expressed by you in the record of [police] interview.

Although . . . witnesses referred to your remorse . . . remorse was not, in my view, an overwhelming feature of the case put on your behalf. There is no direct statement from your mouth or of any act of contrition which might demonstrate substantial remorse for or concern or understanding of what your victims endured at your hands.

O'Donnell looked straight ahead at these words, seemingly taking them in but without emotion.

Judge Kellam sentenced O'Donnell to serve a jail term of up to eighteen months on each charge. There was some celebration and awe in court as each sentence was handed down. But then the judge went on to clarify that some of the terms of imprisonment would be served concurrently.

As O'Donnell was being escorted from the court, one of his victims, a twenty-two-year-old man, only nine years older than Emma, yelled out: 'May you rot in hell, you bastard!' The paedophile did not look back. Instead, he cast a glance at the judge and murmured something on his way out the door. The judge did not hear what he said.

To victims, including Bill Nelson, Jimmy Chambers, Alan Timmons and Peter Taylor, the final three words from the judge – *remove the prisoner* – were a bright moment in decades of darkness. But the prison sentence was a light one and they all knew it. O'Donnell and the cathedral filled lives with pain and the career paedophile got a bit over a year in jail.

I read about O'Donnell's sentencing in the newspaper and thought it was a lenient punishment. But far more pressing to me was whether O'Donnell had harmed my daughter. The facts of his criminal case were screaming at me. Ultimately, however, Emma had said 'no'. I clung to this and temporarily made myself believe that he did not touch her. She, meanwhile, continued harming herself. No matter how hard I tried to fend it off, doubt followed me everywhere.

I walked through Oakleigh shopping centre the day of O'Donnell's jail revelation, when his face appeared on the front page, and felt oddly conspicuous and self-conscious. The guilt-by-association that shrouded my thoughts was astounding. I thought people would identify me as a Sacred Heart parishioner and see me as someone who associated with or supported that malicious priest who molested children.

The next day was dreadful. I forced myself to go to mass. By this time I was ready to explode, bursting to speak to someone from the parish about O'Donnell, the headlines and their implications, all of which were still screaming in my head. I arrived expecting everybody to be shocked and talking urgently about the situation, but found it was business as usual. People didn't look as stressed or concerned as I was; they smiled as usual and acted as though nothing was wrong, as though O'Donnell's face and guilt hadn't been plastered all over the front page of a major newspaper the previous day. Didn't they see it? How could they miss it? It was on every newsstand and in every newsagent in Victoria.

I sat through the mass expecting something to be said during the homily, an unscripted part of the mass where the priest speaks freely, but there was not a word in reference to Father O'Donnell, now officially a paedophile priest who had been sent to prison only two days earlier. What terrible things did he do in Oakleigh? Who knows? Who cares? Not a word. I couldn't believe it. After mass, they all just stood around chatting as if it was any other Sunday. We could have been waiting for a bus to take us for a happy outing to the beach in that atmosphere. Eventually I found a group of my friends huddled together. By this time I was slinking around, beginning to wonder if there was something wrong with me, as nobody else seemed fazed about this huge issue.

I greeted my friends with a whispered hello. Then we all spoke vehemently, albeit in hushed tones, about O'Donnell and his crimes.

'Did you read about all those victims? He's guilty. He admits doing it and he's going to prison.'

'It's shocking.'

'The judge said he stopped molesting children in 1977,' a mother said so quietly I had to lean forward to hear.

'I hope so.'

We all hoped so.

I was relieved to at least vent my feelings to others in the same position of bewilderment and fear. We were young and all had young children who attended the primary school. We had all seen O'Donnell wander the playground in the company of our kids. We had grave concerns but that day the Church's message was very clear – don't talk about it. Or worse – you can still believe it isn't true.

I now know the response well. I have fought it for so long that I can barely remember a time when it didn't confront me. What we were being introduced to that morning was the shameful sound of holy silence.

Chapter 5
A frightening path

Days later Emma was weighed at her next GP appointment. She'd lost another two kilograms and now weighed only forty-seven kilograms. Her one hundred and seventy-three-centimetre body was very pale and weakening.

It was at this time, just as she seemed to be taking her first steps into a dark tunnel, that a faint light shone from her.

Emma had been learning to play the violin since she started secondary school and was a very talented musician. Her teacher, seeing Emma's potential, suggested she have extra one-on-one lessons, which I drove her to two nights a week.

The violin first came into our home two years earlier when Anthony, regularly travelling past a violin shop near the city, decided he would stop and have a look. Inside, the shop was full of instruments in various states of repair, newness and oldness, but all beautifully handcrafted in smooth amber timber with black knobs. He talked a while with the owner, whose passion was obvious, and some of it rubbed off onto Anthony. He bought a modest violin. His plan was to take it home and just leave it lying around, hoping natural curiosity would tempt one of the girls to learn how to play. That's exactly what happened.

I used to listen to Emma practise for hours, the sound filling the house. She became better and better in a very short time, then the pieces she played became more and more complex. I took great pride in her determination and talent.

Often I sat in the room with her and listened to her play, praising her. I admired her ability, considering the complexity of the instrument, to achieve the correct sounds. In the music I was familiar with I could hear that her timing was perfect. Many times she didn't know the tunes but I knew she was playing them without fault, a sign of her ability to read music. She was in her second year of learning and had exams lined up when she became anorexic; still she persisted in her music and only weeks before being admitted into hospital played solo at her school concert.

On stage, she was gaunt but unafraid. Before she started we experienced a powerful moment of waiting, which gave us goosebumps and made us think something wonderful was about to happen. I inhaled, bit my lip and crossed my fingers.

Emma was spectacular.

The audience of about three hundred people enthusiastically gave her a standing ovation. We were very proud of her. I overheard the woman in front of me say to her husband, as she clapped and stood: 'Boy, can that kid play!'

That was one of the last times Emma played the violin.

Finally, we made it through the six anxious weeks to see the dietary specialist on 30 August 1995. The long-awaited visit, where I thought we'd find an answer and a cure, did not turn out that way. There was no quick fix. No fix or answer at all. Just 'carry on'. I had expected so much more. Even the expert could do nothing. It was back to us. How could I prevent my girl from starving herself to death? The week after the specialist appointment, Emma was back at the GP for what were now weekly visits. It was at this time she first revealed to the doctor her suicidal thoughts.

On his referral, we booked her into an emergency psychiatric appointment at Monash Medical Centre, one of Melbourne's major hospitals. Our daughter told the psychiatrist that she had previously attempted suicide with an overdose of painkillers from our house. This was an event we knew nothing about.

It was Friday evening. The doctor warned us to keep a close eye on Emma until the following Tuesday, when she had an appointment to see a psychiatrist at the hospital's child and adolescent psychiatric unit.

Things were escalating so quickly we didn't have time to understand anything. We just looked to the next doctor's appointment with slivers of hope that a breakthrough could be made. In the meantime we tried our hardest to keep life moving forward.

We were at the Royal Melbourne Show with the girls, an annual trip they loved, when we received a call to say a bed had become available at the adolescent unit. Emma was admitted on 25 September for anorexia, depression and the earlier suicide attempt. Initially I was relieved she was going somewhere to get help, as nothing else was helping and she was constantly growing thinner. I remember the first time we walked into the unit with Emma and saw the other teenage patients. They sat around staring. Some laughed at us. Others were making harsh remarks and swearing. Some sat on the floor, their legs blocking the hallway we needed to walk along. We waited until they moved. It was a dreadful welcome. I tried to smile and tell myself that this was the right thing to do when I actually felt like turning around and running away, taking Emma with me. But where would we go?

I felt like I was taking an innocent little lamb into a wolves' den. So, with much heartache, we left our thirteen-year-old in that place as an in-patient. I went home and cried yet again. When was this going to stop?

The psychiatric unit housed about twenty-five adolescent live-in patients and was a safe, lockup environment. We visited Emma as much as visiting hours allowed but there was no improvement in her condition. One day she managed to find a pencil sharpener blade from somewhere to cut and scratch her wrists just to 'see if it hurt'.

Because of that she was then kept in a 'safe' room, which had no windows, electricity or visitors, apart from restricted family members. She was not allowed out of this room for almost a month. I constantly questioned this treatment method. What were they trying to achieve? Were they punishing her? I wondered if they were trying to curb her will. If they were trying to break our little girl, they didn't know Emma at all.

She was born headstrong and if it came to a battle of wills she would not back down. I knew. She was like this as a baby, a toddler, and now. With this knowledge, it was heartbreaking to watch her suffer further. But this was all new to me. We were in the hands of the professionals. Maybe isolation came before improvement. I didn't know. She seemed to be caving in on herself, forever in her pyjamas and constantly becoming thinner and weaker. She was mostly bedridden because the huge weight loss caused her blood pressure to double when she sat up. Anything other than lying down put her at risk of a heart attack — at thirteen years of age.

When she was finally allowed out for reasons known only to the doctors, she was so happy she cried to see the blue sky and breathe fresh air. She was wheeled into the sunlight, unable to walk. Our sweet girl had joined the ranks of the semi-dead; darkness enveloping her young dull eyes and the edges of bones showing as lumps under her skin. Her deep pallor was frightening.

I didn't know how we came to be in this hell. I certainly couldn't understand why. It was an utter mystery. Emma was a quiet, home-loving child. She didn't go out much with friends. She liked simple things. The anorexia and everything it brought with it came out of nowhere. It was just shock after shock. Our shy daughter had been transposed into something else, somebody else. I had never had to deal with a teenager before, although I'd heard many stories about difficulties in raising adolescents. Maybe this was something that just happened.

We had session after session with a psychiatrist, individually and as a family. The subject of anorexia, its causes, effects and potential cures, consumed our lives.

In this strange place and with this strange behaviour any parental authority evaporated. Everything seemed to run past our eyes in fast motion so it was hard to stop and think clearly. I felt I must have done something very wrong to have caused what was happening. My child-rearing was completely out of line, I concluded, but what else could I have done? I was bringing my girls up as I had been brought up – but a modern version, with my own philosophy – and I never caused my parents any worry. Katie and Aimee were not like this. I felt I could say nothing about anything to them now. My confidence was so completely eroded that I could barely speak to my children. Even when dealing with our well-behaved Katie and Aimee I felt at a loss, with no right at all to advise or correct them.

On the last day of October 1995, five weeks after being admitted into the adolescent unit and weighing forty-two kilograms, Emma was transferred to a medical ward at Monash Medical Centre, where she was force-fed through a nasogastric tube for two weeks. While in this ward she had her fourteenth birthday. It was a meagre celebration; the first time she had had a birthday without a cake or photos. She didn't want to see herself or eat.

After these two weeks she was transferred back to the adolescent unit. Five days later, she overdosed on a packet of painkillers and was rushed to the emergency ward of the hospital and given charcoal to drink as an antidote. Several hours later, at three o'clock in the morning, she was discharged into our care. She had broken the adolescent unit's rules and was not allowed back in. This seemed to defy all sense. Emma needed help. She had just tried to kill herself. Her expulsion was contrary to the very existence of the unit.

So with a strange mixture of shame, confusion and a lot of fear, we were sent into the night with our distraught, suicidal and angry fourteen-year-old daughter. Emma's two months in the unit had done no good at all; in fact, she was in a much worse condition than when she was admitted.

At home, she tried to keep her distress quiet but it shouted at us through her behaviour.

Always a messy, hoarding child, Emma became the opposite. She packed up two-thirds of her bedroom contents, including most of her clothes, and threw it all out, cramming smaller things into a stack of shoeboxes, which she stowed away in the bottom of her wardrobe. Her worldly goods were now out of sight. She carried out this mission constantly and obsessively for the first three days. After that, her room was left almost bare. Gone were teddies, dolls and toys from childhood, everything cute and pretty. We took this as a sign of her intention to suicide. We felt desperately isolated, as we had nowhere to go.

So we stuck to her like unwanted glue.

Self-inflicted sleep deprivation was another of Emma's new behaviours. This started while she was in the safe room at the unit. It continued at home. She stayed awake for up to four nights in a row, forever leaving the light on. No amount of coaxing helped.

'Why do you want to stay awake night after night, Emma?' I asked.

'It helps me lose my memory,' she explained.

'What do you mean?'

She looked at the ceiling, angry again. That was the end of that discussion. I screwed up my face and hated the brightness of the light globe.

If she accidentally fell asleep, she considered herself a failure and became angry with herself. After nearly two weeks of this, Anthony went into Emma's room, picked up her mattress, carried it into our bedroom and placed it beside our bed. Emma followed.

'You can sleep in here tonight,' he said.

She did. Our light was turned off and she dozed, finally. We had her sleep in our room for a month until she was able to sleep again in her bedroom.

Sometimes during the day I would go into Emma's room, wondering where she was during a period of silence I thought had lasted too long, or just to see how she was going. I often found her curled up in the bottom of her closed wardrobe.

Other times she would cut and scratch her arms or legs. Once I asked her 'Why?' To my dismay, she answered 'Because I need punishing,' and no amount of questioning or pleading would extract any further explanation.

She continued seeing a psychiatrist from the unit as an outpatient.

The least of our concerns at this point was Emma's schooling, which was a disaster. She'd missed all of the fourth term, save for a couple of half days.

'I hate that school,' she said. 'I don't want to go back.'

Out of the blue, Emma's name appeared on the sick list at church. I used to hear her name read out each week but there was no joy in it. I still felt the sting of accusation and guilt they had bestowed on me. I wondered why they had changed their minds. Emma was still anorexic.

Nearing the end of 1995, as well as seeing a psychologist from the unit, Anthony and I began seeing an independent psychologist, who had been recommended by friends. We wanted a second opinion on Emma's treatment.

About the same time I thought we needed a getaway so we planned a holiday to Queensland. I decided that doing something the girls had wanted to do for a long time would possibly bring Emma back from the edge and get her far away from her suffering. Hopefully it would also be a treat for twelve-year-old Katie and ten-year-old Aimee, who were anxiously enduring their sister's tumult.

We mapped out a plan to travel from Melbourne to Cairns by train, with week-long stays in Sydney, Brisbane and Port Douglas. After our rail journey we would hire a car and drive to the Daintree River, in North Queensland, to see the tropics. At the end of our trip in January we would fly home on Australia Day. It was an ambitious itinerary that the girls had helped plan. We wanted to make their dreams come true. Katie and Aimee were very excited about the trip; they told me all the places they wished to visit. We were to leave on Boxing Day and counted down the days.

I called an ambulance at six o'clock on the morning of 21 December. Emma had overdosed on twenty-five painkillers the night before. She awoke with severe stomach pains and was admitted to the emergency ward at the hospital. Doctors fed her an antidote through a drip then discharged her two days later. This emergency scared but did not deter us and three days later we left for our trip.

From the start, Emma proved to be a constant worry. She was angry and bent on self-destruction. When we arrived at our accommodation in Brisbane, we were given the keys to our family apartment, which was on the eighth floor. Eighth floor! I had not anticipated high-rise accommodation. Immediately fear and dread both grabbed hold of me. I counted the floors and the ways Emma could hurt herself. I shuddered at the deadly possibilities. Then, as we settled in, only an hour or so after arriving and as though thinking about it made it happen, I felt Emma's absence. Instantly, I looked out of the sliding glass balcony doors to see her sitting up on the balustrade – her back was to us and her legs dangled over the edge into eight storeys of air. The lights of the city were mesmerising her, the noises of the traffic helping her drift off again into her world. Our daughter was holding on to nothing but a stare at the horizon.

My heart jumped into my mouth. Should I go out? Would that frighten her and cause her to fall? Should I stay in? Will she put her legs back soon? Will she jump? I stood frozen at the glass door. After a while I gathered my nerve and went out on the balcony, casually saying I thought it was time to come inside. She did.

On the Gold Coast we all went to the beach and were playing in the shallows when Emma quietly turned and walked out into deeper water. Anthony and I had been keeping a close eye on her so he noticed when she turned from us and headed out towards the belly of the Pacific Ocean. He followed and tried to call her back in, but she was swimming now and stroking further out, her father in pursuit. He reached her but she fought him off and kept going. He followed still. He would not abandon her. An undertow surged beneath them and they drifted apart, now helpless, exhausted and bobbing, waiting to drown.

At first, I wondered why they were out so far then realised they were in trouble. Katie, Aimee and I stood in the shallows, unable to help. I fought the panic threatening to wash over me. Before I could move, two teams of lifesavers ran past us, dived under the waves and swam with strength and determination to rescue Anthony and Emma from the surf. After what seemed like a long time they were both returned to the beach, badly shaken. I was so grateful that we had swum at a beach patrolled by these alert and wonderful lifesavers.

Emma was not done yet. Her yearning for inner peace was driving her to self-destruction. On the thirty-two-hour train trip to Cairns the motion of the carriages and the endless tropical green landscape pushed her further into her secret thoughts. That night, she was hanging onto the outside of the train with the door shut behind her. I did not see this. She told me about it later. We had left the girls together in their sleeping cabin for what seemed a short time when Katie and Aimee came to us.

Katie said in her usual calm manner: 'Emma's acting weird.'

I stood and looked from her to Aimee, who was standing behind Katie and saw her young eyes wide open with alarm. The message received, I quickly went looking for Emma but couldn't find her. She was no longer in the cabin, which she had ordered her sisters to leave. I raced through several compartments but she was nowhere.

Then I came across her lonely distraught figure staggering along a passageway, crying violently.

I cradled her into a room and between sobs she spoke of the horrible experience.

'I went outside and hung my body outside the train,' she started. 'I wanted to jump but I couldn't.'

I opened my mouth to offer a solution or a question, so many questions. But there were no right words.

She continued: 'I almost fell but managed to pull myself back in and went back into the cabin. I locked myself in and tried to drown myself in the basin.'

I looked at her, only now noticing the hair around her face was wet, water droplets running down her neck.

'Why?'

'There were voices in my head telling me to do it.'

'Who were they? I mean, why were they saying that?'

'Because I'm worthless, Mum.'

She cried a thousand tears that night and they all fell on me. The train rolled on, faster and faster. It was not stopping for anything. The tracks decided our destination and all we could do was hold each other and hope we arrived safely. I cuddled her in bed, talking to her and calming her down for hours, stroking her forehead as I did fourteen years earlier, urging peaceful sleep to her as a newborn baby. At least for a night, Emma allowed me to embrace her. I was determined not to let her go.

On day twenty of our holiday, we went diving on the Great Barrier Reef. Desperate to keep an eye on her for fear she would jump off the boat, I followed her like a stalker. She walked around the decks then sat perched high on the outside of the boat for a long time, watching the sea. The whole time I was worried she would just suddenly run and jump over the edge. Anthony and I were exhausted.

However, just when we thought we would collapse from fatigue, things picked up. It was this activity – the scuba diving on the reef – that caused a turnaround in her behaviour. Emma enjoyed the tranquillity of the fish-watching, the cool salt water massaging her back to health. For the next ten days she smiled, and although it may have been the reflection of the sun off the deck, I could swear her eyes started sparkling again. It was the happiest we had seen her in months.

By the end of our trip we had been to Sydney, Jenolan Caves House in the Blue Mountains, where Anthony and I had honeymooned, Wonderworld, Brisbane, Sea World, Movie World, Dreamworld, Wet'n'Wild, Cairns and the Daintree rainforest. The girls had all wished for one thing each and we made it happen. After the breakthrough on the reef, we stayed at Port Douglas, travelled to Cairns airport and then flew to Melbourne on Australia Day. It was 26 January 1996. We arrived home brimming with confidence. The improvement in Emma's outlook created a new hope. The school year was about to start, with Katie to join Emma at Sacred Heart Secondary College. Emma was bound for year 9.

With the relief of her graduating to a new level (I didn't want her to repeat year 8 as it would seem to her she was going backwards), I bought her new schoolbooks and a uniform. We hoped the worst was behind us and what had happened was some teenage glitch that was now over and would become something to look back on as one of life's mysteries. We limited Emma's contact with doctors from then on.

Two weeks later, Emma's class was planning to go on a weekend prayer retreat in the country. But only hours after they departed the school rang to say Emma had been taken to a hospital emergency ward. At home, the night before, she had consumed a packet of twenty-four painkillers, then went to bed. Early the next morning, before she left for school, she took a second packet of twenty-four painkillers.

Our new hope melted.

We no longer had painkillers in the house, so we didn't know where she had got them. Frighteningly, each overdose was becoming larger and the fact that she had gone to sleep after taking twenty-four tablets – for a second time – showed a bolder disregard for living. Emma was given the charcoal antidote and eventually discharged from hospital.

Distress and desperation moved back into our house. We were witnessing yet another downturn.

On a doctor's recommendation, Emma had a test to check for liver damage. Nursing staff told us that although she survived the overdose, her liver could be in danger. Our daughter could still die a painful death. Luckily the test came back clear. Eight days later, Emma overdosed on painkillers again, was readmitted to hospital and discharged once more. A week later, she was readmitted to the hospital adolescent psychiatric unit.

Anthony and I spoke to Emma's psychiatrist, expressing our confusion and concern. Emma had been happy . . . and then two overdoses in nine days. We were in the adolescent unit near the kitchen, a chance meeting, not an organised counselling session, when he said almost in passing: 'She's displaying all the symptoms of someone who has been sexually abused.'

Said in this way, his words caused further confusion and my mind fumbled with them. We both fought to comprehend them. In Emma's first admission, this same psychiatrist told us Emma was displaying all the symptoms of anorexia but was not 'a true anorexic'. So when he made this latest assessment we thought it was yet another dysfunction among all the other dysfunctions. But more mind-numbing was the shock of him mentioning the term 'sexual abuse'. The psychiatrist said nothing further to enlighten us, moving the conversation on, overriding our stunned and confused silence.

Anthony and I later discussed his statement (why is she displaying symptoms of someone who has been sexually abused when she hasn't been?) and relayed it to our independent psychologist the same day. On hearing all we said she explained that she believed the psychiatrist was saying he believed Emma *had been* sexually abused, not just showing the symptoms. We were silent again, absorbing her words and meaning.

Without pause she went further: 'I concur with his opinion. I would say that Emma isn't just showing signs of someone who was sexually abused. I would say she *was* sexually abused. In fact, her behaviour suggests it happened repeatedly.'

Repeatedly? We just sat there. Comprehending this was almost impossible. After the shock of hearing this, the psychologist then said we needed to think about who in Emma's life could have been the perpetrator. It seemed unbelievable but we had to start to think. Who could have done this? We had taken such care to protect the girls. How could this have happened? When? We kept our daughters safe.

In life you sometimes have discussions you never imagined would take place. Now, sitting in a room with a psychologist, we started going through names of people. Finally, coming to my senses – I felt this was ridiculous – I told her I could not believe it was any male relative or friend. Still, with a rising feeling of distress and sickness in my throat we then began to sift through old memories and occasions where sexual abuse could have occurred.

Repeatedly?

Old swimming lessons . . . old school holiday activities . . . old what? We didn't know. It was beyond us. We couldn't come up with anyone, any time, any circumstances. I could see no cracks in our diligence, nothing slipping under our security, no opportunity within our sheltering. I believed I had never allowed anyone the chance to get past my protective glance. And yet it had happened.

In the middle of our sickening discussion, Anthony suddenly groaned with realisation, his head thrown back, looking at the ceiling. In a tight voice he said to the psychologist: 'What if I told you Emma was the favoured child of a paedophile who is currently in prison?'

The psychologist replied that it would probably be the man we were looking for. Anthony then explained all about our disgraced parish priest. My husband and the psychologist seemed convinced that O'Donnell was the offender but I was not. I had already processed my fears of exactly this situation and made it impossible in my mind. How could it have been O'Donnell? More importantly, when could O'Donnell have abused her *repeatedly*? Emma never hung around the presbytery like the older boys did. She never went away for the weekend with him to his holiday house. O'Donnell had only twice been to our home in the eleven years we had been part of the parish, firstly when we had just shifted into Oakleigh. Emma was only a newborn baby when he had stood at the front door, a little old man, introducing himself as our parish priest, but he did not enter the house. The second time, almost eleven years later when he was close to retirement, Emma was in grade 5. He visited for a short while but I was with him the whole time he was inside our home. As far as I knew and as far as I could see, she was never alone with him.

Emma was always at home, at school or attending other activities, which did not include Father Kevin O'Donnell.

And Emma had said 'no'. I had clung to that one word. I had built my argument against this heartbreaking possibility of her saying 'no'.

We did not disclose to anyone our session discussions about O'Donnell, choosing to keep such an accusation to ourselves. Emma would have to tell us if this was the case. In the meantime, despite the fact I was still not fully convinced, our independent psychologist contacted the Catholic Church, arranging a meeting for us with a representative, a psychologist priest, to discuss our case. We met him early in March 1996.

Our complaint was readily accepted after one meeting and the Church then paid for our private psychology sessions. They didn't even ask to see Emma or expect a disclosure from her. It was so easily and quickly done. Years later I had to ask myself 'What did they already know that we didn't?'

Even though we had private health insurance, Medicare met all Emma's medical and psychology needs, so the Church at that time did not pay for her medical care.

I still attended mass each Sunday, as I had done all of my forty years, with a two-year exception in my youth, when I tired of the Catholic Church's iron grasp on my life. I prayed in vain for Emma's recovery. Her state deteriorated.

With my half belief about O'Donnell being Emma's abuser, we began to look into paedophile priests and the Church's actions in these matters – such serious, shameful, distressing cases, and the apathetic or sometimes hostile Church reactions.

How could priests behave in such a way? I was sitting on a fence, about to fall. Perched there afraid to move. But still Emma had not named her abuser. At mass I was beginning to feel out of place. Gone was the comfort I once felt, the peace that once enveloped me. Acid rain was falling from the Church onto my parched soul. The words said at mass, once so essential, now eroded into something hollow, which held little meaning. In fact, they had become a form of mockery, a sick joke; I was the first to believe, the first to trust, the last to know, the biggest sucker.

We saw this man O'Donnell as he was, with his grumpiness, his rudeness, his angry and abusive outbursts, his strange behaviour. Yet still we trusted. We did nothing to defend our children because we trusted and were blinded. We all saw the faults but felt obliged to overlook his shortcomings because HE WAS OUR PRIEST. We put up with it because we had no choice. He was our only way to God.

Chapter 6
The disclosure

'*C*oke *makes me drunk.*'

The words sat dormant in my mind for years. Emma had said them happily to other children. I assumed it was a reaction to the drink's effervescence. But those four words, never fully comprehended, stayed with me, accompanied by an everlasting, seemingly inert question: Where did she get the Coke that made her drunk?

I overheard Emma and Katie talking about it one day when they were about twelve and ten.

'Would you like a drink of Coke?' Katie asked her older sister. By then my opposition to sugary soft drinks had lapsed.

'No,' Emma replied. 'I don't like the taste of it.'

'You should like it,' Katie insisted. 'It tastes nice.'

'Okay, I'll have a try.' Emma relented and took a sip. 'Mm . . . it tastes different. It's okay.' She sounded surprised but refused another sip.

A couple of years later, in February 1996, Emma and I were talking late one night when out of the blue Emma said, with a confused look on her face: 'Coke used to make me drunk but now it doesn't.'

That night my subconscious must have gathered all the threads of those strange conversations, maybe even making me dream about them, because early the next morning I awoke suddenly, instantly alert, the series of Emma's comments and actions no longer confusing, their true meaning shining at me out of the darkness.

'Makes me drunk . . . now it doesn't . . . it tastes different.' Fall over drunk; unconscious drunk.

O'DONNELL.

The old man, in private, had laced some of his greatly sought after cans of Coca-Cola. I was sure of it. Or was I? To all appearances he gave the drinks only to boys. O'Donnell was friendly to Emma. I could see he liked her and being a girl, it spoke volumes. But I'd never seen him give her Coke; she had never said he did but . . . suddenly, it was obvious. It all fitted. He had sedated her. The power of this realisation sent icy shivers through my veins. The questions I started asking myself then became sparks in a powder keg. What had he done? What did he use? Had he put alcohol in the Coke? Emma's childhood words and actions now became clear truths instead of child's play, allowing me to further question and make sense of the past. I went to Anthony.

'One day Emma had said to Katie it *tasted different* when she tried it *at home* and last night she said to me that it used to make her drunk but now it doesn't. She was confused by the difference. This morning the penny dropped. I think O'Donnell gave her Coke with alcohol in it to make her drunk while he sexually assaulted her.'

A distressed sound escaped Anthony, as it had done when he first realised O'Donnell was Emma's likeliest attacker.

I added, buoying my argument, 'It all makes sense. O'Donnell and his cans of Coke around the church buildings, giving it to his special boys. Where did Emma get the Coke from that made her drunk? Not anyone I know. She even acted out the effects the Coke had on her by falling over in an unconscious heap.'

Anthony seemed doubtful, but I was convinced. 'It all fits. Poor Emma. What has he done to her? What did she suffer? Maybe she doesn't remember what happened.'

Later that morning, without telling Emma about my realisation, I reminded her about her comments from the previous evening and asked: 'What sort of drunk did the Coke make you feel?'

She considered it thoughtfully.

'Very drunk and dizzy and it made a loud noise in my ears.'

I felt an invisible noose tightening around my throat. A loud noise in her ears . . . the effect sounded serious and hearing those words frightened me. All this time the clues had been there but I didn't even think there was a mystery to be solved. Suddenly I understood Emma had been speaking of her actual experience.

I'm a very curious person. All the way through Emma's illness I asked *why*. Without the why there was no answer and we needed an answer to stop her pain, to save her. Asking *how* was almost as important and that's why the mystery of the Coke dogged me so. A crime was committed and that crime had to be dealt with; not left to fester. I had to unravel the years of secrets, a whole parallel life my girl had had forced upon her. Questions created more questions and I pursued each until I reached a dead end, or no more questions were left. I also had to know exactly what happened so I could understand Emma's suffering and give her the attention she needed. I had to try to counter the damage with my love. I didn't want to know explicit details – that was too hard for her to talk about – but I needed to know what surrounded the assaults, the paedophile's access, all his deceitful tricks, cover-ups and lies. I searched for the truth – it had to be found and exposed.

I waited for a day when Emma's ongoing anger and stand-offishness abated, then pressed her for details of where it was she used to get drunk on Coke. Anger flared instantly at my question. Resentfully, she said: 'In the school hall. All right!' Her reply confirmed what I thought. I had to get everything concrete in my mind and everything led to O'Donnell. But I was making Emma upset and so didn't mention it again. It was difficult to talk to her about anything.

The Savi Report released in 2002 stated that only three per cent of sexual assault victims will ever tell of their abuse, so we were lucky to have as much knowledge as we did, and to know what was causing all this trouble. But keeping the pieces of our family together was becoming more and more difficult. As much as I wanted to know more about her assaults, I resolved that I knew enough to take action. I was convinced Emma would tell more of her ordeal when she was ready.

Following an overdose, a wrist, arm or leg cutting, she was always calmer, as if an internal pressure valve had been released. The act of hurting herself somehow let go of the tension that had been building up. After one particular overdose, when I visited her at the Monash Medical Centre, Emma spoke to me for the first time about O'Donnell.

'He sometimes took me into the school hall and gave me Coke,' she said, looking hopeless and faint. 'Sometimes it was just me and him but sometimes boys from school were there too.' But still there was no actual mention of any sexual assault. I listened, but decided not to push her. She would tell me more when she could.

Four days later, I took her for more blood tests. Liver damage was still a real threat. This was her second such test and the results came back clear. Psychologist appointments continued to occupy us all as we searched for a way to glue our broken girl together. I told the specialists about the connection between Emma, O'Donnell and the soft drink.

Emma's psychiatrist, from the hospital's adolescent unit, stonewalled: 'She hasn't spoken to me about that and I won't be able to ask her about it until she feels comfortable enough to bring it up in one of our sessions.'

It created more frustration because Emma had refused to confide in the psychiatrist all along. Meanwhile, Emma was dangerously out of control and we were fumbling for ideas to keep her safe. We could do nothing to contain her wild emotions. She was always one step ahead of us, walking a tightrope of the unexpected, the unimaginable. Unprepared for anything, we could only react in horror after the event and deal with the consequences. The more controls we put in place, the more complicated and restrictive life became. It felt as if we were trying to contain buckets of water in our ineffectual hands.

Emma was in her second admission at the psychiatric unit for teenagers. At least she would be safe and our frayed nerves, and those of our younger daughters, could find momentary respite.

At the same time, the police were hearing more complaints against O'Donnell and Anthony rang a police liaison officer familiar with the case.

My husband asked the question straight out: 'My wife has told me she thinks O'Donnell might have made Emma drunk when he sexually assaulted her.'

I saw Anthony's face turn white as he listened to the policeman's response.

He paused.

Then Anthony started repeating the words he was hearing, so I knew what was being said.

'He used to *drug* kids, it was part of his MO?' His modus operandi. He was a career criminal, of course.

When I heard this I burst into tears. Anthony had to say a quick goodbye so he could hang up and console me. It was true. The priest spiked the drinks. The shock was in the policeman's use of the word 'drug'; she was drugged, not drunk.

My poor Emma!

Every step was an awakening for us, more crushing than the one before. We embraced each other as we tried to understand the nightmare. The mental picture being thrust upon us was of our young daughter rendered helpless as a grown man did what he liked to her little body. It was more devastating than any sight. If we closed our eyes it was more vivid. Guessing what had happened was very different to having it confirmed. It had happened years ago but I was living the reality of it now. Once something so wrong is made clear, you can never go back, you can never escape the knowing.

Emma drugged . . . It made me remember her inexplicable anger headaches, which caused her to have outbursts of ranting and raving over seemingly small incidents. She used to yell and eventually burst into tears, complaining of intense pain. I looked at them now with some meaning. Was my poor child suffering some sort of drug withdrawal or side effects? How I loathed O'Donnell and the hierarchy of the Catholic Church for choosing to keep him as a priest, despite complaints of his crimes.

I tried to recall other things said and done, delving into my memory, attempting to unravel what had happened, bemoaning what little information I had. I took the policeman's information to my GP. Because Emma had used the term 'makes me drunk' I had assumed alcohol was used but my doctor's opinion, given the symptoms Emma described, plus the officer's brief statement, confirmed that it was something more powerful. Firstly, the doctor rationalised, teachers would have too easily detected the smell of alcohol when Emma was allowed to return to class. Alcohol would have taken too long to cause the described dramatic effect. And such drunkenness would last a long time – longer than any school lunchtime.

'I think it was a sedative,' the doctor said. 'Something in the Valium family would have caused the things Emma talked about.'

I went to our chemist for answers. Drug names were suggested but I could not retain them. Anthony thought it may have been Rohypnol, the so-called 'date rape drug'. I thought about O'Donnell. I knew he was taking medication. Maybe he used prescribed pills as his weapon of choice. But it was a fruitless search. I never found out what he used to drug Emma.

Life continued, regardless of the crises. I did canteen duty, which was a monthly chore, at Emma and Katie's school. The kitchen had a serving counter with two pull-down shutters. At recess and lunchtimes, the shutters would be opened and we would serve the girls who stood in queues waiting for snacks. After morning play break we filled the lunch orders that came to us in coloured laundry-type baskets, removing the paper bags with orders written on them and money inside.

I was making students' lunches when I overheard one of the other mums speaking proudly about the pope and the Catholic Church. She was older, stern-looking and devout. There was zeal in her voice. I listened carefully, my rage boiling at every word, ready to bubble and spill over. All the things I had recently learned the Church had done to victims – silencing them, crushing them – with the selfish intent to save itself from scandal, came to my mind. Hurt children meant nothing to it. I didn't know until then the strength of my disgust at this religious organisation for its treatment of sexual abuse victims, my own suffering daughter looking more like one of its victims with each passing day. I felt like correcting this woman with the truth and adding that Church leaders should be ashamed of themselves. But I held my tongue and swallowed the anger. I didn't dare speak for fear of the tirade I would let fly.

All of a sudden I desperately wanted to leave but felt I was trapped in the canteen. I sensed the distance between these uninformed parents and myself. We were worlds apart.

I imagined their disbelief if I was to utter the words I wished to say and for a split second I experienced what it must feel like to be a victim, trapped by silence, like Emma, harbouring an awful secret that cannot be told. What was happening to Emma was sickening and so was this woman's ignorance. How do you convince the brainwashed that they've been brainwashed? I was now shaking badly and my vision was going dark. I felt as if I was about to pass out. Quickly and almost blindly, I hung up my apron and said I had to go. There was no goodbye or looking at them. Leaving the kitchen was a relief and I regathered strength as I headed for my car. One of the women was concerned and followed me out to see if I was all right. I told her something bad had happened but I didn't want to talk about it. I never returned.

Emma's stay at the psychiatric unit continued and so did the disturbing incidents. We arrived one day to be told that another teenage patient had tried to strangle Emma. The boy was over six feet tall and muscular (he exercised obsessively in the ward). When we saw our daughter she was very agitated but what stood out most were the many small circular bruises around her throat, where the boy had placed his fingers and pressed with great violence. I couldn't believe this was happening. Later, we saw the offender through a glass wall. He was upset, pacing up and down, and had scratches all down his arms, where Emma had clawed at him to escape his grasp. The staff told us that Emma had asked the boy to kill her before she changed her mind and fought him off.

We spent four hours trying to sort this problem out with the nursing staff. They said Emma should go to an adult psychiatric unit, as she was not safe where she was. I thought of the upheaval and disturbance of trying to find another place for her, or having Emma at home in her disturbed state while we searched for somewhere else. It felt too dangerous. I might lose her. I suggested that the boy who tried to strangle her should be the one relocated. Emma was fourteen. I didn't want her to experience adult psychiatric care. I bunkered in for an argument and refused to take her out of there. In the end, we compromised; Emma and her attacker were locked in separate areas.

Late one night, a month after Emma's admission, the unit called to say she'd cut her wrists with a broken bottle she'd found in the unit car park after escaping. It happened as a reaction, after revealing to a nurse she remembered O'Donnell taking her into a room in the school hall. She said the door of the room had a sign on it that read 'SHOWER'. Emma didn't need stitches for her injuries and we made an appointment to visit her the next day and learn more. This sounded like the beginnings of a disclosure.

Anthony and I discussed this possible breakthrough. All along, I had hoped Emma could talk about the assault to ease her tortured mind. I could not stop myself from being hopeful. She could be helped through counselling. Was Emma at long last able to talk about her abuse? Maybe this was the start of her improvement – a turning point. Up until now her resistance to talking was absolute; maybe she could let us get closer to her. We drove with haste the following morning to find out more. 'If she starts ridding herself of these secrets maybe it will lead to a cure,' I said to Anthony.

When we arrived we found Emma with the unit psychologist. Our daughter would not speak to us, her anger and distress apparent. The therapist wanted Emma to repeat her disclosure about O'Donnell's abuse but she wouldn't. When the psychologist asked if it was all right for her to tell the story to us, Emma nodded agreement. She wanted us to know but could not say the words. She sat huddled in a ball, perched on a chair, her arms hugging her legs, a sad mixture of fury and distress, both her wrists bound in white bandages.

The story was finally told, in all its misery.

Emma had said she remembered a door with the sign. She thought it was in the Sacred Heart Parish Hall, beside the stage, off a little corridor. She recalled O'Donnell taking her in there alone. Once inside, the priest sat her on his knee and hugged her. And then awful things happened. Emma had said it was a crime repeated often. She couldn't say any more. As the psychologist relayed this information to us, Emma nodded solemnly.

It was true after all this time; after this debilitating period of half knowing. The worst thing, my greatest fear, was realised. Grief and guilt burst through my mind to attack me. I told Emma I was so very sorry but it fell on deaf ears. Emma saw me as the religious one. I had sent her to that school. I had insisted that she go to mass. She knew it was all a farce. Father O'Donnell made it a farce. I was the one blinded by faith, who did not see what O'Donnell really was. Countless accusations presented themselves, all attacking me. I could take my pick of any of them and they all hurt.

She was ghostly pale and agitated after the revelation. Then she stunned us with her following request.

'Can we go there?' she politely asked. 'To see if the sign is there. To make sure it happened the way I remembered. I want to make sure I'm right.'

We said we would go with her soon enough, then Anthony and I went home exhausted. A cold reality moved in on us from that day. I had suppressed a lot of emotion waiting for the day Emma actually told me that O'Donnell had molested her. Thoughts about the Church's guilt, which I had barely held at bay because Emma had not spoken, suddenly became vivid and undeniable. I was enraged by the betrayal.

Now, many years later, I recognise this moment as the one when my whole Catholic conditioning fell away. When previously confronted with the truth of O'Donnell's criminal acts, instead of natural outrage, I could only turn it inwards and share O'Donnell's shameful guilt – his sinful smear had been wiped on me by the simple fact that he was my priest and I was Catholic. With Emma's disclosure, that all changed. I was now furious with both the priest and the Church hierarchy. It was only then that I saw them as a double-headed monster of deceit, previously masked well by the two-faced priesthood and a successful system of manipulation.

Of course it was just the beginning of years of disillusionment and anger against the paedophile priests who heartlessly molested children and the Church that kept O'Donnell and many others like him within its sacred parishes. My venom wasn't wasted. It was the only thing that kept me healthy for a long time. It liberated me and gave me the strength to fight what the Church would throw at us.

Somewhere just below the rage simmered a feeling of stupidity. I was forty years old and I'd never thought of a priest having a need for sex. No longer blinded, I saw O'Donnell as he really was. Not a holy man, not a representative of God. He was less than a man. He was nothing more than a disgusting paedophile – this was a new insight that changed everything. It was like somebody had thrown a bucket of iced water over me and I had woken up in shock, seeing things clearly for the first time. The truth was obvious to me now, but I had never seen it before. Previously, every newspaper story, every piece of gossip or suggestion of priests being involved in anything sexual, had hit a spot within me and bounced off. Now I could accept it and act. But my old, distorted view bothered and embarrassed me. For some time, I looked inward at this gaping and ridiculously childish fault in my thinking, this black hole in my adult logic and commonsense. I thought long and hard about the defects that limited my seeing the possible reality of sex and priests. Then I remembered where it had started.

It was 1963. I was seven years old and in grade 2 at my Catholic bayside primary school. Our teacher was a nun.

We were about to make our first confession and the nun was teaching us about sin and, among other things, the 'sinful parts of your bodies'. This term wasn't explained. Instead, it was left to our innocent minds to work out. For all of us I'm sure it left an ill-defined, pervasive feeling of discomfort and guilt. Perhaps this was where our 'Catholic guilt' – the guilt we suffer when we are not guilty of anything – was born. Our undeveloped minds were left floundering with menacing threats put there by the nun about something we didn't understand.

She described in a slow, careful voice the ever-burning afterworld, the eternal red-hot flames of hell, and the suffering we would endure if we sinned, broke the rules of our faith and ended up there. It was frightening. We little ones sat cross-legged, with our hands in our laps and our bottom lips somewhere down near the floor.

If we didn't quite grasp the nun's helpful description, we could look at a poster on the wall as evidence of what awaited the unrepentant disobedient boy or girl. Up high above our heads was a picture of heaven's alternative, with people standing in the fire and pain, begging for mercy or a drop of water. In the poster there were children, like us, looking frightened, parched and desperately clinging to helpless parents. But no mercy or cool water was ever going to come.

'No-one will give you water in hell, children,' the nun pointed out. 'So make your confession every week and do everything else you can to avoid going there.' I used to think the vivid picture of hell we looked at was a photo – that's how terrified and believing of the nun I was.

While looking into the eyes of the desperate people in the poster during this religious learning, the weight of the threat suddenly grew heavier. We sat silently in contemplation. Then we had a rare religious question time and one boy dared ask our instructor: 'Why don't priests get married?' It seemed an obscure question, even at the time, but we all listened to the answer.

'Priests have special blessings so they don't need to get married,' came the simple reply.

The only reason I remembered this question and answer, I assume, was because it became one of the cornerstones of my faith. In time, somehow, I came to consider this answer as meaning 'priests have special blessings so they don't need sex'. The lie had been handed to me at such an early age that I never thought about it seriously again. It just became the truth, a fact. For the next thirty-three years, through all my Catholic education and years of attending mass, the subject of sex and priests never again arose and I never reviewed that lesson I received when I was a child. There was no budging this deep-seated, unchallenged belief – it just was. Now, at forty, I recognised it as a lie, a brainwashing, blackmail even, as the taboo subject was tossed back into my lap in the form of my sexually molested daughter.

And all the ignorance was wiped away when Emma nodded as her story about O'Donnell was being repeated in that hospital room.

There is nothing like the sexual assault of your own child by a priest to scour the blinding Catholic scales from your eyes. Enlightenment born of bewilderment, disbelief, torment and heartbreak came over the ensuing years. It was as though we had fallen through Alice's looking glass and come out on the other side of the visible face of the Church; as if we had been transported behind the scenes of the Catholic Church. Gone were the colourful and grand props, the smooth and impressive fronts. Gone too were the values of truth, love and Christianity. They were all just facades. Backstage was a dark and cold void, a scary place that housed ugly and grotesque puppet masters who pulled the strings of all those who would dance to their tunes. We could no longer dance because our strings had been cut. We discovered this place exists only for people like us who won't dance. But it was they who had cut our strings.

It was chilling to understand that O'Donnell did not need my approval or permission to gain access to Emma. He didn't need to charm me or the other 500 parents at the school to secure time alone with a child. All he had to do was charm the principal and intimidate ten or so teachers.

His unfettered access was outside my knowledge – a secret back door – happening when I believed Emma was safe in school, safely dropped off for the day – where I trusted she was in class or watched over by a teacher in the playground at lunch and play times. This breach of trust applied to every child who attended that school, and all the parents who dropped their children at its doors.

I have not attended church since. Leaving was a simple matter. I feared not God. I knew whose side He (if He still existed) would be on, and it wouldn't be that of the rapist priests or their fellow priests and superiors, who protected and secreted the paedophiles. It was completely natural never to go back before them or their altar.

My mind drifts with bitter cynicism to a memory of being visited in hospital by a nun after Aimee was born in 1985. The nun was visiting Catholic patients and giving out communion. She offered me the host but I declined, saying: 'I can't take communion because I missed mass last Sunday . . . I need to go to confession first.'

She said it would be all right, as in my pregnant state I was probably too tired to go to mass. But in my mind I knew I was not sick and had just wanted a Sunday off, something I had not done before – not withstanding I was nine months pregnant, the hot summer weather I had to endure, and the two toddlers I had to chase after. I still could not justify my missing mass. My Catholic guilt told me I had sinned, that I needed to go to confession. I saw my sinfulness harshly and unforgivingly, as I had been taught. No excuses. I had missed Sunday mass when I wasn't sick.

Now I see it as a joke. I discovered priests had freely raped children for years, and their bosses had protected them and still they all participated in communion. Did they go to confession? Did they consider themselves sinful? What a farce. It was all a ridiculous sham. They had taught me to see my sinfulness in the smallest of things and yet they ignored their own damning rules.

I am done with subservience and I do not fear Church threats any longer.

As for hell . . . well, I've seen it. It was a small, deathly quiet room with a thousand shadows. And it had two shower cubicles in it.

The day we took Emma back to the shower room was full of apprehension. We arrived outside the Oakleigh presbytery and primary school and someone I knew was able to obtain the master key to let us into the hall and all its rooms.

Sacred Heart Parish Hall, which we called the school hall, divided the junior and senior sections of the primary school. Pupils in prep, grade 1 and grade 2 were taught in one part of the school, situated behind the hall, while the front entrance of the hall opened up to the playground for grades 3 to 6. The only way to walk from one section of the primary school to the other without going through the hall was via a walkway between the hall and the fencing of neighbouring backyards.

I looked constantly at Emma. She was nervous and silent. The person with the key opened the main door and we walked into the hall foyer, passed through a second locked glass door, and then Emma led the way into the main hall, past the stage and into the slender corridor. We overtook our daughter and went ahead along the narrow walkway as protection, a buffer from whatever was awaiting us. On one side of the corridor there were doors to two rooms. Emma looked. After inspecting the first door she moved slowly forward to inspect the second, becoming more hesitant. Still being ahead of her, I saw the sign that read 'SHOWER'.

Emma saw it too and started to back off, her face a picture of distress. She turned and fled. Anthony pursued her.

I was upset too but didn't move. I asked the person with the keys to open the door. I wanted to see inside. But the master key didn't work – it wouldn't open this one door.

Apologetic, the key-holder remembered what had happened. 'Father O'Donnell changed the lock on this door because he stored his Coke in here. It's a bit silly, isn't it? Who would want to steal his cans of Coke?'

I was left there while the appropriate key could be retrieved. Alone I stood, waiting, thinking, when a sick feeling seized my stomach. Of course the old man wasn't concerned about thieves. The career paedophile was being vigilant in protecting himself against potential witnesses barging in on him while he was assaulting a child. Who knows how many children he had taken into the room? Emma was certainly one. She would have felt trapped.

The bastard locked her in. She couldn't get out . . .

Instantly, my thought triggered a memory of Emma only a few years earlier when our bathroom lock failed and she couldn't get out. She had screamed and cried hysterically, banging violently on the door. She was inconsolable and, to my mind, too old to be acting this way. It was an overreaction but, nonetheless, her terror was real. The unceasing hysteria prompted me to rush and get a stool to stand on so that I could make eye contact with Emma through an etched-glass fanlight window, as my voice had no effect. Only with the eye contact did her terror abate. Anthony had to go outside and open the window so that she could climb out. We didn't understand at the time, but it was another instance of seeing the answer without knowing there was a question to ask.

We never locked our kids in their rooms. The doors were always left slightly open so the girls wouldn't feel isolated or abandoned. All our doors had low doorknobs anyway, so even toddlers could open them. Now I understood her behaviour and great distress at what seemed to be nothing . . . locked in the bathroom – the shower room.

The person with the keys returned and unlocked the door. I looked in. Facing me was a blank wall, a protective partition between the showers and the open corridor. Carefully, I took three steps inside to get a clear view. The whole shower room was very messy. On one side, there were boxes of toys and play equipment for the after-school care group. Centre-left of the room were two showers. The floor was littered with paper. I examined the layout of the room with one slow sweeping look and then departed, concerned to find out how Emma was coping. But I'd had my look and committed it to memory.

Emma was deathly pale and said little as we drove her back to the psychiatric unit. We dropped her off and explained to the staff where we had been. Our daughter later commented only that the shower sign on the door seemed smaller than she remembered.

I couldn't get the feeling of the room out of my mind. It was ideal for O'Donnell. It was secluded, off limits to students and teachers, usually locked and positioned between senior and junior schools. If he was ever questioned about leading children into the nearby hall he could say he had a job for them to do. But, really, who was in a position to question the grumpy old man of God? The room's windows were strokes of luck for the priest who was a paedophile. High and extending some sixty centimetres down from the ceiling, they were glazed with thick-wired glass, the type that cannot be seen through, even if you did use a ladder to reach them. The windows shielded the safe room for his assaults. No-one could see them. No-one could hear them.

Come to think of it, the whole school was an experienced paedophile's paradise. With a room in which to commit heinous crimes and the power to roam free among three hundred students aged between five and twelve years of age, initiating rules whereby he could take any of them out of class or off the playground whenever he wanted, plying them with debilitating drugs inside sugary drinks, O'Donnell was like a bank robber with unabated access to the safe – and no fear of leaving fingerprints. Only he wasn't robbing anyone of cash. He was stealing innocence and trust, the opportunity to live happily. Fifty years of practice will make anyone an expert in a chosen field.

I thought about the nun's lesson all those years ago. I wanted to wind back the clock and shout at her: 'He didn't need to be married because he could satisfy himself in seclusion with children. And it wasn't because he had a special blessing. Goddamn him and all who protected him.'

On the way home, I started to think about crimes against children. The term 'sexual abuse' was annoying me the more I heard it. It was an ambiguous description of what actually happened. Through the seriousness of the abuse and my daughter's grim face, I could better recognise what had crippled her – *sexual assault*! If the same assaults were to happen to a woman at a workplace it would not be called sexual abuse. It would be sexual assault. Too much pain and suffering can be covered up by a lesser term. Unless we call it what it is, we cannot hope to act swiftly and aggressively enough to stop it happening again.

I also started to take offence at attempts to minimise the shock of ongoing child sexual assault by calling the criminal assaults 'fondling', 'caressing', 'affectionate touching', 'over-familiarity' or 'inappropriate behaviour'. Offenders and their defenders use these soft descriptions to mislead or seduce the uninformed. The aim is to cause confusion or win sympathy for their crimes. Some paedophiles even suggest the child has led them astray. O'Donnell did. We need to know enough to be able to reject any such excuses, so that we can act immediately against these criminal offences.

We continued with counselling sessions at the unit. We discussed Emma's disclosure and the cutting of her wrists. It all led nowhere. Emma closed up again and moved back into her silent world.

I was filled with trepidation again when I started recalling two family sessions with the unit psychiatrist. Katie was behaving oddly. I had noticed her in the background when the attention was on someone else. She drew her legs up and sat in a ball, much like her sister did at stressful times but cradling a small toy or building block from the toy box that sat in the corner. She held the toy up to her eyes, rotating it quickly without really seeing it. The first time I witnessed this I was puzzled. I had never seen regression before but had read or heard about it. The second time it happened was in a session with several psychologists behind a mirrored wall, observing our family. As soon as the session was over I went into the observation room to ask the experts what they thought of Katie's behaviour, but none of them had noticed anything; perhaps not a very observant family observation. After Emma's disclosure I worried more about this regression in our second daughter, who was only twenty months younger than Emma. I wondered whether it meant that O'Donnell had also assaulted Katie. We arranged another family session but once Katie found out it was to concentrate on her behaviour, she purposely avoided any regression and denied the priest had assaulted her.

'No. It didn't happen.'

That was that. But I was still worried. Emma had said 'no' too.

Under no circumstances would Emma return to Catholic schooling. Catholic anything was now out of the question – they had done enough harm. Anthony and I found another school for her, eight kilometres from home. But we had to go through an interview before she was accepted. She wore a long loose cardigan, which purposely covered her bandaged wrists. She was as pale as ever and a little nervous. But the discussion was relaxed and the principal showed us around the open school grounds, which were leafy and green. Emma liked the peacefulness. We drove her back to the unit feeling positive, but the staff said there was some unrest with the boy who had tried to strangle her. They advised us to take Emma home and we did.

That evening, we received a phone call from the unit saying that same boy had escaped and was thought to be heading to our house to see Emma. The police were notified and started looking for him. I was scared, so we all stayed up hoping to hear some positive news from the unit.

At about eleven-thirty I went to check on Emma in her room. I stopped dead in her doorway as I saw the teenager from the unit outside her window. It was raining and he was soaking wet, and talking to our daughter through the window.

'Can I come in?' he said, looking at me.

'Go to the front door,' I instructed. We talked through the fly-wire screen and he seemed calm so we let him in. He insisted he would return to the unit without protest but wanted to talk to Emma first. We rang the unit and they said someone would come to pick him up.

The doorbell soon rang and we expected nursing staff but it was four police officers. They had received a serious warning in regards to the youth. We explained the situation to them as they stood on the verandah. The boy was left talking to Emma inside, under Anthony's close watch. The police agreed to stay as long as it took for someone from the unit to retrieve the runaway.

I stood outside, speaking to one of the friendly officers. He listened to my description of Emma's problems. I told him why she was in the psych unit, as I didn't think it fair that people thought there was something mentally wrong with her. The policeman's full attention was grabbed when I mentioned Sacred Heart and Father O'Donnell. He looked at me with empathy. He was once an altar boy at Sacred Heart, he explained.

'O'Donnell used to put me on his knee and kiss me,' said the officer.

'What happened then?' was all I could think to say.

'One day I made a mistake in mass and he took me out to the sacristy and beat me. After that he never came near me again.'

I was relieved for him and he appeared to consider himself a lucky man.

'But he sexually abused one of my friends,' he added. 'We found that out later.'

Within minutes, the unit staff arrived and took the youth away.

The young officer's story was the first of many we would hear from people when we talked about our family's experiences.

The following day I rang our parish priest, O'Donnell's replacement, and invited him to our home. We informed him of Emma's disclosure, and that this had been the cause of all her pain over the past twelve months. He was saddened by the news and concerned, which was appropriate, but on leaving the house, as we followed him down our hallway, he said: 'Don't tell anyone.'

Anthony and I just looked at each other. What? Until when? Forever? But there was no more to the instruction.

It was very much the wrong message to give us because we knew it was the same message the Church was forever telling victims and parents. 'Don't tell anyone' – just like the paedophile whispers into the ear of the child. It was the Church's old reliable form of containment – relying on the faithful to obey the instruction. And it had worked very well for the priests and their hierarchy in the past.

The priest had just undone the compassion that he had earlier shown us. His demand for our silence stirred in me not only anger but a lifetime of influence from my mother to counter my Catholic brainwashing. She had brought me up on the saying 'Evil prevails when a good man keeps his mouth shut'. The priest's and my mother's words now clashed.

The priest lost.

As soon as the Father left, I walked directly to our telephone and one by one I rang all our friends from the parish whose children had gone to school under O'Donnell's reign. We now had a damning reason for Emma's behaviour and the source of her pain and we shared this with people who should know, in case they had something to worry about with their children. It was disturbing to everyone who listened. They knew it meant O'Donnell was sexually assaulting children in the mid- to late-1980s, ten years after the time that his most recent court charge referred to. He could have been assaulting children right up until his retirement in 1992 (which we later discovered was the case). We stressed to parents that they should look for behavioural symptoms in their children.

How could any of these important discussions between parents take place if we obeyed the Church's 'don't tell anyone' instruction? Our children, the children of Oakleigh, would always be more important than any Church secrecy or avoidance of scandal.

I made an appointment to see Emma's old college principal to tell him she would not be returning to this school. When

I explained the reason he took in a deep breath, stood up and began pacing angrily.

'That bastard!' he finally exploded, unable to contain his feelings any longer. 'You know I've written several letters of complaint about that man to the archdiocese.'

'Really?' I asked.

'Not for sexual assault issues but for his downright rudeness and verbal abusiveness towards some of my students,' the principal explained. 'How is Emma now? Poor girl. I really like her. Did you know that when she started school here, I asked her whether she liked our college . . . and she said quite bluntly that she didn't?' He smiled kindly.

'I didn't know that.'

'I admired her honesty.'

We left Katie enrolled in year 7 at Sacred Heart. Aimee was still in grade 6 at the primary school across the road and we decided to leave her there also. They both had long-time school friends and I didn't want to disrupt their lives further by insisting that they move schools. Looking back now, I guess my utter disillusionment at the entire Catholic system was not yet complete.

While Emma was waiting to see whether she was accepted at the new school she wanted to attend, her terrible times continued at the unit. One Tuesday, we picked her up to find that she had been suspended for a night (and sent home) for having appetite-suppressant tablets in her room. She said she hadn't been taking them; they were only for when she went home, where she felt she had to eat to relieve the boredom. Even though Emma was no longer critically anorexic and had put on weight, she was still suffering an eating disorder. She bought diet books and tried to hide them from us, exercised and wrote down everything that passed her lips, how many calories each item contained. Her thoughts on food were distorted; measuring her food intake gave her some form of control over her life.

Emma became experienced and resourceful in other ways too. She knew that to become intoxicated she could consume vanilla essence. Travel sickness tablets gave her a high, an escape. And Epicac syrup helped her to vomit – another method of weight control. These different forms of self-abuse came over time, one after another. It was almost impossible to monitor them. In the beginning I went to our local chemist to ask them not to sell her any travel sickness tablets, painkillers or Epicac but all she had to do was go to another chemist. I couldn't stop every supermarket selling her vanilla essence or painkillers. It was impossible.

We just seemed to be forever chasing after her, trying to help, stop or change what was happening.

In the middle of the mayhem, however, she received some happy news. Her new secondary college accepted her application. Anthony enrolled Emma at the smaller, more peaceful campus. We gladly paid the term fees, again holding some hope of a new beginning, believing we had finally understood and made the right decision to remove her from the Catholic environment. The unit wanted Emma to become a day patient only, over the school holidays, meaning she would spend less time in the nurses' care. The psychiatrist discussed with us the possibility of preparing her for such a progression. We agreed, and maintained Emma's doctors' appointments.

She and I went to her new school to buy a uniform and we bought her books for the remainder of the year, in time for her to make a fresh start at a non-Catholic school.

On a grey, overcast day in April we had to go out some-where as a family. When it came time for us to leave, Emma refused to come. I knew she was not interested in spending more time with us (we had kept a tight rein on her movements) so a decision was made to leave her at home for the short time we would be away. I left her alone with trepidation.

After thirty minutes, I said to Anthony: 'Let's go back. I need to check on her.'

We strode through the front door and I called to Emma . . . No response. With increasing dread, I yelled out: 'Emma. EMMA.'

Nothing.

After a quick look through the house I went out of the back door, shouting. It was cold and on the verge of raining. I scanned the backyard; still no Emma. I ran to the back fence and climbed over it, into a laneway. There she was, sitting on the grass, crying, her sleeves rolled up and lines of blood streaking her arms. I ran to her and helped her into the backyard, onto a seat, placing her down with my arm around her. I looked at her new wounds, multiple long cuts running down both her arms between her elbows and wrists, but the blood was now only dripping slowly and was mostly congealed above the wounds. I knew the blood flow was stopping but she would still need medical help.

Katie and Aimee had followed me in my search for Emma and were trying to comfort her, while trying not to cry themselves, attempting to be brave and supportive for their older sibling but not understanding why she had done this. The situation was almost too much – my three beautiful daughters, all suffering, all this pain, all this damage, just because of that disgusting priest and an uncaring hierarchy who let him be.

I wished someone could witness what we were going through. But it occurred to me that after all the weight obsession, self-destruction, months in a hospital unit, the hours upon hours of appointments and everything else, we had nothing visible to prove our pain. It was psychological torture, so hard to explain. I imagined that the Church would have been pleased no-one could see us now.

Anthony headed back into the house to get the car keys so he could take Emma to the doctor's clinic. I called out for him to bring me the camera. The hardhearted men of the Church would see the pain and tears of this day and the trouble we were in. When he returned, Anthony took three hasty photos as I explained to him why I wanted them. Anthony then drove Emma to our GP, while I stayed home with Katie and Aimee, consoling them.

Emma received three stitches to one wrist, the rest of the cuts were held together with special plastic strips. That afternoon she agreed to attend an already booked appointment with SECASA (South East Centre Against Sexual Assault). She was less distressed after harming herself and wanted to go. But the SECASA sessions were short-lived; after four weekly appointments she no longer wished to attend. Five days after her last appointment she cut her wrists once more.

We were lost again. After her disclosure I believed she would get better, but that was not happening. It was similar to when I'd taken her to the dietitian, expecting a cure for anorexia. I assumed the psychiatric unit would help rid her of depression and suicidal thoughts but that didn't happen either. Now the disclosure had failed to make a difference.

It was around this time I stopped praying for Emma to be cured, relieved, healed – because no matter how hard or how much I prayed she would still try to destroy herself. My whispers to God made no difference at all. It was hopeless.

And somewhere in all of this I began to think I had turned to stone.

Chapter 7
Accountability

The need for justice is vital, the fight for it essential, and the desire for its reward – peace of mind – never ceasing. I don't think anyone can know how unquenchable this desire is unless they suffer an injustice – the greater the injustice, the greater the thirst.

Anthony and I turned to familiar people we trusted in our desperate time. We were helped with love and support, a special privilege we were grateful for then and continue to be grateful for now. We had all known each other for some years, all with different histories, meeting in various ways, through nursing mothers' meetings, playgroups, kinder or just being neighbours, but we were bound tighter when our children started prep at Sacred Heart Primary School. We first gathered as an organised group when we created a parents' committee working to better the school for our children through activities, including weekend working bees and usually ending with a social barbecue. Our mixed bag of mums and dads had different talents and backgrounds but grew to know and trust each other, our relationships flourishing both in and out of school. The glue which held us together has never been pulled apart, and the shock of Father O'Donnell's guilty plea and, later, Emma's disclosure, brought us closer, as crises tend to do to people.

In those fearful times, parents of children who went to Sacred Heart under O'Donnell's cruel stewardship placed their heads on their pillows at night and stayed awake for longer than usual, wondering if they had anything to worry about. Had the priest also assaulted their loved ones?

But there were those in the community who seemingly lost no sleep over the revelations of O'Donnell's crimes. Even as late as 1996, long after O'Donnell was incarcerated, the opinion of some at our local church was that priests could not be sexual predators, therefore the victims must be making up stories. This faith-saving explanation was more comforting for them than the reality of the corruption of the Church; of child rapes and cover-ups; of God and his role in all of this. For the unspoken questions forever remains unanswered: What was God doing while His priests and bishops were committing these atrocities?

We, who knew the truth, started turning our minds to victims' claims. As a group of friends we moved as one and all defiantly took up the pen. Together we fought for victims and accountability. The first thing Anthony and I did was approach our parish priest about making sure O'Donnell was laicised (defrocked), stripped of his clerical status, which the Church had so far failed to do. We didn't know much about this procedure but we believed laicisation was the priesthood's version of sacking one of its own members. It did not sit well with us that O'Donnell, the paedophile, was still referred to as 'Father' – even though he was in prison with thirty-one years of child sexual assaults to his name.

An appointment was made for us to speak with a canon lawyer, a priest expert in the Catholic Church's 'legal' system, who, as it turned out, was from a neighbouring parish. He had white-grey hair and wore his all-black uniform with a white collar. I was anticipating a positive meeting with this man because I knew what I wanted and felt totally justified in making our request. If the Catholic Church had previously not known about O'Donnell's assaults, as it unconvincingly claimed, then now would be a fine time to show everybody that it was appalled by such offences committed by one of its own, and make it clear the Church hierarchy no longer wished to support the criminal. The Church could easily take away his 'Father' title to show the primary school students and ex-students that the Church sided with them, not their tormenter. But of course I lived in fantasyland.

The priest–lawyer entered the room and smiled at us in a formal way.

'We'd like the Church to laicise Father O'Donnell,' I said bluntly, but without aggression. 'His crimes against children make him unfit for the title.'

The canon law expert's smile broadened. He shrugged, saying, 'We can't do that.' I was not impressed.

'Why not?' I asked. 'He's confessed to molesting children for over thirty-one years.' Again the priest shook his head and smiled, as if I was being ridiculous for asking. I wondered why the Church had such a procedure available to it – written in its laws – if it was so preposterous and unthinkable to use laicisation even under these circumstances. When would be a better time?

Getting nowhere with what I considered to be an obvious case for laicisation, I argued: 'If O'Donnell remains a priest then when he gets out of jail he'll have to live in a retired priests' home. I don't think the other retired priests would be too happy to have a paedophile living with them. It wouldn't be a great message to send the public, would it?'

It wasn't as if I was requesting that a new law be drawn up for O'Donnell. It says clearly in The Code of Canon Law that priests should be laicised for committing certain acts, including sexual assaults of minors. The law has been around for a long time (which made a joke of claims from Church officials that child sexual assault by clergy was some sort of recent phenomenon).

My point only prompted more smugness from the canon lawyer. He treated me like a fool. It was a waste of time. The meeting had achieved nothing but irritation for us. I was beginning to despise these men who had made us bow down in awe of their holiness all our lives, but now at this critical point of righting a wrong, bringing about justice, being honest and upright . . . I was faced with this shielding farce, this brotherly protection. I wondered why he would be on the paedophile's side, defending him, denying my legitimate request. It only made me more determined.

I also started to wonder about something else, a curious Catholic Church rule that I had always found perplexing, in which we were told to call all priests 'Father'. My query related to a Bible passage I had read but until now did not possess the voice to second-guess. It was Jesus who said: 'And don't address anyone here on earth as "Father", for only God in heaven should be addressed like that.' (Matthew 23:9, *The Living Bible*.) Yet this is what they called themselves. For centuries, the Church has enforced followers to call priests exactly what Jesus said not to, regardless of the fact they chose not to be actual fathers. I can only imagine it was done to establish themselves as little Gods here on earth, which is exactly how we have had to look at them, treat them, honour them and trust them from childhood. With that title, they placed themselves above everyone who addressed them as such. What hope did any of us have with this set-up?

Soon after the useless meeting with the canon lawyer, our group attempted to gather possible victims' families together. I made a petition entitled 'A meeting of parents whose children attended Sacred Heart Primary School while Kevin O'Donnell was Parish Priest'. This petition was signed by thirty-eight of us and I sent it to our parish priest, Father Ted Teal. We requested that the Church address several issues, including the impact of O'Donnell's crimes on those left behind. Our aim was to let victims know they were blameless and provide them with any help and support they might need.

Our next small attempt at correcting an injustice was to have the child sexual offender's name removed from the 'Father O'Donnell Care of the Aged Fund', a money-raising initiative to look after the elderly in the parish. It was a fund that was talked about at mass – the name read out repeatedly. To know his name was being spoken in front of the congregation without discussing his crimes made me shudder and wonder why nobody else saw it as completely inappropriate and embarrassing. On the same day as the previous petition went out, twenty-two of us signed another petition to have the words 'Father O'Donnell' removed from the title. This time there was no priestly smugness. It was acted upon promptly by the parishioners involved.

As we set about changing the status quo, things at home were not improving. Emma's appointments continued, often three or four a week. She was going to her new school but overdosed again on painkillers and was readmitted to hospital for a few days.

Our next step was to organise a meeting of local parents, which we named the Oakleigh Forum. A preliminary meeting was held to discuss what we wanted to achieve. The Catholic Church sent several representatives to talk to us. One of them was Monsignor Gerald Cudmore, the Vicar General (business and operations manager) of the Melbourne Archdiocese.

By 1996, Monsignor Cudmore was being inundated by victims of paedophile priests from all over his archdiocese. Of course it was not just happening in our city. Cathedrals were being deluged all over the country. They were under pressure to respond to victims' complaints and explain the Church's inaction, not to mention the cover-ups. In Victoria, the police and victims' groups were hearing hundreds of complaints. The State Government had just released findings of a year-long investigation called 'Combating Child Sexual Assault', which came to the conclusion that the Church had covered up instances of sexual abuse and in doing so, was perverting the course of justice. The chairman, Ken Smith MP, said, 'I'm certain there's been a [Church hierarchy] cover-up in these issues and it would be an ongoing thing. I believe it would be occurring right now.' When asked whether he thought some cases involved conspiracies to pervert the course of justice, Ken Smith replied, 'I'd say yes, definitely, because what they're not allowing is a criminal offence to be reported to the police.'

Monsignor Cudmore, for his part, had set up a Church service called the Pastoral Response Office, offering victims counselling but strictly no apology. When he arrived at our Oakleigh meeting, he seemed refreshingly honest and open.

I was still trying to comprehend the Church's position and pressed him about what I saw as a poor historical response to sexual assault. He tried to soothe our anger with his explanation.

'We didn't know the effect it [sexual abuse] would have on children.'

This was their excuse? This is how they justified ignoring the criminal truth?

Was this an admission from the Church hierarchy that the Church knew about child sexual assault, but didn't think it worth stopping because they didn't know the effect it would have? What about the fact that child rape and molestation were against the law? Criminal offences with jail terms attached . . .

I didn't understand their thinking. Our precious children meant so little to these men who chose not to have children of their own, that they didn't lift a finger to protect them. This was an outlandish and damaging admission I thought would be lost without record. But when I reviewed the 5 August 1995 newspaper coverage of O'Donnell's court case, I found Monsignor Cudmore quoted on page four of the *Herald Sun* newspaper saying the same thing. 'I don't think we understood paedophilia, or the extent of the problem, in the spirit of the time.'

The 'spirit of the time' excuse was ridiculous. The establishment knew assaults against children were taking place. That was the point. The Church's claims of ignorance were not fooling anyone. That 'time' was the same as now. It held prison sentences for adults who sexually assaulted children. Such laws have been in this country since its white settlement in 1788 and for centuries before that in England. You can go back one hundred and fifty years in Australian history to find examples of people tried for such crimes.

In 1867 in Beechworth, a country town in Victoria famous for its nineteenth-century goldrushes and bushrangers, a Mr John Kelly was hung for sodomising a nineteen-month-old toddler. Newspaper editors of the era declared the crime unfit for publishing; even the execution was noted in a government gazette, minus the offences.

Sir Redmond Barry, the presiding judge, said, before he pronounced the death sentence, 'In this case there could be no excuse. It was a crime that even the beasts in the forests will not commit.'

The law 'of the time', reasserting itself eighteen years later in the statutes of 1885, listed thirteen offences that you could be hanged for — arson, sodomy, carnal knowledge of a girl under ten, laying logs across train tracks, the rape of a woman, under force or threat. How could educated men of the priesthood, more than a hundred years later, claim they did not understand child sexual assault?

As if this Church official's admission to us was not enough evidence of the Church's ineptitude, I later read a press release statement that the vicar general released on behalf of the wider Church. He described sexual assault and tried to give it a fanciful historical twist.

'Earlier, when the problem in both Church and society was poorly understood, such abusive behaviour was treated as a moral problem.'

This was completely misleading. When did society treat the rape of a child as a moral problem? We knew the police and judges did not excuse rape as a moral problem. And, over time, I understood that the Church knew a lot more about the 'problem' than it was letting on. In fact, if priests and bishops knew anything about the history of the Church, which I assumed they studied in the seminaries, they knew that clergy sexual abuse of children had been embedded in the Roman Catholic Church's culture for centuries. Documents dating back to the *fourth century* stated that the Church had rules against priests sexually assaulting children. Over the centuries, punishments included turning priests over to secular authorities, even execution. Canon laws followed, so priests would know exactly what they were not allowed to do.

An international expert on the subject, United States' canon lawyer Reverend Tom Doyle, summed it up best.

The bishops . . . have, at various times, claimed they were unaware of the serious nature of clergy sexual abuse and its impact on victims. This claim is easily offset by the historical evidence. Through the centuries the church has repeatedly condemned clergy sexual abuse, particularly same-sex abuse. The very texts of many of the laws and official statements show that this form of sexual activity was considered harmful to victims, to society and to the Catholic community.

Church leaders may not have been aware of the scientific nature of the different sexual disorders, nor the clinical descriptions of the emotional and psychological impact on victims, but they cannot claim ignorance of the fact that such behaviour was destructive in effect and criminal in nature.

Rev. Doyle has been a victims' advocate for twenty-five years, since the first United States cover-up scandal broke in the press in 1984. He has used documented evidence to back up his heavy criticisms of the church's ruse of ignorance.

At certain periods in the church history, clergy sexual abuse was publicly known and publicly acknowledged by church leaders. From the late 19th century into the early 21st century, the church's leadership has adopted a position of secrecy and silence.

One document Doyle points to was written in 1957. A priest, the founder of a US clinic that was set up in the hope of curing his colleagues of their psychosexual addictions, wrote to his archbishop:

May I beg your Excellency to concur and approve of what I consider a very vital decision on our part – that we will not offer hospitality to men who have seduced or attempted to seduce little boys or girls. These men [paedophile priests] Your Excellency are devils and the wrath of God is upon them and if I were a bishop I would tremble when I failed to report them to Rome for *involuntary laicisation* . . . It is for this class of rattlesnake I have always wished the island retreat – but even an island is too good for these vipers of whom the Gentle master said – it were better they had not been born . . . When I see the Holy Father [the Pope] I am going to speak of this class to his Holiness.

This priest wrote many such letters of warning to the Church hierarchy between 1952 and 1964.

We know Australian bishops were not in the dark. The Church is a global fraternity. Many of the clerics in Australia studied at the Vatican or colleges in the United States. Their networking is as effective as any politician's or multinational business leader's. They are not isolated by distance from the USA, Rome or Ireland, the world's great exporter of Roman Catholic Church priests.

Also, we were told for a fact that Australian bishops saw priests' convictions, victims' complaints and the subsequent public scandal coming, long before the rest of the nation started reading about paedophile priests and brothers in the daily newspapers. It was revealed in an insurance document.

In the early 1990s, the Australian Catholic Bishops Conference took out 'special issues liability' insurance. The 'Catholic Church Insurance Limited' policy makes for eerie reading. It insured dioceses and archdioceses against 'actual or attempted sexual activity with a child or any other person, which constitutes a criminal act' to a limit of $1 million for a claim against one person or $5 million overall. The Church's excess was $25,000.

The policy was issued from an office in Melbourne. This was proof the Church was concerned about the actions of its priests well before it decided on alternative money-saving initiatives. The insurance policy was terminated when the insurer said it would not cover the bishops against claims involving cases of blatant cover-ups by the hierarchy.

So much was known about all of this in the secretive halls and plush offices of the Australian Catholic Church, yet the paedophile O'Donnell and criminal cowards like him were left to wear the collar of God's representatives and destroy lives.

Our Oakleigh group was quickly becoming expert in hearing the excuses given by the Church leaders.

Not long after our meeting with him, Monsignor Cudmore was replaced as vicar general. In 1996, a documentary was aired on national television, in which he appeared and apparently misspoke, contradicting his archbishop. The ABC's *Four Corners* program, entitled 'Twice Betrayed', investigated from May 1996 the Church's fear of victims' claims financially crippling the Church. The documentary detailed the hierarchy's handling of paedophile Father Gerald Ridsdale. It produced evidence that his superior, Bishop Ronald Mulkearns of the Ballarat Archdiocese, knew Ridsdale assaulted children but did nothing to stop him; rather, he relocated the predator to other parishes.

But the *Four Corners* documentary was not aimed squarely at any particular priests or bishops. It was bent on exposing a disturbingly widespread pattern, detailing how the Church had offered victims a heartless national statement of regret, a letter read out in all parishes, but withheld promises of justice.

The statement said: 'We cannot change what has happened in the past, undo the wrongs that have been done or banish the memories and the hurt . . .'

It seemed a legally prepared non-apology. Monsignor Cudmore honestly interpreted the statement to the pressing journalist questioning him during the filming of the program.

'Perhaps you're highlighting a distinction between express-ing regret and saying sorry,' the vicar general said. 'And I think there's perhaps a difference of opinion over what those words really mean. I suggest, on the one hand, there may have been advice legally that says if you say you're sorry you could be held to blame.'

Later in the program, the vicar general contradicted his boss, Archbishop Sir Frank Little, when questioned about who was responsible for the criminal behaviour of priests. No less than thirty-five victims of sexual assault were suing the archbishop. The archdiocese, through its lawyers, was using typically hard-nosed defences to avoid paying compensation. In particular, the Catholic Church was claiming priests were not under the control of their superiors.

This was news to anyone who was Catholic! We had lived a lifetime of observance to the Catholic Church pecking order. The journalist on 'Twice Betrayed' asked Monsignor Cudmore how Archbishop Little could make that argument.

'Um . . . err,' Monsignor Cudmore struggled to answer. 'I'm not sure I understand what he said and why he said that. It's . . . ah . . . I can't explain that.'

'It doesn't make sense to you?'

'No, no.'

'And it's not a tenable argument as you see it?' asked the journalist.

'I don't think so. And I think that's been misunderstood because clearly a priest of the Archdiocese of Melbourne is under the jurisdiction of the Archbishop of Melbourne.'

Within weeks of the documentary being aired, Monsignor Gerald Cudmore and Archbishop Sir Frank Little were no longer serving in their positions of power. The archbishop announced his retirement and the Vatican promoted Bishop George Pell to replace him. Archbishop Pell then installed his long-time friend Father Denis Hart as the archdiocese administrator, the new Vicar General of Melbourne. Gerald Cudmore was sent back to resume serving as a parish priest. Although he was dutifully peddling to us the misleading line about naivety involving clergy sexual assaults, he was otherwise too honest about legal liability. I assumed he was being seen as potentially damaging to the Church.

Chapter 8
The Oakleigh Forum

While the Vatican sorted out its promotions and demotions in the Melbourne Catholic headquarters, we parents of Oakleigh eagerly prepared for our forum. We wanted a clear statement from the Church recognising, among other things, that Kevin O'Donnell *was* guilty of the sexual assaults he had been sent to prison for. We arranged for a psychologist to speak to us about situations that lead to child assaults, signs to look for in children that may indicate a history of assaults, where to get help and so on. This was to be followed by an open discussion.

The Church's Pastoral Response Office wanted to run the event. The Oakleigh Liaison Group, as we now called ourselves, was being sidelined. I was reluctant to hand over control of our forum to a Church department but I was under pressure to do so. The Church had ignored us for a year and offered no assistance to those suffering. We'd been cut loose to float about in uncertain waters. Now the Church would only help with postal addresses for our mail-out to parishioners – if we agreed to allow the Pastoral Response Office to stage our first big meeting. I finally had to let them do it for without the addresses, we couldn't notify anyone. They kept up their end of the deal and a thousand letters were posted out to all parishioners, giving notification of our Oakleigh Forum, the time and the date.

Broken Rites is an action group set up to demand justice for victims. In the four years it had been running it had received one thousand complaints from victims and was seen by the Church as an adversary. It was at this time that Anthony and I met with Broken Rites so we could learn and better prepare. We found the group's volunteers to be greatly experienced and informed in Church matters. We attended one of their meetings in an old disused railway station converted into a community centre. We listened to their stories and their aspirations. It was Broken Rites that first instructed victims to go to the police and not the Church with complaints. However, despite our common goal, we wanted to remain independent from other groups, for fear of the Church labelling us as the enemy. It would perhaps be a way for the Church to discredit us. We wanted to be part of the Church telling the Church. At that point I was still hopeful of a fair hearing.

In the meetings we held, my mind often went back to the rumour that O'Donnell had given to Church officials a list of ninety children he had molested. It was barely believable, but if true it could quickly identify victims, perhaps some of them still children, in need of help. We did not want to see or know the names but thought the Church could have used the list to assist individuals or, depending on their ages, inform parents of child victims. They could address the issue; take some positive steps before traumatic, self-harming lifestyles became ingrained.

The Oakleigh Forum took place on 29 July 1996. It was a large meeting, held in the parish hall and attended by two hundred and fifty people. We were well prepared and tape-recorded the whole proceedings. Later, members of our group painstakingly transcribed seventeen pages of notes and distributed copies. Vicar General Cudmore did not attend. We were expecting him but were told at the meeting he was overseas. Disappointment and mistrust were felt, as no high-ranking

Church official took his place and came to talk to us. Even the priest who chaired the meeting wondered why he was there and could not answer any of our questions. It felt as if it were a good ploy by the hierarchy to sabotage our efforts, and it generated even more angst.

Presentations were delivered from a social worker and a family therapist on child sexual abuse. Then, during question time, one of O'Donnell's victims rose to speak to us about his ordeal at the hands of our paedophile priest some fifty years earlier. With a flood of tears, he expressed his heartbreak at how many victims followed his horrible experience.

He blamed himself unjustly.

The vastness in ages of O'Donnell's victims was stomach-churning. The man speaking was close to sixty years of age and Emma was fourteen.

We sent our first letter to Archbishop Pell after that forum, informing him that we had received twenty new victim disclosures. We also gave him a list of twenty-four questions and points we would like addressed, including:

- How does the Pastoral Response Team feel that the healing process will be attended to in months when it has taken some victims ten, twenty, forty years to find their voices?
- When will Sacred Heart Parish/teachers come to me as a parent and tell me that Kevin O'Donnell had my child go with him during school hours without my knowledge?
- Why is the Catholic Church looking at pastoral healing and not the central crime? This is sexual abuse – a criminal offence.
- Why are priests who have been found guilty of sexual assault still priests?
- Why is the Catholic Church spending our donated money on expensive lawyers to fight our fellow Catholics, who, when little children, had fallen prey to a paedophile priest?

We submitted those questions with covering letters three times in the following months without reply.

Even though we received no response, at least the Oakleigh Forum started people discussing O'Donnell and his crimes. It was important. The Church called it 'gossip'. We called it learning.

Among the many stories being told about O'Donnell was one involving the 'cottage'. When I heard that word, my brain jumped on it. The story, I soon realised, was the missing piece in a puzzle from many years ago. Thirteen years earlier I had attended a playgroup in the cottage, the house with a room that had a mysteriously boarded-up window, a low-wattage light globe and a dirty bed. I listened to a friend tell us of her family's stay in the cottage, before O'Donnell retired.

The family had nowhere to live as their rented home was being renovated. It was the primary school principal who kindly offered them refuge. O'Donnell agreed to let the family stay in the empty house for a week. Seven days passed. The renovations were dragging on and so was their stay in O'Donnell's cottage. The old man was getting testy about it.

'When are you leaving?' he asked. It became a daily enquiry that he or his secretary asked the family.

The cottage had only two bedrooms. One was locked. It was the small bedroom I had viewed years earlier. The large family asked if they could use it but the priest said no. The children had to sleep in the lounge room. When the family was in bed with the lights out, at around one o'clock in the morning, a gentle but persistent knocking, described to me as a 'familiar knocking' at the door, woke up the parents. This happened on at least three occasions during the short stay. Each time, the dad turned on the porch light and opened the door to find a different young man standing there, aged in his late teens or early twenties. The light and the dad surprised the young visitors.

'Is Father O'Donnell there?' each of the young men requested with some hesitation.

'No. He lives in the presbytery,' came the confused and slightly annoyed reply. 'And it's the middle of the night.'

'Okay, sorry.'

I believe O'Donnell had a longstanding prearranged night-time rendezvous with young men. The parish cottage served for many years as one of his safe lairs. I can only guess why these young men went to that boarded-up room in the middle of the night, out of sight, the weak light globe telling nobody on the street that people were inside. Perhaps some of them were previously O'Donnell's child victims, who had turned to drugs and needed the cash.

I know now that O'Donnell repeatedly raped a child both orally and anally in that cottage during school hours. Just a year older than Emma and only seven years of age when the assaults began, O'Donnell sexually assaulted the child for four years. This child has suffered similarly to Emma in subsequent years. The secret remained unspoken for 22 years and the suffering continues.

A number of months after the Oakleigh Forum, four of our group attended a Parish Council meeting. One of us had organised to speak at the meeting. We stood just inside the doorway, having received an icy reception. There was no invitation to sit down. We made a simple, peaceful request: if any victims came forward could they be given our details to receive support and information? Our concern was only for victims and how they would be otherwise treated. Then one of us mentioned 'the cottage' and was immediately cut off by a nun, who had lived there since O'Donnell's departure. The once-vacant and neglected house had since been renovated for nuns to live in.

'We know about that room in the cottage and it's disgusting,' the irate nun said. 'It was a long time ago and we don't want to be reminded of it.'

We had made no mention of 'that room', nor were we going to, but it seemed the nuns had discovered the purpose of that dark, boarded-up room for themselves. There was silence. The other twelve or so Parish Council members showed no surprise or confusion at her words. Perhaps they had all discussed or discovered for themselves some of what O'Donnell got up to in the cottage. It made it even harder for us to understand why we received the icy looks, a cold reception and opposition to our efforts to help the victims, who may not be able to help themselves. Deeming it too uncomfortable or too 'disgusting' to talk about, then forbidding others the freedom to discuss it, does not make it go away or assist anyone who needs help.

After the Oakleigh Forum, a psychologist hosted a sexual abuse educational follow-up session at the parish/school hall, which I attended, as I did all other meetings relating to the issue. Still concerned about what I saw as Katie's regression, I asked the psychologist whether it was possible my daughter's independence could have protected her from the paedophile. As a baby, Katie had basically just fed and slept for the first few months of her life to the point that she didn't get to see or interact with many adults other than us. I often questioned whether that period formed her insular personality.

'Would the fact that she didn't take to other adults make her less vulnerable?' I enquired, hoping Katie's reticence meant she would not have gone anywhere alone with O'Donnell. But of course O'Donnell was not a stranger. He was somebody to be trusted and obeyed. The psychologist gave me no comfort, insisting few children, if any, could protect themselves if targeted by a sex predator.

My heart sank for my precious Katie. I hoped O'Donnell had not touched her.

My mother was distraught about the source of the abuse, having grown up in a strict Catholic household and lived a life of fearful obedience to Church and God. Feeling cheated, and mystified at the do-nothing attitude towards paedophile priests, she wrote an angry letter to Archbishop Pell, who replied to her three weeks later. In his letter he referred to 'a few errant priests who abused the trust placed in them'.

Errant priests? There it was again, such soft language. He made it sound like the priests made a typo or took a wrong turn down a street.

Archbishop Pell ended his letter to my mum with this sentence: 'I can only trust that through this trial, you and your family might find new depths of faith.' His letter only served to inflame already bitter feelings. Mum was furious and so was I.

Late in August 1996, Emma overdosed on medication and spent two days in hospital. Her education was suffering and during the third term she left the new school. We took her to an inner-city adolescent psychiatric unit, searching again for a new beginning. She joined a psychotherapy group and attended five days a week. We had gone from the public health system at no cost, to the private health system, where the sessions were expensive. We had health insurance but I believed the Catholic Church should pay for Emma's medical care and told the hierarchy so. I advised the unit to bill the Church, not our private cover. This was the first time we would approach the Church for medical expenses since Archbishop Pell came into power. So began a waiting game.

There continued to be a flurry of public activity over clergy sex abuse. Information sessions were running often. The Pastoral Response Office invited some of us to become part of the Victims' Advisory Group in preparation for the Melbourne Forum, to be held on Saturday 19 October 1996.

They sought our 'expertise in this development process', whatever that meant.

A week before the forum, we attended a two-day seminar. It was held at the Corpus Christi College, where priests were educated. A guest speaker was the late Ray Wyre, an international expert on paedophile behaviour and child sexual assault. Mr Wyre was brought to Australia by the Church to present a series of educational lectures. I studiously sat through all of them. Other mothers from our group also sat in on them. We were a band of women travelling around Melbourne, learning what can easily happen to children and about the profile of those who could stalk them. Those lectures provided a wealth of knowledge that all parents should possess, to enable us to properly protect our children against the paedophile we might know, for only five per cent of child sexual assaults are committed by strangers (CCPCA 1992), the other 95 per cent of offenders are known to us and our child. Mr Wyre stated in one of his books: 'It is heroic that any victim ever discloses.' I was again thankful that we knew as much as we did about Emma's assaults. I imagined many teenage children suffering for behaviour their parents neither recognised nor understood. The deadly secret would weigh upon those teens, further ruining their lives, but with nobody to comprehend their pain. My heart went out to them. They were like Emma.

At the end of a particularly gruelling and distressing lecture in the Corpus Christi lecture theatre, I felt physically sick. I would gladly have not listened to any of it but I owed it to Emma. Ignorance had let us down once and I was determined it would not do so again. I was waiting to catch up with a friend as all the seminar attendees started filing out. Most of them were priests. Looking past the sea of black, I could see my companion walking towards me, looking pale and distressed.

'What's wrong?' I asked, noticing he was shaking.

'I was sitting in the back row . . . beside three priests,' he blurted. 'After the lecture I looked at one of them and he had a strange look on his face.'

He explained that something in the priest's demeanour – a lack of revulsion, a lack of empathy for what we had all just heard – made him look closer. He inspected the priest up and down and saw in his lap the outline of an erect penis, right there in his priestly black pants. My friend was a child sexual assault victim of a priest.

'I can't believe it,' he continued, with eyes full of distress.

It was a shocking indictment. I felt like reporting the priest, but to whom and for what? A Church official would have just thought that I was disgusting to even utter the complaint.

The next month we held four well-attended information sessions for Oakleigh parishioners. Night after cold night, meeting after meeting, our friends left their warm homes to give of their time and effort to fight for justice. For all our children. We conversed, debated and learned, wrote letters, made phone calls and endeavoured to move forward a public consciousness through awareness.

With that in mind, one of our members had the idea of bringing in the local press to cover our efforts. A journalist turned up to report on our meetings and other events. Several days later our plight was on the front page of the *Oakleigh Times*. The headline read: VICTIMS FIGHT BACK.

Chapter 9
The Melbourne Forum

The biggest meeting of all was hosted by the Catholic Church at its city headquarters. Three hundred and fifty people attended the Melbourne Forum.

Surrounded by friends and family, I still felt nervous. After all, I was going to confront an archbishop. This in itself was a quantum leap for me. Never before had I done anything remotely like this.

Archbishop George Pell strode out onto the stage and took his seat before us, as did his companions, other Church leaders, all dressed in black with white collars.

All eyes went to Archbishop Pell. He had been enthroned as Archbishop of Melbourne two months earlier. He was rumoured to be doing a clean sweep of the archdiocese, creating a fresh start.

A man in the front row approached Archbishop Pell, who seemed startled, if only for a half-breath. 'Are you George Pell?' he asked.

When the cleric nodded, the gentleman extended some papers, a subpoena. He was a lawyer engaged by a victim of a paedophile priest. The archbishop did not accept the document and it was placed at his feet. The solicitor, who would spend several hopeless years opposing the mighty Church on behalf of clients, retreated and the audience fell silent, expectant.

A lot of people spoke that day. A young man, a victim, spoke of the sexual assaults he suffered in primary school at St Alipius, in the large country gold-mining town of Ballarat, the headquarters for a diocese that covered half the State of Victoria. The victim bravely explained to the audience that his nightmares began in the 1970s, during the reign of the merciless paedophile ring, which included Brother Robert Best, Brother Edward Dowlan and Father Gerald Ridsdale (among others). Each of these men was a prolific abuser of children. Ridsdale went on to become one of Australia's most infamous paedophile priests.

The victim said that he had been assaulted by Brothers Dowlan and Best. He later went to the Ballarat Cathedral Presbytery for counselling. Father Ridsdale answered the front door, welcomed the fearful child in – and sodomised him.

'Ridsdale!!' I whispered to Anthony as a curse, loud enough for a few people around me to look in my direction.

George Pell and Ridsdale had lived in the same Ballarat presbytery for a year in 1973. Ridsdale was a chaplain at St Alipius Primary School. George Pell was a curate priest at St Alipius Parish, but also worked part-time as Episcopal Vicar of Education, advising Bishop Ronald Mulkearns on educational issues.

In 1993, just three years before he was appointed archbishop, Bishop Pell walked into a criminal court side-by-side with Father Gerald Ridsdale (dressed in a hat, over-sized dark sunglasses and a religious cross on his tie) who was finally being brought to justice, about to plead guilty to thirty charges of sexual assault. The prosecution outlined crimes against only nine victims but there were hundreds more out there, quietly haunted by memories of their innocence being stolen.

After public complaint of his escorting the paedophile to court, Archbishop Pell stated he did not know his housemate was a paedophile when they lived together in Ballarat. He would much later explain his support of Ridsdale in court was given out as priestly solidarity. He said he had no idea of the gravity of the offences.

In his first sentencing, Ridsdale was given an amazingly light twelve-month jail term, with parole after three months. But more victims found the strength to go to the police and the following year – 1994 – Ridsdale was up on another forty-six child sexual assault charges, including buggery (rape). This time he was sentenced without Bishop Pell's supporting presence and he received an eighteen-year prison term.

The presiding judge, John Dee QC, wrote in his 2009 autobiography:

> Ridsdale was the very worst offender I ever had to deal with. I thought I had heard just about every terrible thing one human could do to another. Ridsdale, however, horrified me. What I found difficult to comprehend was that the hierarchy of the Catholic Church, being well aware of his sexual perversion, had never sacked him, but merely moved him from one parish to another.

A third court appearance in 2006 saw Ridsdale plead guilty again to thirty-five more charges, including buggery, sexual assault and gross indecency upon children. He has hundreds of long-suffering victims.

We sat in the audience at the forum trying to work out how Archbishop Pell could have supported such a heinous criminal. But we had to try to look past it for now.

The next speaker was Chris MacIsaac, of the victims' support group Broken Rites, which was determined to expose the behaviour of sexual predators within the clergy. She echoed the thoughts of many when she said: 'I still want to believe in God but I no longer believe in the Catholic Church.'

Heads nodded.

Archbishop Pell's face didn't move. He seemed determined to ignore the stares and pursed lips of the crowd. But he was listening.

When he rose to speak later he smiled deliberately and noted dryly: 'I'm glad you still believe in God.'

But did *I* still believe in the Almighty?

It was a difficult question to answer. Faith had been a big part of my life. As well as being raised and educated in Catholic schools, from my late twenties until my late thirties I continued to read the Bible almost daily. It was pretty heavy reading but certain phrases and quotes made me feel capable of dealing with troubled times. I believed God would look after my children and me.

I had read the New Testament more than once and was three books into the Old Testament when Emma was thirteen and started suffering from the crimes committed against her as a five-year-old. The Bible's passages that I had learned and studied suddenly seemed to mock me. I had trusted and believed in God, the Church and the bishops who ran it – and look what had happened behind my back. A priest had raped my child.

Now I was too busy trying to prevent my daughter from harming herself through painkiller overdoses and starvation. The Bible now sat on the shelf.

The new Victims' Advisory Group held its initial meeting in September 1996, five weeks before the forum. During this period the group put together ideas for the big day, one being a recording of our own verse or words to be played during a meditative pause. Each of us had a sexual abuse complaint against a priest, a nun who had given up her vows, another child victim (now grown up) and a teacher, whose job was lost because of trying to protect primary school students from their predator priest.

I tensed up when I knew my plea was about to be played aloud. It had taken six attempts to record. Each time I started, my mouth became dry and the words tripped over each other. I had never really had a 'voice' and this exercise confirmed it. Still, I persevered and finally expressed what I was feeling. Now it was time to replay my message to the packed hall of people.

'Sins of our fathers . . .' my voice began cracking and shaking from the PA system. The audience was hushed. It tore holes in me to listen to myself. 'By the parent of a victim . . .'

As I listened, I focused on the Church leaders to reduce my embarrassment. They appeared to be listening but did they believe me? Did they believe us? Did they think we were liars, inventing complaints? This forum was our chance to make real contact: to touch the hearts of the untouchables. If they heard our voices, saw our pain, maybe then they would believe. This is why I had come. I said:

It used to be that I went to mass every Sunday.

It used to be that I was a Special Minister of the Eucharist.

It used to be that I read the Bible almost every day.

It used to be that I believed with God's presence we would make it through life.

It used to be that I could believe in the celibacy of priests.

It used to be that people complained to Church leaders about our parish priest's paedophilic behaviour over the decades.

Nothing was done.

Now I stand in the blood and vomit of my suicidal child.

Now I find this priest has victims aged from sixty down to fourteen.

Now I know this priest is in prison and he is still a priest.

Now I read that there are many of these priests and brothers to be found.

Now I understand that the leaders of the Church, by leaving this priest in his position of trust, allowed him to retain his freedom of access to Catholic primary school children, providing him with a victim pool for up to fifty years.

People are dying.

Now I am told in the press by a Church leader that 'one or two lonely voices have suggested that the Catholic Church is in a state of crisis'.

Now I am told by the same Church leader that he trusts 'that through this trial my family and I might find new depths of faith' within ourselves.

We have been so deeply betrayed.

Now all I can say is – my God, my God, why have you forsaken me?

My words trailed off and the moment was frozen. I held my breath and slumped a little in my chair. There was no reaction from Archbishop Pell up on the stage.

There were more presentations; then questions from the floor. Victims stood, took the microphone and quizzed the archbishop about his response, crying out for his compassion. Under-the-breath grumblings grew into raised voices, all of us stunned by the lack of reaction from the hierarchy before us. The forum became adversarial. I remained quiet, for my part in the proceedings had not finished and I was becoming nervous again, awaiting my final contribution. I had written a letter on behalf of parents from our suburban parish in Oakleigh. They were parents whose children could have been assaulted in the 1970s and 1980s, and as late as 1992, by Father O'Donnell. In many cases, children were yet to admit they were victims, trapped in dark tunnels of shame and confusion. I asked someone else to read my letter aloud because I didn't trust my composure.

My writing was steeped in a deep sense of betrayal, with my love for Emma in mind. I wanted the letter to alarm those it was addressed to and inspire everyone else who heard it.

'*Dear Archbishop Pell and other Church leaders*,' it began. The audience was quiet again. The room seemed to be charged by electricity, as if a thunderstorm was fast approaching.

> In recent years . . . we have learned that although you oust priests who marry, you unflinchingly retain, protect, secrete and repeatedly forgive and forget the sexual abusers of little children.
>
> In expelling priests who marry and retaining priests who sexually abuse children you are increasing your concentration of sexually dysfunctional men within your ranks.
>
> You are gathering greater numbers of those who seek asylum and social credibility as someone who can be trusted immediately, without qualification, hence gaining access to the children they crave.
>
> Intentionally or not, you have been aiding and abetting these men in their atrocious crimes.

It was at this part of the letter that the audience began to clap enthusiastically. The tension of the words made the room shrink a little. I was sorry I was not reading it. I had arrived at the meeting frightened of my voice and now I longed to hear it. The reading continued.

> Because you refuse to oust, expose or be honest about offenders, we do not know who is guilty and who is innocent of these crimes within the priesthood. Your holy men have lost credibility through your secrecy, inertness to right a wrong and acceptance of these felons – the more you deny and remain silent, the more parishioners you lose.

We seek honesty and action to remove all known paedophiles within our Church for the sake of past children, present children and future children.

With the Church's knowledge of these paedophile priests, and leaving them in parishes with Catholic primary schools, you have undermined our authority as parents by removing our choice of exposing our children to paedophilic abuse or saving them from it. You have sabotaged our efforts to bring healthy, balanced and effective Christian adults into being.

The clapping increased. Everyone around us was applauding. Some were even standing and many were cheering. The reading had to stop until the crowd calmed. I again had the urge to take the microphone and read the letter with the passion and energy I had written it. I knew what was coming. I had created the sentences. I knew the words and wished to say them to the men I saw as responsible. But I contained myself and remained seated as the reader continued.

To these criminals, and they are criminals, you offer asylum so their offences are not brought to light. You offered support and counselling – ignoring the victims. You have made it, and done your best to keep it, a secret and not warned us – the Church and our little children have become victims. We, the Church, do not understand why you tolerate and keep blindly forgiving these priests who are nowhere near Christianity or its teaching. Many of them are not sorry and can see no wrong in their deeds.

We, the Church, say we don't want them anywhere near our little ones because it destroys them. We, the Church, are frustrated and outraged because we have no say in this matter. You, the Church leaders, seem to be unwilling or unable to say or do anything about this situation. You, the Church leaders, act and speak on our behalf to the outside world when we neither agree with your words nor commend your actions. Perhaps it is time for you to listen to the people of the Church instead of your lawyers; to listen to what has happened to our children, to listen and believe and weep with us.

Up on stage, halfway through this paragraph, the entire Church leadership stood up and walked away.

There were no nervous smiles, no acknowledgement or goodbyes as they left. I hoped they had been listening and that my letter had found its target. Maybe now they could understand a little of what we felt.

This unresponsive behaviour was repeated when I later posted copies of this letter (signed by twenty-two Oakleigh parents) to Cardinal Edward Clancy of Sydney; Father Ian Waters, Judicial Vicar of Melbourne; Most Reverend Franco Grambilla, Apostolic Nunciature of Canberra; Cardinal Carlo Martini Palazzo Arcivescovile in Italy; and Pope John Paul II, Vatican City. Not one of them ever acknowledged receipt of the letter, let alone made a reply.

The noise from the audience reverberated for a long time in my mind. I was mute witness to these remarkable scenes but I knew I had found my voice. From that moment I stopped fighting myself, my hope, my faith, my past. For the next decade and beyond, George Pell and the Catholic Church would be my opponents. Anthony and I promised each other to chase justice in time to save Emma's life. The pain we would endure would multiply as other emergencies and tragedies happened. But if we could rescue her from the trauma caused by that priest and his bosses then we would win.

It became apparent, after the event, that the purpose of the Melbourne Forum was not to facilitate an opening up of communication between victims and the hierarchy, for the establishment of supportive contact or ongoing dialogue. It was a one-off meeting for George Pell to announce the formation of what would come to be known as the Pell Process (or the Melbourne Response), a scheme for compensating victims. It restricted every Archdiocese of Melbourne claim of sexual abuse by parish priests to be handled by a system, installed and controlled by Archbishop Pell.

He brought in this new scheme just six weeks before the national scheme, Towards Healing, commissioned by the Australian Catholic Bishops' Conference, was introduced. It was a similar model but without the cap on payouts that made Archbishop Pell's scheme so unique and shrewd.

In stark contradiction to his statement less than three months earlier, at his enthronement, that there was no crisis in the Catholic Church, Archbishop Pell had managed in that short time to put together the Pell Process. If there was no crisis, why establish a system to deal with complaints about paedophile priests? If what we had seen so far was the full extent of the paedophile problem, if the problem had diminished, why set up a process to deal with it? Did they know how big this problem was going to be? Surely they had solid information before establishing both the Melbourne-based Pell Process and the Australia-wide Towards Healing. And if indeed it was a bigger problem needing two complete processes, wasn't it a bigger crisis rather than no crisis at all?

Both schemes are still active today.

Confusion and cynicism met Archbishop Pell's address but he had not yet laid out his entire plan. That came in subsequent weeks. Basically there were three platforms to the new strategy. Firstly, a victim's complaint would be directed to a Church-appointed 'independent commissioner', who was to investigate and decide if the allegation against the priest was valid. If he found it was, the victim would then move to the second section of the scheme, a compensation panel, which was to decide on the amount to be offered, of no more than $50,000 (although it was rarely that much – the average payment was $24,000, minus legal costs). Money paid was ex gratia, meaning it was given freely and had no admission of responsibility or liability of damage attached. The final section was Carelink, where victims would go to receive counselling or counselling costs.

I read about the new strategy in the newspaper and was instantly enraged by its limitations. How dare Archbishop Pell say that the sexual assault of my daughter and the lifelong damage it caused could be valued up to only $50,000? It was a paltry amount considering the crippling damages it was supposed to atone for.

But where else was there to go?

The Pell Process seemed to be hurried. It was now obvious to me that it was a financially motivated system that would save the Church millions of dollars. Of course, if the Church deemed you were to receive a payment, the amount would be determined by the archbishop-appointed compensation panel.

The 'Application For Compensation Form' states:

> The Archbishop will offer to me such an amount as may be commended to him by the Panel, provided I execute appropriate releases and discontinue any relevant legal proceedings.

Not only that, the signing of the document releases the archbishop from all further claims arising out of the sexual abuse 'or any other sexual abuse by a priest, religious or lay person under the control of the Archbishop of Melbourne'. So any future sexual abuse is written off forever; before it even happens.

By the mid-1990s, although many people had tried, no-one in Australia had ever successfully sued the Catholic Church. One particular solicitor (the one who used the Melbourne Forum as an opportunity to serve a writ on Archbishop Pell, placing the papers at his feet) was David Forster. He tried to take the Church to court with civil claims of negligence and found it extremely frustrating.

'The difficulties are enormous,' Mr Forster expressed in 1996. 'There's an argument being run by the Catholic Church lawyers that the Church doesn't exist as a legal entity. That's the legal position. They're not a company; they're not a registered incorporated body in the usual sense. It's saying it's above the law and [with] that approach it's acting as though it's above the law.'

The lawyer and many other solicitors could see no way around it. 'What the Church is effectively saying to victims is sorry . . . we're sorry it all happened, we know it happened but we're not going to pay any damages, we're not going to be responsible for it.'

And that was why the Pell Process was so effective for the Church. So many victims felt compelled by impossibility of choice to take whatever one-off payment the Church panel offered, even if it did stipulate it was 'for any amount of abuse, by any number of priests for the rest of their lives'.

Anthony and I were not satisfied with anything Archbishop Pell announced and did not lodge a claim for Emma. However, I still believed the Church should pay for counselling at the new unit she was attending as a day patient.

Another initiative that was being held up by the Church as a cure for its crisis – even though the Church still wasn't calling it a crisis – was the creation of a Code of Ethics. It was lauded as a corrective measure for abusive priests, but I failed to see the difference a code would make to a paedophile. In the past, no common decency, no mercy, no concern for any child, no threat of prison for their crimes, not even the promise of going to hell for their sins nor the wrath of God, had stopped the paedophile. What difference would a few more words on paper make? My concern was that the Church was standing on a soapbox and declaring it was fixing its longstanding problems by introducing this new ethics code. I thought parents who didn't understand paedophiles would believe the code would make things right and safe. Yet in private, the Church was telling victims and their families something vastly different.

I continued to find out what I could about O'Donnell and the Church's new systems of dealing with complaints, and in doing so I made a shocking discovery. I was talking to an official on the phone about O'Donnell's plea hearing in the County Court and the name Professor Richard Ball was mentioned. Ball was a witness for the defence of paedophiles. He gave the opinion in O'Donnell's case that the priest's diminished libido would prevent him from harming children if he were set free. He said nothing would be gained by treatment and O'Donnell had no inclination to offend again. However, the most recent accusation against the paedophile was that he had assaulted an eight-year-old girl two weeks before he was sentenced in 1995. A lawyer acting for the victim mentioned this complaint when he wrote in May 1997 to the leader of the State Government, pleading in vain for a royal commission to be established.

I was alarmed by Professor Ball's contention that O'Donnell was not a threat to children because he was old (and that he had not offended since 1977). Age does not weary paedophiles. In 2009, the Australian Bureau of Statistics stated that the most common offence for males aged fifty-five and over is sexual assault.

Professor Ball's other claim – that O'Donnell was contrite for his past behaviour – was also inaccurate and rightly rejected by the presiding judge.

Professor Richard Ball, as well as giving evidence for the defence of O'Donnell, also provided reports to lawyers acting for other prolific paedophile priests in Victoria – the worst of the worst abusers. I was told the Church paid Professor Ball for all these defence reports. The Church's lawyers used Professor Ball's clinical assessments to try to obtain lighter sentences for their clients.

I was furious to find out that Carelink, the counselling arm of the Pell Process, was run by the same Professor Richard Ball. I couldn't believe it. I grabbed the Melbourne Archdiocese brochure and there he was – Professor Richard Ball – or Dick Ball, as the Pastoral Response Office called him.

The Church thought it appropriate that the man they paid to write defence reports for their paedophile priests, to achieve more lenient sentences for the men who raped and molested our children, was put in charge of seeing to the psychological needs of those very same raped and molested victims.

Professor Ball gave expert evidence that O'Donnell had not offended since 1977. Why would O'Donnell stop in 1977 when he had enjoyed having sex with children for the previous thirty-one years? Our daughter's shattered life blew his professional opinion out of the water and here I was being urged by the Church to go through the Pell Process and to see Dick Ball about Emma's sexual assaults. I could not be in the same room as this man, let alone talk to him as though he had not worked towards a more comfortable sentence for the child rapist O'Donnell.

There was no way Emma, in her state, could have dealt with this system. I felt for victims who had to fight for justice alone. They could not achieve peace of mind. I no longer felt like I was living in fantasyland. I was seeing very clearly the reality of our dire situation.

I objected to Professor Ball's position as head of Carelink but was met with a reply along the lines of 'we have every trust in him' or 'we are happy with him'. They may as well have slapped my face.

The things we had to endure from the Church were both unjust and inhumane. Sometimes I think the whole push from the Church was to make us go away, make us leave in disgust, one by one, until they could claim there were no more complaints or victims.

I declared I would never go to see Professor Ball.

After the Melbourne Forum, our Pastoral Response Office meetings continued until I began to feel that we were wasting our time travelling into the city – only to vent our anger and frustration to someone who would then carry our complaint in a diluted form to the archbishop, someone we could not speak to directly. It wasn't through lack of trying. We had requested a meeting with Archbishop Pell for some months to no avail and we were left dealing with the Pastoral Response Office. We were caught in a bottleneck of energy, words and feeling. I was close to calling it quits when, in mid-December 1996, we received notification that Archbishop Pell would visit Oakleigh to meet with thirty of us on Tuesday 18 February 1997. We were surprised to find out that Archbishop Pell would meet with Anthony and me at seven o'clock that same evening, then meet the larger group immediately after, at seven-thirty.

FINALLY.

Meanwhile, Emma turned fifteen.

At the end of November she sank very low and was admitted for depression into an intensive care unit, a secure twenty-four-hour monitored suicide prevention ward. Our daughter was locked in there for five days. After that, she resumed daily psychology sessions.

A friend suggested we send Emma to a community school in the inner suburbs for the following school year of 1997. He spoke highly of the principal, who was running the school well and making a difference for the students who attended. We looked into it; Emma liked the school so we decided to send her there. The school had just two rules – no drugs and no violence. Only thirty students were enrolled and they all, like Emma, looked as though they had had an unfair start to life. The teachers were great and the students stood by and defended each other like they were family. Part of the school site was an old partially-demolished factory, adding to an atmosphere of it being something different. Most importantly, it was a *different* environment and at last Emma wanted to go to school.

Chapter 10
An evening with Archbishop Pell

I endured anxious days leading up to Archbishop George Pell's arrival at Oakleigh by studiously collating Church-related information about myself to present to him. It was my religious résumé to convince him I had been a committed Catholic – before all of this happened.

I gathered documents that I had compiled over several years, the written proof that I had given a great deal of my life to our Church. The curriculum vitae I would present to him included several copies of old Church newsletters, which named me as a 'Special Minister of the Eucharist', from the long period when I helped the local priest give out communion on rostered weekends. But I wanted to do more than prove I went to mass on Sundays. I wanted him to know I was a contributor on various levels, so I included my tax statements, quantifying the extent of my 'sacrificial giving', sums of money I donated weekly. I also threw in papers that illustrated I was an active member of organising committees. There were letters with dates outlining my position as secretary of the Oakleigh and District Inter-Church Council over five years. I had other paperwork that would show the archbishop I loyally went to the local minister's fraternal lunches, was one of two people who ran a baptismal program for young parents, and was an editor of our parish magazine *Heartbeat*. When I was pulling out past editions to show to the archbishop I thought the magazine's title was quite appropriate, for whenever I thought about his visit my pulse quickened.

I had donated my time and energy and I was able to prove to Archbishop Pell that I was on the side of the Church, not a troublemaking outsider. I wanted to convince him our case was real and that what was happening to many other children was the truth. These victims had suffered, were suffering, and I wanted to make the hierarchy understand what was happening. I wanted to enlighten them, starting with their boss.

The day of his visit went slowly. I counted down the hours until it was early evening. Dusk started to throw some streaks of colours across the blue sky and I knew it was time. I was ready.

Standing on the freshly cut lawn at the Oakleigh presbytery, I held my pile of papers, my proof, and tried to forget the butterflies in my tummy. I felt like I was waiting to be interviewed for an important job, rehearsing sentences and phrases in my mind, hopeful they would be well received. My questions were reasonable and my discomfort with the Church's position and attitude justified. Up until this point it seemed the archdiocese was standing by paedophile priests, supporting them instead of the victims. O'Donnell had not been laicised, although he had admitted his guilt, had been convicted and was in prison for his crimes. It was hard to comprehend the difficulty the Church was having in understanding the plight of victims. The new compensation and complaints scheme from Archbishop Pell seemed so very cruel.

I looked at my watch. Seven o'clock.

It was time to go in.

I sighed nervously as Anthony and I walked to the presbytery door. Anthony was silent, maybe also rehearsing sentences in his mind. Our parish priest, Ted Teal, heard us knock and opened the front door. He issued a welcome and ushered us into a small room at the front of the house. We believed Father Teal was there to help us, but I wondered whether he was a supporter of the archbishop. It was no secret George Pell had polarised the opinions of priests in Melbourne. His time as rector of the Melbourne seminary was controversial because he was a stickler for traditional methods and advocated a stricter curriculum. The Church, from Rome to Melbourne, was wrestling with relevancy and some priests were supportive of a less formal mass to attract a broader, younger audience. Archbishop Pell was not.

It turned out Father Teal *was* his boss's friend. They'd played football together decades earlier, while studying for the priesthood, and more recently lived at the same parish in suburban Mentone.

Father Teal left us standing in the small cramped room, strewn with old chairs and a dusty office desk – a real furniture graveyard. It was a peculiar choice for such a meeting because the rest of the presbytery, a large house, appeared to be otherwise unoccupied. We took stock of our surroundings. The only uncluttered space was one step away from the door, an area cleared for a small timber bench and a large grandiose chair. We squashed up on the wooden bench, assuming it was for us. I placed my pile of proof on my lap, ready to reference it when needed, probably at the beginning as an introduction to establish the foundation of our discussion. I sighed again as we waited for The Most Reverend Archbishop of Melbourne DD, STB, STL, Med, DPhil (Oxf), FACE.

Within minutes, a squeak in the floor made us aware of a presence on the other side of the slightly ajar door. Suddenly the handle shifted and the door was opened a little further. Then it paused. We still couldn't see anyone but knew a man was there because he asked in a booming voice of another unseen man: 'Are they friends?'

Seconds later a voice further away replied: 'Yes.'

We sat there puzzled, staring at the doorknob. It was Archbishop Pell of course but why was he asking his colleague Father Teal, at that late moment, for a short character reference on us? We had been asking for this meeting for months and the archbishop had plenty of time to research or briefly enquire about our character. He obviously knew about our case from the forum and our letters. The reason for his *Are they friends?* question was plain. It was his first power play. Pure theatrics.

Archbishop Pell stepped into the room and sat in the big, padded leather chair. There were no polite introductions and the mood in the room darkened. A discussion ensued that was both gruelling and unpleasant.

We had come for compassion but were handed confrontation. Anthony and Archbishop Pell argued, not with raised voices, but with sternness and determination. I interjected to make a point every so often. It was very intimidating.

I was glad my husband wasn't Catholic because he was able to speak his mind and demand answers. I was compelled into silence, being challenged and mortified by what was bordering on a hostile exchange with a person I would have once bowed before. At that moment I reverted to being a docile Catholic, my proof sitting on my knee as useless as it was heavy. I had not even had the chance to open my mouth before the verbal jousting took on a life of its own. I felt for my dear husband defending our daughter as he fought to get words out, trying to finish sentences under a bombardment of legalistic grenades, thrown so freely and confidently.

Anthony said softly, almost whispering: 'What if my daughter dies? What if my daughter harms herself in such a way that she has a terrible life from now on? Shouldn't the Church look after her? The Church caused this.'

George Pell countered by saying the Church's liability would be defended in court.

When Anthony mentioned the Church had known about O'Donnell's paedophilia for many decades, Archbishop Pell said: 'That was before my time.'

Here sat a doctor of philosophy, who studied the history of the Church at Oxford. Did this mean that now, as he sat with us, he no longer cared about the Church's past? He had been the archdiocese boss for a year and was saying that whatever went before was not important enough for him to discuss. By that rationale, every time a new archbishop sits at the altar, all wrongdoing is forgotten forever, or at least never spoken about.

The seemingly good traditions of the Church and the people it helped along the way are still welcome, but the vile acts, the cover-ups, the victims are forgotten or hidden from view.

We believed Archbishop Pell knew O'Donnell assaulted Emma. But Anthony repeated the facts for him, just in case.

'I hope you can substantiate that in court,' came the words that shook us most. Anthony winced.

'We are victims,' my husband pleaded. 'Can't you understand we feel that way – can't you understand that many people feel that way?'

The discussion moved quickly to the new scheme for complaints and compensation. Anthony said it was a cost-saving measure, unfair and to the victims' detriment.

'It might look good on paper but as people involved in this, as victims, it all looks very shallow. Part of the reason is we see this cap and we see these restrictions . . .'

Archbishop Pell interjected: 'If you don't like what we're doing, take us to court.'

'We don't want to. We don't want to drag the Church through the courts. We don't want this,' Anthony explained.

Anthony then outlined our opposition to Professor Ball's place at Carelink. 'The man who assesses whether we get Carelink facilities is the man who wrote the defence report [for O'Donnell and other paedophile priests] saying . . .'

Pell interrupted but Anthony wanted to finish: '. . . there is a conflict of interest there . . .'

I worked up the courage to speak but could only manage to say: 'Why is he in charge?'

'Because he was the best man available,' was the curt reply.

Anthony was pleading again but also demanding: 'This will go on forever. Now will the Church come to the aid of Emma?'

'I don't know,' the archbishop muttered.

'You don't know? Almost all the emotional problems Emma will have for the rest of her life will stem from this,' said Anthony.

I was anxious, feeling almost claustrophobic, but couldn't work out why. I wriggled again in my seat.

Archbishop Pell, like a tradesman who comes to fix a leaky roof, arrived at that meeting with a handful of trusted verbal tools. He used phrases such as: 'I hope that you can prove what you are saying in court . . .' and '. . . take your evidence to court'. He used them to attack, deflect and interrupt. Meanwhile, we tried to defend the innocence of our daughter. The archbishop's tools were very effective, for they eventually exhausted Anthony. The man of the Church was used to confrontation and we were not.

Truth and justice were what we wanted from him, but did his views of right and wrong match our moral standards? We felt like we'd been hit on the head and bullied into submission. The archbishop's threatening words ended all avenues of conversation. I believe this was his aim.

Two of the items I had gathered as evidence of Emma's suffering were photographs. One pictured her receiving her confirmation certificate only two years earlier by none other than what was then Bishop George Pell himself. The other photograph was taken just a few months before the meeting, when she had cut her wrists in the laneway behind our home. To maximise the impact this photograph would have on the archbishop Anthony had enlarged it to A4 size.

When the meeting was almost finished, Anthony passed to Archbishop Pell the confirmation picture, to which he commented: 'That's nice.'

Then Anthony gave him the image of Emma with bloodied wrists and arms. I held my breath, hopeful that we could reach this man on a deeper level and he could offer us some sympathy, or a display of surprise perhaps, something, anything . . .

Archbishop Pell, however, peered at it for a moment and with an unchanged expression said casually: 'Mmm . . . she's changed, hasn't she?' He handed the picture back to us. We couldn't believe his response. He was the first person we'd shown the image to. It was too distressing for anyone we knew to see. But it did not disturb the archbishop. Not a grimace or a frown.

What sort of people does he mix with, what sort of life experiences did he have, that allowed him to feel that his comment was appropriate? This man was Archbishop of Melbourne, leader of Australia's biggest archdiocese. He was partly educated in Rome, and had studied Latin, Italian, French and German texts. He had written books and academic papers. He edited *Light*, a Catholic news journal, writing editorials and book reviews for years. He had a seemingly decent grasp of language, had travelled the world, witnessing vastly different cultures. Why did he react the way he did to Emma's distressing photo, without emotion?

'*She's changed.*'

I'm nobody special. My family are just ordinary people, just like anybody else. But were we that worthless and dispensable?

This was the man who had taken it upon himself to be in charge of correcting the paedophile problem within the priesthood. How could he change the status quo when he appeared to feel nothing for victims?

After these brief words about Emma, his rejection of her pain, there was little left to say. We were stunned and sat trying to comprehend how our long hopeful wait to meet George Pell had been for nothing.

As I sat listening to Anthony lose the last moments of the battle, the uncomfortable feeling I had experienced through the meeting, the cramped sensation, recurred. Apart from the stress and near nausea I was enduring, another awareness was beginning to break through. Time and again I had sat stiffly upright, thrusting into the hard wooden back of the bench seat, feeling as if I needed to be further away from the arch-bishop, sitting up straighter but to no avail.

Once again, I was ramming my backbone into the hard timber, trying to sit up, only this time I spotted the source of my irritation. I looked down to see what I was instinctively trying to get away from – it was the toe of Archbishop Pell's shoe. His long legs were crossed casually and stretched out towards me, his shod foot protruding to just two or three centimetres from my knee. All this time he had been impinging on my personal space, spreading himself out in the cramped confines. My anger spilt over. It was ridiculous that we were even in this position, not just the horror movie our lives had become but in this tiny, obsolete furniture storage room, opposite this confronting man in his big padded chair.

Unable to restrain myself, I interrupted their futile conver-sation without excuse or politeness.

'Get your foot away from my knee,' I ordered.

They both looked at me in silence. I repeated my instruc-tion and this time pointed at his intrusive foot. I was furious. We stared at each other until he complied. As pathetic as it was, this was the only point we won during the whole meeting.

It is so hard to understand people talking about innocent, molested children without compassion. Perhaps priests, bishops and archbishops don't have that connection with children because they can't or rather, according to their vows, shouldn't father them. But that's no excuse. They were once children too. Surely we are not so many worlds apart that we can't share a sense of loyalty and protection of young people, humanity's future. Even the Bible tells us to be childlike and to protect children, especially their faith.

'But if any of you causes one of these little ones who trusts in me to lose his faith, it would be better for you to have a rock tied to your neck and be thrown into the sea.' Matthew 18:6, *The Living Bible*.

The seabed must be littered with clergy.

When the meeting finished we left, me carrying my pile of proof, which could now be thrown into the bin for all it meant and represented to the hierarchy. It was irrelevant. We were irrelevant. It appeared to us that the most important thing was to silence us and avoid scandal. Not yet comprehending what we had just been through, we stood fuming on the lawn outside the presbytery, looking back at the door we had just exited, as it slowly and firmly closed on us.

Two of our friends came to us at the front of the presbytery, enquiring about the meeting. Out of dismay Anthony showed them the photo of Emma with her wrists cut and repeated what Archbishop Pell had said about her. They too were shocked by both the image of Emma and the words of the archbishop.

There was still the large group meeting to attend. We had only minutes to recover from our failure to convince the archbishop that victims were telling the truth and were not the enemy.

Maybe more people would mount a stronger case.

There were forty-five of us. Anthony and I didn't want to speak to anyone else at that point and put our heads down to walk across to the school hall and take our seats. A U-shape of chairs was set out, with the end dedicated to members of the Catholic Church's Pastoral Response Office, the South Eastern Centre Against Sexual Assault (SECASA), the Catholic Education Office and the archbishop. There wasn't much noise as people took their places. This meeting was the apex of our group's efforts, achieving a visit from the Archbishop of Melbourne. We had wanted the press there but unfortunately the Archbishop's office had insisted on a media ban. For some time we had harboured high expectations that we would finally receive some answers to our questions. It is such a frustrating and energy-sapping exercise writing letters to a high office and awaiting a reply but receiving nothing but side-stepping and avoidance. We had written to Archbishop Pell three times following the Oakleigh Forum, without receiving the promised answers to our forum questions. But now he was here, right in front of us. No more letter writing, just him and us. Catholics all.

Even after the bitter disappointment of the past half hour, I had a sense that this meeting was a chance for a break-through. There were so many of us. We wanted an assurance that the hierarchy was taking steps to make sure history would not repeat itself, and that all known paedophiles (we knew of several) were removed from parishes, as well as some account-ability for the actions of past paedophile priests and Church leaders who supported or protected them.

My mind was still stinging and I was too busy repeating the private meeting in my mind to form any new arguments for the group session. But I listened and paid close attention to the archbishop's manner. Anthony sat beside me, brooding quietly. It dawned on me that we were sitting in the same hall O'Donnell took Emma before he raped her, luring our little five-year-old under the false pretence (as I later learned) of helping him stack cans of Coke in one of the rooms not far from where I was sitting – a snug, safe paedophile hole, which no doubt saw many children molested over his seventeen years with us.

And we were here to discuss the man himself in the very place he committed his criminal deeds. I doubt anybody else felt as Anthony and I did at that moment.

A little prayer table had been prepared. One of these popped up at every meeting Church officials attended. Months earlier, we had requested *no* prayer tables but the officials of the Church could not understand our opposing point of view. This time, whoever set it up positioned it between the visiting archbishop and us, the support group – a God-buffer to protect them, to calm our outrage, and a display of the power invested in them.

The prayer table was resplendent in a white cloth, a candle and a flower, symbols of life. It was not so much the prayers themselves that irritated us, but that the hierarchy appeared to be hiding behind the prayers – the words of the Almighty – carefully chosen and said by them to control us. Still, prayers were said and we did not comment. There were important matters at hand.

SECASA began with an introduction. Then a spokesperson for our group welcomed the archbishop, announcing that for the duration of the meeting we would call Archbishop Pell 'George'. It was supposed to be an equaliser.

'Oooohhhhhh,' came the gasp of horror from one of the archbishop's aides, sitting near him.

The deliberately loud intake of breath – a theatrical protest of sorts – caused a momentary halt in proceedings as the echo made its way around the cavernous hall. It embarrassed everyone present, except perhaps 'George', whose face didn't move. Our speaker continued.

A chronology of our activities over the past eight months was laid out and then we moved straight to questions. Archbishop Pell sat ready.

People stood and spoke, some with tears, about their experiences and feelings of disillusionment. The archbishop, all our eyes upon him, was unmoved. His head was down and he never even looked up when people spoke and cried. A man stood and explained that he expected a Christian response from the Christian Church. Again the archbishop did not reply; rather he still had his head down, writing. The ignored man, having poured out his heart, slowly sat down looking around at others in the audience, not sure what to do. A woman stood and held back tears as she recalled her life's terrible moments, this time framing questions in her address to the archbishop – still no reply. He just had his head down, writing more. By now we were looking at each other in furious confusion, unrest stirring the air. The proceedings came to a standstill.

One mum bravely challenged Archbishop Pell.

'What are you writing?' she demanded to know. 'Have you heard any of this? Do you know how much pain we are in?'

He stopped scribbling and looked up.

'I'm writing everything down so I can reply to specific points,' he offered.

But even with the help of his notes he did not reply to anything that was asked of him at that meeting. He still hasn't. However, at least he was now talking.

Questions then flowed; questions that had burned inside, real questions to try to understand the Church's stance on the paedophile issue. Anger simmered beneath every response from the esteemed visitor. He seemed put out.

It was the same brave mum who picked him up on his tone.

'Why are you so angry?' she asked. 'The people in this room have a right to be angry because their children have been abused. They should be angry. Why are you angry, Archbishop Pell?'

He muttered something about his Irish blood getting the better of him.

We didn't need this. We were just mums and dads trying to do the right thing; protect our children. We hadn't done anything wrong. We were not on any criminal register. Why were we facing such resistance from a Church that should have been doing the right thing – siding with the innocent children and not their molesters and rapists – without any input from us?

The discussion continued down the paedophile trail. We asked about the paedophiles we knew of who were still serving in parishes in suburbs of Melbourne.

Someone said: 'Have they been removed from those parishes?'

And then Archbishop Pell turned on his hosts. His reaction indicated he knew what we were referring to.

'It's all gossip until it's proven in court,' he boomed. 'AND I DON'T LISTEN TO GOSSIP.'

There it was again, that legalistic tool being used, those bullish, belittling words.

We were talking about children! Protecting children. What was so hard to understand?

There has to be something between the moments when a reticent child whispers a disclosure and having to prove the actions of the offender in court. And the Church hierarchy had the power to implement that something – removal, a desk job at Church headquarters . . . anything to disallow further contact with children. The 'it's all gossip' attitude won't heal anything. I was hearing the archbishop's defence for the second time but now I was listening on behalf of my daughter. He was, after all, speaking to the victims. I took every one of his callous words to mean he was calling Emma a liar, reducing her disclosure to 'gossip', imagining or inventing the assaults that had driven her to repeatedly attempt suicide. I felt for all the victims; knowing their innocence, what they had lost, and their inability to speak about what was done to them. It made me determined to fight. Only three per cent of victims disclose, and only a small fraction of those get to see their offender convicted in court. Sometimes it takes them decades to tell. And then they are met with this cruel opposition?

We spoke to the archbishop not only about Sacred Heart but parishes throughout the archdiocese. During a previous meeting with the Victims' Advisory Group, one of the members began researching the history of a parish on Melbourne's outskirts. That particular church was presided over by five suspected paedophile priests or assistant priests consecutively. We had all the offenders' names and demanded the Church do something about these still-serving clerics. We could do nothing but drop leaflets, general information about paedophiles, onto church porches. We were warned that to publicly name the offenders would be an infringement of *their* rights.

'It's all gossip until it's proven in court.'

In subsequent years, those offenders were recognised by authorities. Three were found guilty (two on child sex charges and one on child physical assault charges), a fourth caused a Church payout to a victim, and the actions of the fifth priest prompted a letter of apology from the Church to victims, after the cleric died. I had to wonder why one outer-suburban parish had so many criminal priests. The priests didn't choose to work there; a board within the Catholic Church allocates clergy positions. This parish, with so many paedophiles, was in a poor community. Perhaps that was why. The board receives knowledge of complaints then dumps the child-molesting priests in a place where their damaging actions would be camouflaged by life's other struggles.

But Archbishop Pell would not discuss our problems in depth, let alone the pain being inflicted upon others elsewhere. Moving along, we tackled the question of O'Donnell being laicised.

A long time before the meeting, after Anthony and I first failed to have the sexual predator defrocked, we drove to a Catholic bookshop in the city, right next door to St Francis' Church, where my great, great, great-grandmother Mary Lee was married one hundred and forty-five years before, and bought a copy of *The Code of Canon Law; A Text and Commentary*.

I turned to Canon Law 1395.2, which stated: 'If a cleric has otherwise committed an offence against the sixth commandment of the Decalogue with force or threats or publicly or with a minor below the age of sixteen, the cleric is to be punished with just penalties, including dismissal from the clerical state if the case warrants it.'

After purchasing this volume, I showed my friends. One of them now stood up in front of the archbishop and asked whether O'Donnell would be laicised. Archbishop Pell gave a half-smile, the placating apologetic smile I had seen when I asked the same question of another cleric months earlier, then said in a less than clear voice that he wasn't that up on canon law, it wasn't that easy to say, as canon law was difficult to interpret.

This response prompted a strong reply from my friend, who fired back: 'But it is stated clearly in the Queen's English that he can be laicised for interfering with a child under sixteen.'

The archbishop looked uncomfortable at this part of the grilling and mentioned he would look into it. It was unconvincing and we never did hear back from him.

Many years later we were to discover that Archbishop Pell, at that time (February 1997), was a member of the Vatican's Congregation for the Doctrine of the Faith previously known as the Inquisition. He served on this body from 1990 to 2000 with Cardinal Ratzinger, the future Pope Benedict XVI. Part of the Congregation's function is to laicise priests. As a member of the Congregation, surely Archbishop Pell, of all people, would have known about bringing an offending priest to laicisation, but he never declared this knowledge nor offered to help us in our request.

The only unclear part of that law was its open end.

'. . . *if the case warrants it.*'

Who decides if the case warrants it?

Another escape clause is 'to be punished with just penalties'? Who judges and decides what the 'just penalty' is? The victim or the senior cleric trying to contain the scandal?

This canon law has clauses that leave important rulings open to individual hierarchical interpretation. This is the only confusion Archbishop Pell could be talking about. Maybe 'just penalties' could be interpreted as the recitating of a few 'Our Father prayers' – but surely not for such a crime.

No, Canon Law 1395.2 is fairly straightforward. Only in the eyes of some men who wear white collars do the words not make sense.

The meeting was winding up. When hard pressed about the Church's inaction, the archbishop told the group the same thing he told Anthony in private.

'*Take your evidence to court.*'

It silenced us all. We were good people, loving parents of children, and parishioners of Oakleigh.

As I listened to all of this, again I remembered where I was sitting, in the very building where a seventy-year-old priest raped my five-year-old daughter. My eyes went to the closed door beside the stage, behind which lay the shower room, just down the passage – the room with the changed lock that the master key could not open, lest someone caught him in the heinous act. He was still a priest – fifty years of raping and molesting children and he was still a priest!

I wondered where O'Donnell was now. The last I'd heard was that he had claimed to be sick and was moved from prison into a secure prison ward at St Vincent's Hospital. He would die and be placed in a fancy casket one day, I thought. They would chisel the title 'Fr' into his tombstone.

It was a miserable position to be in. In desperation, with nothing else to say to George Pell, we pleaded again for O'Donnell to be kicked out of the Catholic Church. And then Archbishop Pell all of a sudden changed his tone. He offered us a sob story, sympathetically and sadly describing how Father O'Donnell was close to death.

The archbishop told us he'd visited the semiconscious priest and stood by his deathbed.

We heard how O'Donnell was muttering something incoherently over and over again. He explained how he leaned closer to the dying priest and listened and how he believed O'Donnell was saying '"I'm sorry . . . I'm sorry . . . I'm sorry".'

I couldn't believe what I was hearing. The whole story seemed farcical. Sorry for what?

Certainly it wasn't for his crimes. O'Donnell was last quoted in a newspaper, arrogantly saying he didn't think his behaviour had hurt anyone. His police statement showed the same heart of stone and denial. Even the judge in his case didn't believe he was remorseful. That all fitted with the personality of a lifelong paedophile and his behaviour in the parish.

And why, why, was the Archbishop of Melbourne visiting a convicted paedophile in a prison hospital? Was George Pell supporting the vile man, just as he had supported the paedophile Ridsdale? Why would he want to talk to O'Donnell? What did they talk about? All we knew was what Archbishop Pell told us.

This story from the archbishop, that O'Donnell was a dying priest begging forgiveness, his mind tortured by guilt, confessing on his deathbed didn't seem plausible. But how could we challenge Archbishop Pell on it? It was a clever strategy. As Christians, we would feel heartless to continue attacking a dying man – even a paedophile – by demanding he be laicised. The leader of the nation's largest archdiocese knew the right strings to pull. We were silenced as one, again.

So the meeting wrapped up, with us feeling some kind of instinctive guilt. We felt flat, empty, defeated – as if we had achieved nothing.

Two members of our group got to work transcribing eighteen pages of extensive notes from the meeting to keep as a record. For me the battle continued internally. The final guilt trip the archbishop sent us on, making us the enemy of the institution he defended, sapped me for three days, making me feel like a bad child. But it wasn't long before my spirit returned. I replayed the conversations in my mind endlessly.

One thing that kept gnawing at me was Archbishop Pell's confidence.

'Take your evidence to court.' During the two meetings, he had repeated it several times.

He believed we had no evidence. And, indeed, what child gathers proof of an assault? What evidence could there be? The Father took them out of class and off the playground, led them to isolation – just the child's word against his. The priest raped children, orally and anally. He put his hand inside their underpants and touched their genitals while he masturbated. He lay on top of them. He pressed his erection against their little naked bodies. He left few physical scars. Instead he left them emotionally tortured and spiritually ruined. He irreparably altered their development as humans, so their relationships, their ideas of love and connection to others, were always strained and sometimes impossible. O'Donnell and the Church stole a part of their souls. What evidence did Archbishop Pell expect us to produce? Their stories, their pain and their torment were all they had. But to him that was 'gossip' until proven. No wonder those victims were cutting themselves, taking drugs, getting drunk, suffering depression and even attempting to kill themselves, some with success. If the sexual assaults didn't destroy them, then the reception they received from the hierarchy might.

I began to wonder whether the archbishop's confidence stemmed from a second source. Did O'Donnell write down a list of victims' names after all? What was the purpose of that last visit by Archbishop Pell to O'Donnell on his so-called deathbed? Did he give more information to his superiors about the assaults? This is how my mind wandered after the Pell meetings. His verbal grenades had left me momentarily speechless, but my anger still smouldered. Slowly I deconstructed the archbishop's arguments. The phrases he used – 'prove it in court', 'take your evidence to court', 'take your proof to court', 'I hope you can substantiate what you are saying', 'it's all gossip until it's proven in court', 'I hope you can prove what you're saying in court' – had me questioning how Archbishop Pell believed in a God he could not see in the witness stand, until declaring Himself present on oath.

The tale about O'Donnell's deathbed confession was very convenient, but he still hadn't died. We had been hearing for months now that O'Donnell was dying, always thrown at us by the hierarchy to put us off our demands. It annoyed me the more I thought about it, so I rang the hospital to check on his condition and spoke to a nurse in the prison section.

'Hello?'

I froze.

'Um,' I started. 'My name is Chrissie and I was just wondering how Father O'Donnell is . . .'

I hesitated, not sure how much or what next to say.

The nurse cut me off.

'Just a moment, I'll put you through,' she said matter-of-factly.

Put me through – to the non-compos mentis priest in the throes of death? I was out of my depth now. I thought the nurse would just give me the standard non-committal speech about the condition of the prisoner/patient. Instead, I was about to talk to him. I prepared to hang up but stayed listening, mortified.

'Hello?' O'Donnell said, in a clear voice.

I hung up.

The following month he was dead. I read about it in a newspaper on 14 March 1997. The headline read: 'Abuse priest dies'. I asked the Pastoral Response Office what would happen to his diocesan file and was told it had been burned. For twelve years I did not know where he was buried, as the Church hierarchy would not release any details. I assumed his priestly colleagues and the hierarchy held a grand funeral, away from the public glare, a full Catholic Church tribute and farewell he did not deserve. Even the informed and investigative Broken Rites did not know where O'Donnell was laid to rest. Then, one day, I had it confirmed to me by a spokesperson for the Melbourne Cemetery that O'Donnell was buried at the city's oldest graveyard, in a special, private underground crypt with all the other dead priests. I would like to know what is written on his plaque or tombstone. Is it something gushing and falsely celebratory? I will never find out. A request was made to inspect the crypt but the Church hierarchy declined.

'The crypt only records basic details such as date of death,' a spokesman for the Church replied, without specifying what those other details were. 'It is not possible to provide access.'

At the end of our group's Oakleigh meeting Archbishop Pell had told us he would return to our suburban parish to meet us again and answer our questions, which he spent so long recording in his notes. Much later, we heard from a member of the Pastoral Response Office that the archbishop would not be returning because we 'were too angry'. Actually we kept a lid on our anger that evening in the church hall. He had not yet seen how angry we were.

At last, summoning up the courage, Emma went with her psychologist to make a police report about the assaults against her. Only after O'Donnell's death could she bring herself to make an official report. I hoped with all I had that she would realise that the police and society recognised what happened to her was wrong and against the law.

Also on 14 March I wrote a letter to the Suicide Prevention Task Force, which was seeking submissions, outlining what I believed were connections between childhood sexual assault, depression and youth suicide. They wrote back asking Anthony and me to come in and make a presentation to the Task Force when it visited Melbourne, which we did. The Task Force was not unfamiliar with the sexual assault and suicide connection. In 'The Victorian Government Response to Suicide Prevention Report' under the heading 'Targeting High Risk Groups' the highest funding of $500,000 was allocated to 'expand services to victims of sexual assault . . .'

The Oakleigh Liaison Group activities became fewer. We had been to the top and achieved no changes, no account-ability and no answers. Leigh Murrell, an artist friend to some of the members of the group, created five large paintings in support of our cause and efforts. We organised an art exhibi-tion. One of O'Donnell's victims read a heartbreaking poem, which concluded with the line . 'Remember "Father" the greatest sin of all is the denial of sin'. We nodded our heads and wiped away our tears. Leigh was quoted in the local paper, saying of his paintings: 'They portrayed the brutality needed to drive home the horror and shame of clergy sexual abuse.' It was a very emotional event.

By the end of June 1997 I was still battling the Church to pay for Emma's psychology bills and other medical accounts. The Archdiocese of Melbourne, learning I had private health cover, wanted me to use it, offering to pay only the gap, if there was one. Months earlier, it was suggested to me by the Pastoral Response Office that the Church would even pay my insurance premiums. I replied that it sounded somewhat illegal. I really just wanted the Church to stop avoiding its responsibilities to a victim it had failed to protect.

We received a letter from Vicar General Denis Hart, stating the Church would not pay for Emma's treatment. The invoices were returned to me to forward on to our private health fund with the explanation, 'If there is a gap between the fund payment and the invoice, the invoice should be resubmitted to Carelink.' The Church was offering to pay only the gap again.

By this time the psychology bill was several thousands of dollars. Defiant, I returned the invoices to the Church. I explained to the private hospital I could pay the account any time but was holding out on principle. The hospital understood and did not pressure me. Another four months passed and I was almost ready to pay (I don't like having outstanding bills and it was not fair to the hospital) when I received another letter from Denis Hart, stating the archdiocese had paid all of Emma's outstanding accounts. In holding out I had twisted the Church's arm. The letter also stated it wanted me to claim the accounts against my health insurance and give the Catholic Church the refund. Hell would freeze over before that happened. To this day I have not made the claim. Accompanying Vicar General Hart's letter were documents from Church lawyers and the Health Insurance Commission backing his argument.

It was part of a new push for me to claim payments through Medicare. I was against this, as taxpayers fund Medicare, while the Catholic Church has a government tax exemption and pays no taxes. Yet the Church showed no shame at using the public's money – while saving its own. I believed the Church should be responsible for the damage caused by its paedophile priests who it decided to harbour, thus creating victims – not the taxpayer.

After the year-long standoff over paying Emma's adolescent day programme accounts, I contented myself with my minor win in making the Church do what I saw as the right thing. And from then on claimed Emma's accounts on my private health cover. The Church paid none of it.

Meanwhile, we were lurching from one emergency to another at home. Emma continued to suffer. Nothing improved, not even after the police report was made. The anger inside me was overwhelming. Many times I had the urge to flatten the accelerator on my car and drive into a power pole. I thought of this often, imagining the impact, the snapping pole, the crushing of metal. I did not want to harm myself and I believed the four-wheel drive I was in would protect me. What I wanted was the impact, a physical expression of the rage that lived in me, like a lion in a cage.

I had used swear words maybe twice in my life but when I looked at Church leaders, who expressed no guilt at leaving child rapists among us in parishes and schools, I had to swear. Whenever I drove past a primary school and I saw the children, how small they were, it reminded me of just how little my daughters were when sexually assaulted. I cried every time. It took me years to curb this reaction. Sometimes I wanted to scream until my lungs bled. Sometimes I wanted to rip my hair out. Sometimes I wanted to tear someone apart. I was a candidate for road rage – any hint of arrogance from another driver would have me fuming, as it reminded me of the arrogance I had to put up with from Church leaders.

I played loud music so I didn't have to think the thoughts that plagued, even stalked, me. Sometimes the songs incited in me the strength to defend my children and myself. None of my urges for violence were acted upon. I didn't know where to go or what to do with my blind fury, so I just continued fighting to live as a daughter, wife and mother.

Chapter 11
The Pell Process

The school Emma went to in 1997 was something completely different. She had gone from a suburban Catholic girls college, just across the road from the church and primary school that hosted her rape, to a non-Catholic but still conventional school, and finally to the last resort of an inner-suburban community special school. It was a more relaxed way of learning, but also an introduction to the darker elements of city life; this is where our precious Emma was introduced to heroin.

Years later she told us about the day she first tried the drug at the back of a shop in a grungy alley. She was crouched low, staring at the needle, when she lost her nerve and decided not to. The man she was with insisted and injected her anyway. Emma's mind and body were then lost to the sensation of that initial hit. She said it felt great. But never again could she recapture the high, no matter how much heroin she used. Addiction sank its teeth into her in that shadowy laneway in 1997 and never let go.

While Emma was taking awkward steps into a world that would leave her strung out and desperate, Anthony and I were doing the same. Three weeks after our meeting with Archbishop Pell we decided to go through the Catholic Church's Melbourne Response, more commonly known then as the Pell Process, seeking justice for our daughter through the three-step scheme, which included a decision on whether the abuse was conceded, an amount of compensation and counselling. Up until then we had resisted the Pell Process because of what we saw as inequities in the system. Finally, on 11 March 1997, we met the overseer of complaints, Peter O'Callaghan QC.

Mr O'Callaghan is a prominent Queen's Counsel in Melbourne, having been educated at Catholic schools in country Victoria, and graduating from Melbourne University in 1958. He had appeared in many royal commissions and acted as an arbitrator, as well as a mediator in many high-profile commercial cases and associated litigation. He was recommended to the archdiocese and duly accepted the appointment in 1996. His terms of employment specified that he be placed on a retainer 'for the period of six months', which the 'Archbishop shall extend . . . for a period of six months' if enough complaints kept coming from victims. Almost fifteen years later, he is still in that role.

The archdiocese released a promotional booklet when it launched the scheme and described the role of the Archbishop's Independent Commissioner:

> Peter O'Callaghan QC has been appointed to enquire into allegations of sexual abuse by priests, religious and lay people who are, or were, under the control of the Archbishop of Melbourne. In much the same way as a royal commissioner appointed by a government the commissioner will operate independently of the Church.

The advertising material did not say that unlike a royal commissioner, Mr O'Callaghan had no power to force all witnesses to give evidence, nor were his hearings or findings accessible to the public. So, really, it was very different to a royal commission. But it sounded impressive and that was the point.

The brochure went on:

> He will be subject to the rules of natural justice and the relevant provisions of Canon Law. The Commissioner will be empowered by the Archbishop to require the attendance before him of priests and religious [sic] the subject of complaints, and the Commissioner may conduct hearings at which there may be present the complainant, the accused and relevant witnesses. The Commissioner will interview the complainants, the accused and relevant witnesses, and provide the Archbishop with both interim and final recommendations for appropriate action.

This is the wrong way to investigate crimes. The Church should go to the police with allegations of sexual assault. By conducting such interviews, the priest is made aware of the accusations and can start preparing to defend himself. Also, by the Church-appointed commissioner not referring complaints directly to the police, Mr O'Callaghan becomes the initial investigator. That job should always belong to the specially-trained police officers and Director of Public Prosecutions. In one case, many years after his appointment, Mr O'Callaghan decided a priest's conduct was 'inappropriate, equivocal and suspicious' but NOT criminal. He was wrong. That same priest was later found to be guilty of criminal charges.

The police always know better, but the Catholic Church sees itself above the law. The Pell Process is proof of this.

Emma was not yet sixteen. With our help, she signed and lodged with the Melbourne Archdiocese an 'Application For Compensation Form'. Because Emma would not speak further about her sexual assaults, I submitted with her application reports from various psychiatric professionals, including a report from the Monash Medical Centre regarding Emma's disclosure in the adolescent unit.

About that time, we also made our first official contact with a firm of solicitors, who had represented an O'Donnell victim in a civil case. That suit dissolved after the lawyers discovered there was no such entity as the Catholic Church. It was like that for everyone.

It's impossible to sue the Church, we were again told.

Because of those precedents, we engaged the same lawyers to instead look into the State Government's crimes compensation fund, which compassionately exists for those who have no other legal claim for damages. We filled out the forms and lodged them but we never claimed crimes compensation. I just wanted to wait a while. I didn't like being told our rights and choices were limited. Maybe there was a way to take the Church to court after all. I had no legal grounding for my thinking, I just wasn't ready to give up on the prospect of it.

Six months later, we received a letter from Mr O'Callaghan stating: 'I propose to make a formal finding that I am satisfied that Emma was the victim of sexual abuse by Kevin O'Donnell.'

We were neither pleased nor dismayed that Emma had made it through the first step of the Pell Process. The Church had already conceded that O'Donnell repeatedly sexually assaulted Emma. A year earlier, we received that recognition when we first contacted the archdiocese and the Church paid our psychology expenses, so to read about it on official letterhead was not a breakthrough.

It took us a long time to even act upon Mr O'Callaghan's letter. Our next task was to front the compensation panel and plead Emma's case for anything up to $50,000. We were sceptical about the whole business. But we were also flat out trying to save our daughter's life. Thoughts of the panel were left behind for almost a year.

I kept a diary of events in those torturous, tumultuous years, witnessing the disintegration of my daughter. I look back at my entries now and wonder how any of us survived.

March 1997

3rd	Emma to GP, Oakleigh, diagnosed with glandular fever
5th	Emma to Moorabbin Radiology re CT scan for complaints of headaches since 1987 – scan is clear
11th	Anthony and I meet with Peter O'Callaghan, independent commissioner
13th & 14th	9 am–12 noon Emma to psychology day program
13th	Anthony and I to Emma's psychiatrist and psychologist
13th	Emma to unit adolescent psychotherapist
17th	9 am–2 pm Emma's send-off from the adolescent psychology day program she has been attending up to five days a week since her 15th birthday in November
20th	Emma to unit adolescent psychotherapist
24th	Emma to unit psychologist
27th	Emma to unit adolescent psychotherapist

April

3rd	Emma to unit adolescent psychotherapist
7th	Emma to unit psychologist
8th	Emma to unit adolescent physician
9th	Emma to Melbourne Pathology for extensive blood tests and an ECG re possible heart damage from anorexia. Placed on iron tablets.

17th   All of us to family session with unit psychiatrist and psychologist

22nd   Emma to unit adolescent physician

24th   Anthony and I to our solicitor re Crime Compensation for Emma

24th   Emma to unit psychologist

24th   Emma and unit psychologist to S/Constable at Prahran Community Policing Squad and made police statement re Emma's sexual assault.

24th   Emma to unit adolescent psychotherapist

29th   Emma to Monash Medical Centre for total body and lumbar spine bone density scan in regards to anorexia damage. Scans show bones are okay.

We were fighting spot fires every day. Some days were better than others. Sadly and worryingly, Monash Medical Centre diagnosed Emma with tachycardia and arrhythmia, heart conditions related to post-traumatic stress syndrome.

Despite her health problems, Emma spent an entire school holiday period getting drunk on vanilla essence bought from supermarkets. It was around that time authorities ordered the cooking ingredient be taken from store shelves because it was becoming fashionable for young people to abuse it for cheap thrills. Emma did it to escape her own thoughts and to forget what was done to her. Three times we picked her up from school because she was drunk. One afternoon she was picked up near a bus terminal by an ambulance and rushed to hospital. She had taken a combination of vanilla essence and travel sickness tablets and was found unconscious in the gutter. While I stayed at home to care for Katie and Aimee, Anthony rushed to the hospital for yet another bedside vigil, waiting for Emma to recover. He arrived home at 3 am, without Emma, in time to grab a few hours' sleep before the start of another work day. While she was hooked up to a drip and heart

The Foster family *(left to right)*: Emma, 6, Aimee, 2, Chrissie, Katie, 4, and Anthony, January 1988.

Katie, held by her godmother, being baptised by O'Donnell at Sacred Heart Church, Oakleigh. Looking on are *(left to right)*: Anthony, Emma, Chrissie and Katie's godfather, September 1983.

Emma, 6, January 1988.

Katie, 4, January 1988.

Disgraced: *pedophile priest John O'Donnell, 78, who is set to become the oldest person jailed in Victoria. Picture: MARK SMITH*

Pedophile priest locked up

By CHRISTINE GILES and GEOFF WILKINSON

A 78-YEAR-OLD pedophile priest who admitted child sex offences dating back almost half a century has become the oldest person jailed in Victorian history.

Fr John Kevin O'Donnell was remanded in custody yesterday for the indecent assault of 10 boys and two girls between 1946 and 1977.

But one of the 10 boys, now in his 50s, said he and another man had found 165 more victims in 48 hours by phoning 300 former classmates at two Catholic schools from the 1950s. And several of the victims said outside court yesterday they believed the Catholic Church was "just as guilty as O'Donnell".

CONTINUED Page 4

Front page of the *Herald Sun*, 5 August 1995, announces Father John Kevin O'Donnell pleaded guilty to sexually assaulting 12 children between 1946 and 1977. The Foster girls were assaulted between 1987 and 1992.

Bishop George Pell blesses Emma during her Confirmation ceremony, May 1993.

Outside court: Bishop George Pell *(right)* lends his support to charged paedophile priest Fr Gerald Ridsdale *(left)*. The pair are walking into the Melbourne Magistrates' Court, August 1993.

First day of school *(left to right)*: Aimee and Katie in their primary school uniforms and Emma in her new secondary college uniform, January 1994.   © Foster family

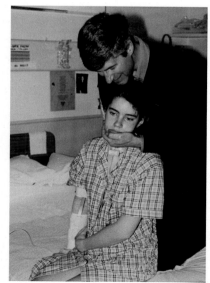

Katie's 16th birthday. Anthony supports Katie in a sitting position, for the first time, while she is still in her coma, 7 July 1999.

© Foster family

Cardinal George Pell kisses the hand of Pope Benedict XVI during the Dedication of the Altar service at St Mary's Cathedral, Sydney. The mass was celebrated with Australian bishops, seminarians and novices at St Mary's Cathedral as part of World Youth Day celebrations, July 2008.

Chrissie and Anthony Foster during the press conference at Sydney Airport after their 40-hour trip from the UK for World Youth Day. They pleaded for the Pope to treat victims with compassion and justice, July 2008.

Emma Foster in 2007, aged 25, just months before she died of a medication overdose.   © LF

Aimee Foster in 2009, aged 24. Having experienced the pain and loss of her sisters, she is now studying Arts/Law at a Victorian university. She is the brightest light in her parents' lives.   © NT

The Foster family after Emma's death. *(left to right)*: Anthony, Aimee, Chrissie and Katie, January 2008.

monitor in hospital, I found thirty-one empty bottles of vanilla essence hidden in her room.

On another occasion, Anthony and I were at a neighbour's wedding celebration when someone whispered hurriedly that an ambulance was outside our house. Alarmed, we instantly left the backyard reception and rushed out of the gate into our street. Blue and red flashes lit up the usually dark street, full of wedding guests' cars. There was little room for an ambulance so it was parked in the middle of the road. The ambulance doors were wide open and nobody was in sight. We ran to our house. Katie and Aimee followed.

Dread filled me. Had Emma hurt herself badly? Had she killed herself? I hadn't even noticed her missing from the reception. We opened our front gate, ran up the path and through the front door. At the end of the hall were ambulance officers crouched over Emma lying on the floor. We edged closer. It was like a horribly frantic emergency scene from a movie. All we could do then was stand and watch.

'She's overdosed on heroin,' said an ambulance officer.

Heroin?

We didn't even know she had begun using the drug.

It was the beginning of another nightmare.

It was an awful sight to find Emma being resuscitated, lying like a beautiful doll on the family room floor, her long, fair hair spread everywhere, in her good clothes from the wedding, now partly torn to have medical sensors attached to her skin.

Only hours earlier, a photo was taken of a proud Anthony and his three daughters all dressed up for the wedding. It was the last photo taken before we entered the dark tunnel of Emma's heroin addiction.

Afterwards Katie, Aimee and I were all crying at the shock of what we had seen and the reason for it, especially Katie and Aimee. Aimee was only twelve years old and badly shaken by it. We all sat on the couch under blankets, trying to banish the coldness of shock. Emma was treated with Narcan, a drug which negates the effect of heroin, and given oxygen and left at home, out of danger – for now. The ambulance officers gave us the simple instruction: 'You need to wake her continually by pushing firmly with a knuckle in the centre of her chest.'

Four of our kind friends came and sat with us. One of them had seen the ambulance and told the others – they came to see how they could help. Their very presence was appreciated. The ambulance officers were also very caring, as always. I have only admiration for both ambulance and police officers. Without exception over the years, the various officers treated our family well.

The emergencies didn't stop.

Emma spent the first day of 1998 in hospital after she was found unconscious at our New Year's Eve party. Paramedics couldn't tell whether she had overdosed on heroin or alcohol, so at the hospital she was given antidotes of both Narcan and charcoal.

She could not settle into a consistent education. We took her out of the inner-city environment and enrolled her at a public secondary college closer to home, but Emma suffered anxiety attacks and so we were forced to send her back to the community school. Within a month of resuming she was found using heroin on school grounds.

She spoke to me about wanting to stop using. Our poor daughter had been addicted to heroin for four months. We contacted the Outreach program for help. Outreach provide drug withdrawal assistance and referrals in your own home. Emma courageously undertook to try to kick her habit but suffered greatly from withdrawal. Outreach personnel took her to a doctor and arranged for her to be given three bottles of natural medicines to help relieve the pains of her symptoms. It barely helped. Often, Emma was doubled up in terrible agony, crying, 'It hurts. It hurts.'

Stomach cramps and body aching continued for weeks. We thought they would diminish but they did not. On top of all of this Emma was prescribed antidepressants and sleeping tablets. For many years she had suffered from nightmares and waking in fright for seemingly no reason in the middle of the night. Later she was placed on Doloxene, which was administered to help with withdrawal pain and cravings. I could barely comprehend a teenager, my teenager, having to take thirty tablets of prescribed medication a day, just to keep living on an even keel.

In March 1998, Anthony and I visited, for the only time, Professor Richard Ball, the head of Carelink. I had declared never to talk to him but he absolutely insisted we meet. In fact, we felt we were being forced to see him. He had intimated to us through a colleague that he was upset we would not discuss anything with him. We were still angry that this man had been put in charge of the Church's victims' assistance section and I had so far refused to deal with him, communicating only with a psychologist and hands-on manager at Carelink. The meeting with him achieved nothing. I went in with so much anger that I can't even remember what our conversation was, only that I questioned his assessment of O'Donnell and his suitability for his new position.

My mind was constantly racing. As well as worrying about Emma, I couldn't stop thinking about how many other victims may be suffering in silence, not yet able to disclose the crimes against them. I drove to Sacred Heart Girls College to point out to the new school principal that at every year level in her college, and the next three years of intake from Sacred Heart Primary School, just across the road, there were girls who had been exposed to the presence of Father Kevin O'Donnell.

'It means there could be girls at every year level for some years who could have been sexually assaulted by him and counselling should be made available,' I insisted. The principal made all the right noises and was very concerned. I returned soon after with another woman from our group, armed with information about an existing program, which went into secondary schools to talk to all students about sexual assault and counsel those who needed it. Again, I heard all the right reactions from the principal, but there was no action. I rang her on two occasions over the next couple of weeks to see if she would implement the program, but she would not take my calls and so far as we know, she did nothing for the students.

After Emma suffered withdrawal symptoms for a month, seeing no relief in sight, we arranged for her to be admitted to another adolescent psychiatric unit, as a last resort. It would give her some respite. She felt safe when her movement were restricted at difficult times. While awaiting her placement I took her to a doctor, who finally helped ease her pain by arranging to place her on the methadone program. The next problem arose the same day when I took Emma to the unit for admission, only to be refused entry because she had started taking methadone that very morning.

'The unit doesn't admit people who are on methadone,' we were instructed.

'But she only took the first dose this morning,' I argued. 'Could she still go in without taking another dose?'

It was very frustrating. I had rushed out especially early that morning so Emma would have relief before being admitted to the unit. If I had known, I wouldn't have let Emma begin the methadone. The person who was denying admission was someone who had seen Emma repeatedly for counselling over previous weeks. He didn't explain the rules to her. She was there with bags packed, ready to stay.

'One dose!'

He wouldn't budge.

We picked up Emma's bags and left. Emma and I were both passionately complaining about the situation and timing. It was so aggravating. We had both been under a lot of stress, Emma with the pain for so long and me trying to manage her and the torment. The admission would have been a relief to both of us. Still fuming, we got in the car and I drove onto the main road to head home. It was the early afternoon but the city-bound traffic was still heavy. Not far from the unit, we rounded a major road that changes the flow of the centre lane from north to south, depending on whether it is morning peak hour or afternoon peak hour. The overhead gantries displayed either green arrows or white crosses. I was all of a sudden facing a white cross and had little time to merge into a lane that had cars flowing in our direction. Otherwise, we would have smashed head on into cars coming the other way.

I was driving our Supra. We were moving fast, too fast, my foot loaded with a weight of anger on the accelerator, the car's bonnet running low to the road, low enough to fit right under the large truck I was heading for. The thought of ending it all was a very real temptation. In a moment of madness I said to Emma: 'I may as well drive under that truck.'

Instantly Emma turned to me excitedly and said: 'Yeah, do it, Mum, do it.' Her excitement at the fatal prospect completely snapped me out of the state I was in. I quickly diverted, shooting out of the wrong lane and away from the oncoming truck. It frightened me how close I had come to going under that truck and ending both our lives.

After we arrived home safely, life went on. This is what my diary recorded for the next three months:

April 1998

2nd	Methadone – Emma remained on methadone or its equivalent
3rd	Emma to doctor Bentleigh
7th	Emma to psychologist
7th	Emma to doctor, Bentleigh
9th	Emma to psychologist
11th	Emma to doctor, Bentleigh
14th	Emma to psychologist
14th	Emma to doctor, Bentleigh
17th	Emma to Monash Audiology Service re hearing test
17th	Emma to doctor, Bentleigh
17th	Emma to psychologist
18th	Emma to doctor, Bentleigh
20th	Emma to psychologist
21st	Emma to psychiatrist – stated he thought Emma should only be seeing one therapist i.e. the psychologist
22nd	Emma to psychologist
22nd	Anthony, I, Aimee and Emma to meet psychologist
23rd	Emma to doctor, Bentleigh
27th	Emma to psychologist

May

1st	Emma to psychologist, Bentleigh
1st	Emma to doctor, Bentleigh
4th	Emma to psychologist
4th	Emma to doctor, Bentleigh
8th	Emma to psychologist
13th	Emma to psychologist
15th	Emma to psychologist

18th	Emma to psychologist
18th	Emma to doctor, Bentleigh
20th	Emma to psychologist
20th	Emma to doctor, Bentleigh
25th	Emma to psychologist
26th	Emma to psychologist
27th	Emma to doctor, Bentleigh
29th	Emma to psychologist

June

2nd	Emma to doctor, Bentleigh
3rd	Emma to psychologist
4th	Emma to doctor, Bentleigh
9th	Emma to psychologist
9th	Emma to doctor, Bentleigh
10th	Emma to psychologist
12th	Emma to doctor, Bentleigh
16th	Emma to doctor, Bentleigh
16th	Emma to psychologist
17th	Emma to psychologist
19th	Emma to doctor, Bentleigh
23rd	Emma to psychologist
24th	Emma to psychologist
30th	Emma to doctor, Bentleigh

And so it went for the next nine years.

In July, Emma broke the routine by overdosing on prescribed medication. She took approximately one hundred and twenty antidepressants and antipsychotic tablets. Soon after that, she was released from hospital. And we started grinding out our existence again. From September 1995 to September 2004, I kept records of Emma's appointments, some with more concise comments than others. The pages of treatment details numbered twenty-five. I did my best to record them all but there were some I would have missed. This was the degree of Emma's plight and our devotion to helping her recover from what was done to her. It wasn't until 11 August 1998, almost a year after receipt of Mr O'Callaghan's letter, that we attended a sitting with the Catholic Church Compensation Panel. Making a gap in our schedule, we rang for an appointment.

It was early evening; very cold and dark when we arrived at the front door of the East Melbourne office, where the panel sat. The building was an old Victorian two-storey terrace house, one of many stretching the length of the street. We were welcomed in and escorted up the carpeted stairs to what seemed a larger than necessary meeting of people. A roomful of blank faces greeted us. They were seated around a large rectangular table, mainly men but a couple of women. I wondered how a lone victim would have felt confronted by this gallery of assessors. We sat in the chairs left empty for us. Of our hosts I only remember two. One was the panel chairman David Habersberger QC and the other, although I don't remember his name, was a young lawyer from Corrs Chambers Westgarth lawyers, who acted for Archbishop Pell and for the Catholic Archdiocese of Melbourne.

Some innocuous speech or introductory talk commenced the proceedings, but I remember only what Anthony said. We had not planned what we would say. But now Anthony spoke clearly and simply.

'You have the reports of what has happened to Emma, I do not want to upset myself further by talking about it now,' my husband said. 'I believe you should pay Emma the full compensation amount of $50,000.'

That was all. I sat there in silent agreement. It could not have been said better.

Mr Habersberger agreed we did not need to go over Emma's sufferings and we were grateful for his kindness. 'A letter at a later date will inform you of Emma's amount of compensation,' he added.

With the brief proceedings completed, people milled around, talking over cups of tea. I had something else on my mind so Anthony and I did not leave straight away. Before the meeting with Professor Ball earlier in the year I had done some sums on which costs the Church should reimburse us for. In my mind the Church still had to pay, if only in monetary terms, for its wrongs. Being a fair person, I included only costs I had receipts for. They were school fees from Sacred Heart Girls College, the private school Emma went to for a couple of terms (the last term of which she did not attend at all, but I was still expected to pay as a form of severance notice); the new school uniform at Sacred Heart; the summer and winter uniforms from the other school; and the two lots of schoolbooks for both schools – all of which added up to about $15,000. I did not include the more than five thousand kilometres I calculated, to that point, I had travelled driving Emma to various appointments around Melbourne, nor the hundreds of work hours I had lost.

I approached the young lawyer, believing he was the man I would have to speak to. We sat together at the far end of the rectangular table. He was full of confidence and very cheery. I spoke about costs incurred, basically money thrown away in our attempts to correct the causes of Emma's wasting life. I stated how much it was and that I had receipts. He lifted his happy face up at me and cheerily said: 'Oh, the ex gratia compensation payment Emma receives will cover that.'

Not sharing his cheeriness, and certainly unimpressed, I looked directly into his eyes and replied: 'Do you mean to tell me, that if you decide to give Emma $30,000 compensation, for instance, you then expect me to take my $15,000 from her?'

Instantly the grin left his face and his eyes looked down at the tabletop. He had nothing else to say.

And so you should be ashamed of yourself, I thought.

Perhaps he had been given that parrot line from his bosses. By now I had heard it many times – how the compensation would fulfil every aspect of recovery, a show of the Church's great generosity. The Pell Process' 'up to $50,000 compensation' was going to change the world for poor victims struggling to breathe without choking on awful recurrences of shame and degradation. It was pathetic and at that moment the young lawyer understood just how pitiful his words were. Caught up in the same circumstances as we were, I'm sure he would be dissatisfied with the 'generous' offer as well.

I then moved on to David Habersberger with my request for reimbursement of abuse-related costs. He listened and suggested we ring a more senior Church lawyer at Corrs Chambers Westgarth.

'What you're requesting is not covered by Carelink or the ex gratia compensation,' he explained.

Anthony and I then departed down the carpeted stairs.

A letter addressed to Emma arrived at our house ten days later. It was signed by Archbishop George Pell and said:

> . . . the payment of compensation raises difficult and complex issues. It is my hope that my offer, based on the Panel's recommendation, will be accepted by you as a preferable alternative to legal proceedings and that it too will assist you with your future. On behalf of the Catholic Church and personally, I apologise to you and to those around you for the wrongs and hurt you have suffered at the hands of Father Kevin O'Donnell.

The language of the letter suggested the panel was acting independently of the archbishop, just like the archbishop's 'independent commissioner'. But Archbishop Pell chose the panel and placed a cap on payments. It was not an independent panel, as far as I could see, because the archbishop controlled how much money it awarded (in most cases it was far less than the maximum).

We didn't know it then, but that letter would be a key in our civil case against the Church in future years.

Accompanying the archbishop's letter was a letter from the Church lawyers Corrs Chambers Westgarth. It restated the amount being offered to Emma ($50,000) but this time with not a hint of warmth, declaring, 'The compensation offer [is] a realistic alternative to litigation that will otherwise be strenuously defended.'

In one hand we had a piece of paper carrying an apology from Archbishop Pell, and in the other hand we had a document that seemed like a threat from his lawyers. The Corrs letter continued:

> If she wishes to accept it, it is proposed that the amount will be placed in a trust fund, to be jointly administered by you and the Archdiocese, until Emma's eighteenth birthday.

A trust controlled by Archbishop Pell, the Roman Catholic Trusts Corporation for the Diocese of Melbourne and us. It went on:

> At that time, Emma will have the choice of ratifying her acceptance of the compensation offer and signing a document releasing the Archbishop from all further claims arising out of the sexual abuse or any other sexual abuse by a priest, religious or lay person under the control of the Archbishop of Melbourne.

A copy of a third letter accompanied the others. It was from David Habersberger QC to Vicar General Denis Hart, addressing him as 'My Lord'. I looked at this privileged title, realising I was dealing with men who lived with the expectation of being addressed as Your Eminence, Your Excellency, Your Grace, My Lord . . . even of having their rings kissed when proffered. The letter stated the panel's recommendations of the ex gratia compensation and how he had advised us to approach the senior lawyer directly about my abuse-related costs.

This reminded Anthony to follow the advice and ring. I was in his office when he made the call. Anthony began by way of introducing himself. It was obvious the lawyer knew of our enquiries about reimbursement.

He asked Anthony: 'How can I help you?'

Anthony told him of the school fees.

'I'm sorry, I can't help you with that,' the senior lawyer said. 'What else can I help you with?'

Anthony told him of the school uniforms' costs.

The lawyer repeated: 'I'm sorry, I can't help you with that. What else can I help you with?'

Anthony told him of the schoolbooks.

'I'm sorry, I can't help you with that. What else can I help you with?'

It continued like this until Anthony ran out of items. There were no reasons or explanations given. In the end, Anthony quietly put the phone down without saying goodbye. During the conversation I could see by the look on Anthony's patient face that something was wrong but didn't know what it was. Confused by his silent hanging up of the phone, I asked what had been said. He then told me. According to Anthony, the lawyer's behaviour did not warrant a goodbye. When I heard the full conversation relayed I thought it was all just another cruel game.

Chapter 12
The dreaded late-night call

When we brought Katie home from the hospital as a seven-day-old baby, swaddled safely and comfortably, she was a joy to look after. Once she was fed and changed she would go back to sleep until it was time to get up again, which was exactly what I needed when I had twenty-month-old Emma running around. One day, when Katie was about three weeks old, I went into her room while she was asleep. Looking down into her crib I saw my tiny little baby was sucking her thumb; I had not seen her do this before. She had managed to wriggle her arm out of the tightly wrapped blankets, her thumb, only two centimetres long, delicately placed in her mouth. If I didn't think I could love that little baby any more than I already did, I just found I could. She was so sweet. Because she did little more than eat and sleep in her first few months, she only ever wanted to come to me. I enjoyed it.

When Katie was twenty months old and Aimee was born, visitors came to see Emma and Katie's new baby sister and their most common comment was: 'Oh, she's got big, beautiful eyes.' After some weeks of this, when visitors arrived to see the baby, Katie would rush around the legs of the adults, look at the baby, look up at the visitors and say excitedly 'big eye, big eye', until someone agreed with her.

If Anthony or I lost our car keys and said to each other we couldn't find them, Katie would often run off and return with our keys. At this stage she was barely talking. When Emma started three-year-old kinder, I would take the other girls too; Katie would sit at one of the tiny tables, doing jigsaw puzzles, holding the handles on the little wooden pieces, placing them in the right positions and loving every minute of it. One of the other mums, who saw this talent, said Katie would probably be an architect. We both laughed. We thought Katie was pretty clever.

As she began to talk, using short sudden sentences, I noticed that most of her words began with the sound of the letter D, even when they shouldn't. As time went on, it became difficult to understand her. I tried very hard to comprehend what she was trying to say. I would ask her to point at what she needed or wanted and I learned the difference between statements and questions. Sometimes, however, I just could not figure out what she said. At these frustrating times, I looked at that beautiful, innocent and trusting face, trying so hard to be understood. The last thing I wanted to do was to hurt her feelings or destroy that trust and hope. When I had tried everything, I simply hugged her and kissed her face and told her I loved her. Not long after, I took her to a speech therapist. Within a year she could speak clearly.

From age three or four, if we were going away, Katie would pack her own bag unassisted and perfectly, even leaving enough space for Yellow Teddy, her favourite soft toy. Katie was very capable, independent, instinctively knew right from wrong, and always did her very best to behave well. I told her something once and I would not need to repeat it. It was all inbuilt; this was Katie's personality.

She went to three-year-old kinder, four-year-old kinder, then Sacred Heart Primary School. In about 1992, a new teacher arrived and suggested Katie should attend some

Saturday morning courses for children at Monash University. There were a number of different subjects and over the years Katie attended most of them. The one she enjoyed most was an Australian dinosaur course. The teachers brought a load of soil from a dried-out ancient lake in Gippsland, country Victoria, to the university. The lake was supposedly a place where small dinosaurs had gone to drink. The children had the opportunity to take a bucket of the earth and slowly sift through to find a fossil. The dirt was full of bone fragments, with few large pieces. There were many loose teeth and pieces of jaw. When I returned two hours after dropping Katie off, the class was finishing and the children's finds were laid out on large mats of cardboard. They had been taught to document and catalogue their discoveries. Katie proudly showed me the piece she had been lucky enough to find. It was a section of jaw about five centimetres long and, more importantly, it had two teeth still attached. It was the largest jaw remains of that particular dinosaur found to date, and it ended up in a museum somewhere in Victoria with Katie's name attached to it as the finder. She was starting to make her mark on the world.

In 1996, Katie started her secondary education at Sacred Heart Girls College, just as Emma had done two years earlier. In the middle of the year she entered, with the rest of her class, the 'Mathematics Talent Quest'. She was no novice to academic competition, having competed in a primary school quiz tournament, but this was a new challenge. Much to our delight she was a state finalist and awarded an honourable mention. Her achievement provided a bright spot in our lives.

Halfway through year 8 we moved Katie to a grammar school. It was more than a year after Emma disclosed her O'Donnell assaults and we were finally fed up with the Catholic system. Katie did very well in her new classes. While still in year 8 she entered The University of New

South Wales Australian Schools English Competition. She was now taking on broader challenges. Her performance won her a distinction certificate. Katie's school marks were exceptional, well above our state's average, and we believed she would have a great future.

However, within months, she fell mind–first into depression, spending many hours alone in her bedroom. It was difficult to speak to her after school and on weekends. At the worst times, when I went to see if she was okay, I knocked on her door and she barely opened it. I peered through the gap to see one dull eye looking back at me, her flat, lifeless voice asking me what I wanted. No encouragement could make her come out or do something different.

'I'm all right,' she said, still wanting to be the child who caused no problems.

I was particularly worried about her one day. It was Sunday, 16 November 1997 and I kept knocking on her closed door to check on her. One time I didn't wait for an answer. Instead, I opened the door and stuck my head in to see what she was doing. I noticed Katie was writing or drawing. She saw me enter and quickly stopped, desperately trying to hide her sheets of paper under her bed. Later in the afternoon Emma and a friend asked Katie if she would like to go for a walk down the street.

'Sure,' she agreed and left with them.

I had always respected my daughters' privacy but because I was so concerned about Katie's state of mind I decided to read whatever it was she was writing. I thought maybe it could explain why her mood was so low. I went into her room to where she had been sitting. Under her bed was a large shoebox. It contained several covered school exercise books and what she had been writing. I picked it up and read the words. To my horror, it was a suicide note.

'By the time you read this I will most likely be dead,' it started. 'I just find it too hard to be here . . . I just want to die . . .'

It was a long letter in delicate handwriting. In cold dread, I read on.

'I hate only two people. They are myself and Kevin O'Donnell . . . he raped Emma continually for years. I suppose I should tell you that I remember him doing it to me . . .'

I sat on her bed absorbing the shock. My heart was breaking. Again. He raped Katie as well . . . This malignant man, this worthless piece of humanity – even though he was dead, his toxic legacy lived on. How I hated paedophile priests and the high-ranking bishops, who allowed O'Donnell and others like him to stay in parishes and maintain their access to primary school children. To my knowledge, he had never even looked at Katie; didn't know of her existence. As far as I knew, he had never even breathed her name. It was impossible to put the two of them together. There was no connection. I had no idea.

The silence that enveloped me in that moment, on my daughter's bed, was so profound.

In the shoebox was a piece of loose paper, looking like it had come from her school folder. Written seventy-eight times in two columns, in her small neat handwriting was the sentence: 'I hate myself and want to die. I hate myself and want to die. I hate myself and want to die . . .'. This is what he did to her; this is what he made her feel about herself, her life and future. I grieved for Katie, felt the pain in those words, knowing her dreadful secret, one that made her want to give up on living, just like Emma.

My thoughts jumped to Aimee. Was she a victim too? It had been fifteen months since Emma's disclosure and Katie had said nothing of her own sexual assaults. In another fifteen months would I find this disgusting old man had raped Aimee too?

What do I do now about Katie? How do I save her from killing herself?

I returned the letter to the box and flicked through a couple of the exercise books. It was clear they were diaries, filled to the brim with her delicate writing, thousands upon thousands of words on hundreds of pages. I didn't even know she kept a diary. I could see from the copious amount of cursive script that she had been consoling herself through the written word, but now it no longer worked. She had had enough and needed help.

I flicked through a diary and read Katie's thoughts on one of the pages. She wrote of the primary school and how she had been playing at lunchtime in the senior playground near the hall's front entrance, near the back of the church. Playing in the senior playground – and O'Donnell's presence – could only mean she was in grade 3, making it 1992. O'Donnell retired in August that year.

Katie wrote that the priest was leading some children through the yard, heading off to do a job. He saw Katie, stopped and asked her to come with them.

'. . . The adult priest who we were taught by parents and teachers to be a special follower chosen by God, who we were taught was good and real,' the diary explained.

She obeyed. Katie was always eager to do the right thing. I brought my children up to be obedient and polite. In the past, many adults complimented me on my lovely, well-behaved girls. Now I cursed my actions, as I could see it paved the way for a paedophile, their obedience accommodating his control, then gratification.

The selected group of pupils followed O'Donnell into the church. He instructed: 'Look for pencils around the church.' He waved the children away, but with the other hand he held tightly a child's shoulder.

Occasionally at Sunday mass, charity collections were taken up; envelopes and pencils were provided to write details of your donation for a receipt, if you wanted one. These were the pencils the children were asked to collect.

Katie and the others looked all over the church floor but there were no pencils to be seen. While they searched O'Donnell took the child he had retained into the sacristy. When O'Donnell came out with the child, the other children approached him and said: 'We can't find any pencils.'

They did not understand why they had to keep up the hunt.

O'Donnell crankily told them to 'keep looking', waving them away again but holding back a different child to take into the sacristy, the door closing behind them. This scenario was repeated several times until all of the children in the small group had spent time alone with him in the sacristy.

Katie eventually found two pencils. She was very diligent and took her task very seriously. She was holding the pencils when O'Donnell came out and let his eyes fall on her.

'Come in here and put the pencils in the box.' She complied. He shut the door and sexually assaulted her. He was about seventy-five years old but his eagerness to attain sexual gratification from very little children was not diminished.

The school bell went and he told them all to go back to their classes. They ran, confused and disoriented, and never spoke to each other about what had happened in that room.

Katie never uttered a word. I learned then, by reading Katie's awful diary entry, more about how a paedophile works. The crime was frighteningly easy to accomplish: get them to follow under false pretences; isolate them; take them one at a time into a closed-door room and display a hint of anger as a threat, so they obey and don't run off or complain. Make each of them think they are the only one, shamed and embarrassed, unable to speak of the soul-destroying minutes when their little minds and bodies were frozen. They don't even know what sex is, let alone whether it should or should not be happening to them. Children are like empty blackboards when it comes to sex. Do not allow a paedophile to come into your child's life and write damaging things on that precious blackboard. Teach your children proper names and respect for their bodies – where people are and are not allowed to touch them. That way, they will know when something is improper, enabling them to tell you. This, combined with parental education in paedophile behaviour and abuse symptoms, are our only tools for early detection of this life-crippling crime, which can so easily and invisibly befall our children.

What did O'Donnell tell Katie as he molested her? What foul lies did he whisper in her ear to silence her? Did he make the threat real and menacing so she wouldn't or couldn't reach out for help to her own mother or father? What twisting of the truth did he use to make her believe it was her fault, or that she enjoyed it, or that she made him do it?

It was a game to him. The well-honed perverse adult mind versus the natural innocence of a child. How simple. How debased. Our school children were at his mercy. He could choose whatever child appealed to him, five days a week.

I felt so weak.

Parents need to learn what paedophiles do, and how easy it is for them to operate within our trust, in order to protect their children. Children can't protect themselves against adults like this. They cannot predict what the adult has in mind when they are lured to isolation. Then it is too late. The paedophile will win every time, if parents are not informed or remain unaware of such subtle but lethal manipulation and its effects.

I left Katie's room, careful to make it look as though I had not been there, deciding all I could do for now was keep a razor-sharp eye on her and ring the psychologist the following morning to making an appointment. I felt if I spoke to Katie about the letter, she might just go off and kill herself. If I took her to the appointment and told her I knew about the suicide note during the session . . . well at least she would be in a safer environment to discuss it.

I told Anthony about Katie's note and watched more of his world fall apart. I hated that I was Catholic and had brought this curse upon my family.

When Katie returned from her walk she was happier and more relaxed, which made my decision feel like the right one.

I rang on Monday to make the appointment but couldn't get in until Tuesday. It was during this harrowing wait that I noticed my hair was falling out. I'm not sure if I was pulling it out or it was just dropping out through the enormous stress. Either way, it was coming out in my hands.

We told Katie about the psychology appointment but she didn't know why. I picked her up from school and took her there. During the session I owned up.

'Katie, I read your suicide note on Sunday and that's why we're here today, to talk about it.'

I watched her face for the critical reaction. Relief was written on her expression. I instantly knew I had done the right thing by intruding on her privacy.

'I'm sorry about what happened to you,' I added, mere words that fixed nothing.

She nodded and I left her to talk to the psychologist.

From then on Katie saw the psychologist every week. Unlike Emma, who I drove to every appointment, Katie wanted to go by herself. So, once a week, she would catch a train into Melbourne from school and then hop on a tram to her appointment, and then catch another tram and train home. For a year she did this, without fail.

In a way, Emma was gladdened by the news, as she was no longer alone in her plight. The two girls did not know of each other's sexual assaults – such is the hold the paedophile has over each child in silencing them. Two little sisters, who were such good friends, did not tell each other of their shameful secrets; years of deadly secrets.

I thought long and hard about whether I'd missed signs or symptoms of the sexual assaults against Katie. Had I missed anything like I had with Emma? I thought back over her life and could recall only two possible giveaways. Both were things that had struck me as out of the ordinary at the time. Again it was the oddities, the little mysteries that should have prompted from me questions asked aloud, not silent queries.

The first was around 1991, when Katie was about eight. It was night-time as I walked past her closed bedroom door and heard her crying loudly. I went in and was taken aback by her level of distress. I gave her a big hug and asked: 'What's wrong, my darling?'

Between sobs she told me.

'I don't want to go to the dental van because last time the nurse kept telling me to open my mouth wider and wider.' She showed me how wide she had had to open her mouth. 'And I can't open it any wider.' She sobbed so hard she could barely speak.

I insisted we wouldn't go back to the dental van and she slowly calmed. But I could not understand the intensity of her overreaction. Normally nothing fazed her; she always managed to sort things out without help from me. I had never seen her so upset.

Now I thought about that bizarre distress, her howling and her emphasis on being told to open her mouth 'wider and wider'. This was the part that made her sob most violently.

O'Donnell . . .

It made sickening sense. He may have orally raped her. While she couldn't complain of O'Donnell, she could complain about the visit to the dental van. Another part of me died.

I didn't want to imagine my dear little Katie enduring such a repulsive thing by that disgusting old man, only chasing selfish gratification, forcing himself upon her, angrily ordering her to comply, with no sense or care for the delicate little angel he was defiling. I cried at the thought. I didn't want it to be true, but I believed that is what happened. Did this happen to Emma as well? The only person I told was Anthony. Again I would have to wait for Katie to tell me of her assaults. I could not ask such a disturbing thing.

The second sign was in 1992 or 1993, when Katie soberly came to me and said: 'I'm evil.'

'You aren't evil!' I replied. 'You're a very good girl, why are you saying that?'

Without answer she retreated.

I had pondered why she would say that about herself. The use of the word 'evil' was unusual. She had never used it before and it was not a word we used in our home, although other family friends did as a joke.

I wondered whether O'Donnell told her she was evil while he sexually assaulted her, to make her feel guilty. This would be a crushing thing for a little child who always loved to do the right thing. Being described as evil by a priest, who would know what evil was . . . she could only believe him.

Unlike Emma's many oddities, those were the only two I could identify in Katie's behaviour. There were other things I can now view differently through hindsight. Katie mentioned a few times she had trouble sleeping. This grew until she suffered insomnia in her early teens. Nightmares were also a problem, but she never mentioned them until much later.

In 1998, Katie entered year 9. Her class was to travel to a new campus that the progressive school had just opened in Nanjing, China. Our daughter was worried about being away for five weeks without counselling, so we arranged for a teacher to meet her psychologist and be made aware of the situation. The school was wonderful, the safety nets were set up – Katie was told she had to tell the teacher if she needed help, felt unsafe or wanted to go home, and the teacher would ring Anthony at any time. We had several meetings at the school and by the end of it we all felt happy and confident with our emergency plan.

The trip went very well and a very happy Katie returned. She was so excited to see us and had so much to show and tell us. We were overjoyed at the positive change in her. But only hours after her return she crashed back down into a deep depression. It was so sudden. I went into her room, still delighted about her return. She was kneeling beside her open suitcase, just staring into it, still and sad. I helped her unpack but she was so down. It was returning to Oakleigh that depressed her, particularly her room. While she was away, she must have felt like all her memories were left far behind as she was caught up in a different culture, with fellow wide-eyed schoolmates for company. Now she was back in the mire.

Katie never really recovered from this depression. She was placed on medication by a psychiatrist but it didn't work. Her mood was so dark she stopped getting up in the mornings. She took more and more coaxing just to climb out of bed. She would arrive late to classes or completely miss school. She had never been like this. She was about to turn fifteen.

We spoke to the school about her depression and organised a meeting. Seven of us met: our family psychologist, Katie's psychologist, the head of campus, the school counsellor, Katie, Anthony and me. We all agreed, given Katie's emotional state, to be flexible with the number of days a week she would attend school. It varied over time, but at the lowest point she was going only two days a week, although she persisted with her regular psychology sessions.

On one of the days Katie had off school I returned home from work to find her drunk. She had been drinking from bottles kept in our liquor cabinet and I lectured her about it. I knew my admonishment and carefulness didn't work because weeks later I found her drunk again. This time she was semiconscious and vomiting-drunk. We put a lock on the liquor cabinet, which appeared to fix the problem.

I grimly compared Katie's drinking with the way Emma harmed herself. I could list the mind-numbing techniques. Sleep deprivation, vanilla essence, travel sickness tablets, alcohol and now heroin. Emma was trying to forget. Now Katie looked as though she was beginning to travel down a similar path, trying to escape her mind's house of horrors. More alcohol or drugs were needed for another piece of respite. It was a vicious circle that had no end or cure. I dearly hoped we had stopped Katie's binge drinking before it became a habit and that the counselling would work to prevent her from harming herself.

By the end of the year I thought we should go away again on another family holiday. This time we flew to Fiji, leaving on 9 December and returning on Boxing Day. We all agreed we didn't want to be home for Christmas. It was too difficult trying to be happy in front of extended family. There was no joy and we were all too exhausted to pretend. We flew out of Melbourne and into the hot sticky tropics of Fiji. The girls all enjoyed themselves, had their hair finely plaited on the beach, took part in a few local tours of village life, sightseeing, horse riding and swimming. It did us all a lot of good to get away and enjoy ourselves.

We got back after Christmas. Ten days later, early in 1999, our family was back on the endless rounds of appointments. Katie was offered a place at the adolescent day program that Emma had attended two years earlier, but she was feeling better after the holiday and declined. Instead, she opted to return to school full-time. She put her mind to her studies and began once again doing well academically.

We had been seeing and communicating with our Crimes Compensation case lawyers for eighteen months. They had become our Catholic Church case lawyers and were beginning to think that maybe we could issue a civil writ. Our solicitor had engaged a barrister, who we were about to meet. His name was Tim Seccull and he would become a very important man in our lives. Emma, Katie, Anthony and I travelled to his city office to see what he thought of our legal standing. Statements were taken individually from Emma and Katie about their assaults. Anthony and I were not included in their discussions. I knew the girls did not want to talk to us or want us to know about what had happened to them, so we respected their wishes and did not find out what was said.

After the girls' interviews Anthony and I spoke to Tim Seccull. He was a kindly man and younger than us. He explained how he would often travel to country Victoria to represent clergy sex assault victims going through the Church's Towards Healing compensation process. He spoke generally about how many of the victims were now living broken lives and unable to speak strongly for themselves, or withstand the will of the Church and its heartless scheme. He felt that it was his duty to ensure these victims received a maximum payment.

'It's something they can't achieve on their own,' our new barrister modestly explained.

He expressed himself with genuine compassion. I was almost in tears over this man's integrity and commitment to righting the wrongs these Church victims were further burdened with. Tim was a well-spoken and gentle person and his sense of justice and caring for his broken clients humbled me. I knew my girls were in good hands.

The next step was to have Emma and Katie assessed by a post-traumatic stress disorder expert.

While all this was happening, I saw an article in *The Age* newspaper in 1999 about heroin. The headline read: 'Depression under Attack'. The Victorian Premier Jeff Kennett was exploring social issues, in particular the link between drug-taking, depression and youth/adult suicide. When I read the report I had a clear knowledge of the topic he was writing about. I knew sexual assault was a common link. I thought, here is someone with the power and authority to help ease the suffering and encourage understanding.

I immediately wrote a two-page letter outlining our family's story. Early in 1996 I had begun collecting newspaper articles concerning child sexual assault by priests and anything related. Three years later I had many such clippings. I looked through them and photocopied all of those dealing with childhood sexual assaults, depression, drug addiction, alcoholism and suicide thoughts or attempts. My daughters were living examples, I wrote to Mr Kennett. In the end, I compiled seventy-six articles of many different people saying basically the same thing – that they had suffered ongoing sexual assaults as children, then presented with one or more of the above symptoms. I found a big bulldog clip, bundled the newspaper extracts neatly together and posted them with my covering letter to the premier.

A week later, I was at work when one of my employees, who used to listen to the radio in his office, excitedly called me in to listen. I heard Jeff Kennett reading my letter.

I was almost in tears.

He was speaking at a press conference about his defamation case against a newspaper. Mr Kennett was telling the reporters why he went into politics. It was to help people like us, he explained.

A couple of my friends rang, knowing our story and guessing the identity of the anonymous letter writer. I then thought of my mum and hoped she wasn't listening to the radio.

I hadn't yet told her Katie was a victim of O'Donnell. I didn't know how to tell her that the old priest had set upon another of her grandchildren. I had not expected my letter to be in the media. It had been fifteen months since we'd found out about Katie's abuse and only some of our friends in Oakleigh knew.

Mum did hear it on the radio and assumed it was her family but wondered why Mr Kennett had spoken of two daughters being sexually abused. I went down to see her and explained. More heartbreak.

That night the girls and I watched the news and saw Jeff Kennett, the Premier, reading my letter about them. He became emotional towards the end, struggling to hold back the tears. Emma and Katie were so moved that such an important person cared so much about what had happened to them. They stared with intense wonder at the screen. They were happy for days after that.

If only the Catholic Church cared as much.

His reading of my letter got the issue of child sexual assault talked about in the newspapers the next day and for a short time thereafter.

Jeff Kennett sent me two letters, expressing his sympathies. Some months later we had a chance encounter with the premier. I was driving the girls home and had exited a freeway, waiting at some traffic lights, when another car pulled up beside us. The girls recognised it was our state's leader.

'Can we get out and say hello and thank him, Mum?' they excitedly asked.

'No,' I said. 'It's too dangerous.' The lights might change, I feared.

We received word from our solicitor of an appointment with the post-traumatic stress disorder specialist, who was in Melbourne on other appointments and had kindly agreed to see Emma and Katie, saving us an interstate trip. He was an international expert on the subject, a person whose opinion could not reasonably be disputed. I organised the girls and left work to travel to the inner-city appointment. I was running a little late and driving too fast. We were pulled over and I was given a speeding ticket, the first in twenty-five years of driving. We made it on time, even with the delay. Emma saw the specialist, as did Katie.

It would be another nine months before we sighted drafts of these stress reports. When I viewed Emma's eleven-page report and Katie's seven-page report, the heart-wrenching details of O'Donnell's sexual attacks against my children were laid out before me. My mind had limited the assaults to the ones I had learned about, but the only limitation to their sexual assaults occurred when the priest retired. He had sexually assaulted them for years.

I read also the professor's clear assessment of the effects of these assaults – Emma and Katie's bleak prognosis. He wrote of Emma: 'Even with effective and appropriate treatment this woman's prognosis is poor . . . Her physical health is also likely to be severely disadvantaged. She already is involved in a series of risk-taking behaviours that are associated with premature mortality.'

Of Katie, the professor found: 'She tries not to think about the future, as she is not sure that she will be around. She does not think about having a family and she is worried that if she had children they would also be sexually abused.' Katie's prognosis, although better than Emma's, stated: 'She remains at a significantly increased risk . . . of suicidal preoccupation in her adult life.'

The following day, Emma had an interview for admission to a community residential drug withdrawal service, as she wanted to withdraw from both methadone and heroin. We wanted her to do that too but didn't know how difficult it would be.

The last activity of our Oakleigh Liaison Group was to organise a petition, taking our complaint to a higher level – Parliament. The Oakleigh International Fiesta, an event promoted by the local traders, was coming up and a few of us saw this as an opportunity to collect signatures. I approached our local member of parliament and told her of our intention. She generously helped with the correct wording for a petition and I set about making copies.

The fiesta ran over a weekend. We sat at a table both days, displaying a small sign. Almost a thousand people approached us and gave their signatures. In what was to become a recurring theme, many of them stopped and talked of their own stories of sexual abuse. Others thanked us sincerely. Some just signed without a word.

I handed in the petition to the State Parliament. It was submitted formally to the Legislative Assembly on Thursday 25 March 1999 and read:

Victorian Petition in Relation to Childhood Sexual Abuse

To The Honourable Speaker And Members of the Legislative Assembly in Parliament Assembled:

The humble petition of the Oakleigh Liaison Group . . . pray the Government immediately enact the following recommendations, that:

1. The criminal offence of sexual assault against a child be vigorously prosecuted.
2. Protocols be developed within religious organisations to ensure that the option of the criminal justice system is pursued to ensure evidence is not contaminated by internal investigations.
3. Educational programs to be funded to increase knowledge for parents and teachers about the physical and emotional indicators of physical and sexual abuse of children.

Our submission appeared in Hansard, the Parliament's official record.

Emma was admitted to the residential withdrawal service. Two days later I picked her up. She was crying and wanted to go home. Coming off heroin was no easy matter.

I arranged for a community health centre nurse to visit Emma at home and help her beat her addiction. That night my daughter again cut her wrists. I took her to a GP. After a short series of appointments with specialists she was readmitted into the child and adolescent psychiatric unit, which she knew so well.

It was as if she was stuck on a never-ending, dark carousel. No matter what she tried, she couldn't jump off it to safety. Three days later, she was discharged and I brought her home. The following day there was terrible news. A beautiful young woman who volunteered her time at Emma's community school to cook students' lunches had been brutally murdered in her own home. The violent death sent a shock through the tiny school and the whole community. Emma was broken-hearted, as she knew the young woman well. She was so angry that someone so wonderful could be stalked and killed in such a way. Together they would often prepare the lunches, talking and laughing together.

In distress, Emma was readmitted to the psych unit but stayed only a week.

Peter O'Callaghan, the Queen's Counsel appointed to head up the Pell Process, made an appointment to visit our home to discuss Katie's application for the ex gratia compensation from the Church, which had accepted that the sexual abuse by O'Donnell had taken place. Earlier I had submitted to Mr O'Callaghan a copy of Katie's suicide note stating that both she and Emma had been repeatedly raped by O'Donnell; the diary description of O'Donnell taking her into the church to look for pencils; and other accounts of assault. On this evidence, Mr O'Callaghan stated he would be making a finding in Katie's favour.

As with Emma, I was neither pleased nor displeased by his decision. We knew the assaults were real and did not see how the Church could disagree.

Mr O'Callaghan also wanted to talk privately to Emma about her accepting the archbishop's earlier offer of $50,000. Emma had not yet signed the paperwork for the money to be held in trust until her eighteenth birthday, just seven months away. We had told Emma not to sign, as we were taking legal steps (unknown to the Church), which would be negated forever if she signed her acceptance of the Church's offer. We refused his request for a one-on-one meeting with our daughter.

'You can speak to Emma in our presence,' we offered.

He chatted to her in front of us and left on good terms.

Two weeks later Peter O'Callaghan rang me at work to ask about our lawyers. He had somehow found out we were considering alternative legal action. I did not confirm one way or another what we were doing. Regardless, he did not send his written findings of Katie's case.

Throughout this whole hectic struggle, Aimee, our youngest daughter, continued her education. We had taken her from Oakleigh's Sacred Heart Girls College and enrolled her at Katie's grammar school. On 25 May 1999, she prepared to hop on a plane with her classmates, bound for their school's China campus as Katie had done the previous year. Aimee packed up her bags with great excitement. We all took her out to the airport and waited with the other thirty students and families to wave her away on her big adventure.

She had suffered through her sisters' trauma and seen so much agony. Her life was such a great burden for one so young and it weighed heavily upon her. It was a relief to think she was about to have a positive experience and a few weeks of respite. It was a joy to see her smile and be able to smile back at her.

She was gone for three days before all our lives were damaged beyond repair after another horrifying incident.

We thought Katie had stopped binge drinking. She hadn't.

It was Friday night. Katie travelled to a friend's house to stay the night. At ten-thirty our phone rang. Anthony answered. He looked pale and serious as he hung up the phone. He'd been talking to the father of Katie's friend.

'There's been an accident, Katie's been hit by a car,' my husband said. 'Get Emma up.'

I looked at him. 'Is she all right? What happened?'

He was silent, rushing up the hallway, getting ready to leave. I could tell he was in emergency mode. It was a look I had seen many times. I hurried into Emma's room, anxious but trying to stay calm for fear of panicking her. She was still awake and turned to me.

'You have to get up, Katie's had an accident.'

Within minutes we were in the car, backing down the lane. Again I asked what had happened.

'What did they say?'

Anthony said: 'The ambulance is taking her to the Austin Hospital.'

Ambulance?

The first feelings of serious dread began to pass through me. My husband gave me his mobile phone and said to ring Katie's friend's dad and find out more. I punched in the number and waited for it to pick up. I heard his voice.

'How's Katie?' I asked. He didn't answer the question. Instead he started talking about the ambulance, where it was going, how they were following it. It was all rushed and there was a lot of background noise.

'She's all right, isn't she?' I pressed. But still no answer.

Anything but the answer.

I repeated. 'She's all right, isn't she?' This time I was demanding an answer. I waited, my anxiety choking me.

No reply.

Beyond his silence I heard my answer. The background noise suddenly became recognisable. It was the wailing of Katie's friend, the mournful wailing of bereavement.

I hung up the phone and sat in the car, my face now feeling as ashen as Anthony's looked. We sped the many kilometres to the hospital in terrifying quiet, each of us battling individual thoughts.

We arrived before the ambulance. It had been travelling very slowly so as to cause no further injury. The other family was soon there and told us what had happened.

Katie and her friend had visited another friend and they were all leaving that house when Katie ran out on to the road. She was following the others and didn't look properly. A car struck her. She was flung high into the air and landed flat on her back, in the emergency-stopping lane of the divided dual carriageway. The impacts, of both the car and then the road, had stopped her heart. Her friends could see she was not breathing.

After a while, nobody knew how long – Katie's friends were hysterical – one of them started attempting to revive her. The roadway was not busy but several cars had stopped. The driver behind the car that hit Katie began to help with the CPR. This man later said he had witnessed two other fatal accidents and never tried CPR. He decided this time to try. Then another driver, an off-duty nurse, took over from the person doing heart compressions that she said were not being done properly. The police and ambulance arrived. The ambulance officers treated Katie, then drove carefully to hospital.

We waited many hours to see our injured daughter. Anthony had called my parents, his mother and my older brother, asking them to come to the hospital. I wanted them with us. Eventually Anthony and I were led into a large room. Katie was lying alone. It wasn't the emergency room. No-one was rushing anywhere. It felt more like a morgue. There were no nurses or medical equipment, just Katie on a low metal bench. When I got nearer, I could see she looked dead, her eyes a quarter open. I saw an unconsciousness that went beyond sleep. Above her left eye was an impact injury, which was a bit swollen but not bleeding. I saw no other injuries. I went to her and touched her hand and said her name. There was nothing. Anthony and I stood. Looking.

I hoped with all my being she would be all right. Hope was the only thing to cling to and it was all we had for the next couple of years.

We were allowed to stay only a few minutes, then had to leave the room. We lingered a bit longer in the waiting room then went home, into the dawning light, without our girl.

The nursing staff had assured us they would call if anything happened. I got into bed, and cannot remember thinking anything as sleep took over. I awoke some hours later, instantly alert. The phone had not made a sound.

Katie must be okay, I thought.

I rang the hospital.

'Yes. She is stable.'

We showered, dressed and returned to the hospital. Katie was now in the intensive care unit. After a wait, we were allowed to see her. This time, walls of medical equipment surrounded her and a nurse sat at the foot of her bed. Katie wore a pink hospital gown and lay there like a pretty doll, except for a breathing tube down her throat and sensors of many kinds attached to her, with wires running to a bank of beeping machines behind her. There were about eight sensor plugs. Monitors flashed or glowed their mysterious readings and graphs. I could decipher only the heart monitor, which blinked away at us.

We sat beside Katie and looked at her, wondering if she was thinking anything, feeling any pain, hoping she would wake up soon.

We stayed until late that night. Just before leaving we spoke to a doctor.

'She will be all right, won't she?' I said to him. 'She made it through last night.' He replied: 'The danger's not over. She could die tonight from brain swelling.'

It was as blunt as that.

We left even more distressed. As we drove down the hill from the hospital we both began to cry. Since the accident we were clinging to the hope she would be all right and were holding it together. But now the doctor's words removed this hope. The horror of losing Katie was finally real to us. Anthony and I had cried many times, one comforting the other. This was the first time we cried together. There was no comforting us now.

Again I fell into a deep sleep and awoke with a start the next morning. The phone had not rung. She was still alive! Anthony rang to make sure.

'She's still stable.'

We returned again to the hospital; it was Sunday morning. Our vigil was only just beginning. Emma was greatly affected by Katie's injuries. She quietly sat by her bedside, holding her sister's hand, waiting for a response.

Friends were there for us during that desperate period. The previous evening, at the end of a dinner attended by about forty people, most of them from the Oakleigh Liaison Group, an announcement was made about Katie's accident. During the next four months, the women in our group kindly left meals on our front verandah for us to have when we returned home late from the hospital each night. It was a caring and concerted effort that we were grateful for and will never forget. Other neighbours, family and friends all helped us too.

X-rays showed that the blow from the car to the side of Katie's head had caused three bleeds to her brain, two minor ones near the centre and a large bleed behind the forehead. The impact on the road when she landed had fractured the back of her skull. It was later found that some bone had been chipped off the corner of her elbow. She also had two minor grazes, one on her leg and one on her wrist.

To our horror we discovered that Katie had been drunk when the car hit her. The driver had also been drinking and was over the legal limit.

Anthony contacted Katie and Aimee's school to notify them of Katie's accident and ask that Aimee be returned from China. A teacher escorted her for the whole trip.

Again Aimee was thrown into an emergency. She sobbed when she saw her comatose sister.

We were given Katie's clothes and jewellery in a big, clear plastic bag. All the clothes had been cut off her after the accident. Her favourite velvety maroon jeans were split up the centre of both legs and cut through the waistband. The material on the upper leg had melted with the friction of being rubbed against the car body during the sixty to seventy kilometres per hour impact. I saw the red paint of the car on the jeans. I held the remnants of her clothing in my hands, imagining the impact, the force that could have melted her clothing, fusing the red paint to them . . . the force that must have travelled through her body.

I later saw the police investigation photographs of the car and noted that the front passenger side hit her first. There was a broken headlight. Streaks of white – or missing red paint – ran along the panel, right up to the side mirror, which shattered upon Katie. Her head smashed the windscreen before she was flung high into the air . . .

'Fifty feet,' estimated a witness, who thought our daughter was a kangaroo being hit into the air.

The ambulance officers who tended Katie at the scene of the accident caringly rang to find out how she was. They followed up several times, wanting to know how she was progressing.

Katie's body didn't like the breathing tube in her mouth. She bit hard on it until they put a mouthguard in place. Still she continued to bite down, with less effect but enough pressure to separate her two front teeth. Her previously perfect teeth were beginning to form a noticeable gap.

Katie's brain continued to swell. Doctors decided to place her in an induced coma to reduce brain activity. When they brought her out of the coma, they were still concerned so they decided to take over her breathing, again to reduce brain activity. A tracheotomy was performed. Once all the equipment was in place she was induced into a deeper coma.

She was helpless and so perfectly still. I wondered if she would ever wake up.

Chapter 13
Katie's struggle

I noticed a white fleck inside Katie's mouth. When I looked closer I could see it was an ulcer. There were lots of them. The following day, her mouth was almost full. There were hundreds of sores on her gums, tongue and lips. One mouth ulcer is painful, but so many would be torturous. I hoped she could not feel the pain.

The doctors weren't sure what was best for our daughter. They again brought Katie out of the induced coma, only to place her back into it. The pressure mounting inside her skull was dangerously high. The usual pressure inside your skull triples for a second when you sneeze. Katie's skull pressure was constantly ten times that of a healthy person. It would not go down.

While she was back in the induced comatose state, surgeons drilled a hole just above her hairline and inserted a probe to take pressure readings. It protruded from her skull like an iron pencil. We followed these readings with great angst. More swelling meant more brain damage. She was induced into three comas until the dangerously high pressure began to abate.

Police had taken statements and accident investigation officers collected evidence, searching for the cause of the serious accident in the event that Katie died. Like us, they were not sure whether Katie would survive and often rang to check on her condition.

Anthony, Emma, Aimee and I all visited Katie every morning and stayed until night-time. She was soon attracting up to thirty visitors a day. Relatives, schoolfriends, our friends, Emma's friends, Aimee's friends all came to show they cared. But only very few were allowed into the intensive care unit. They went in one at a time for a few minutes to sit solemnly next to our motionless daughter.

We waited and waited for positive news from the doctors. A specialist came to me five days after the accident and I could tell he was not about to raise my hopes. 'We believe Katie will remain as she is,' he declared. 'In a coma, in a vegetative state.'

Minutes later, still trying to stop my head spinning, I was approached by two young women from the Transport Accident Commission (TAC). They wanted to discuss insurance. I was hardly able to speak to them and could barely hear what they were saying.

All I could make out was: 'You have nothing to worry about. Katie's medical costs were fully covered.'

I was still floundering with the news that Katie would never recover. Anthony wasn't around to talk to. Anger and denial began to take over my thoughts.

I thought back to the doctor who initially said Katie would die. 'He was wrong about her,' I thought defiantly. 'She's still alive.' I decided not to believe the specialist who said my daughter would not wake up.

He might be wrong too. It felt better to tell myself that. When Anthony arrived, we discussed Katie's prognosis and he too chose not to believe the experts.

'How can they tell someone that when they don't know it for sure?' I said.

A week after the accident, a physiotherapist came in to plaster Katie's legs. I didn't understand why until she explained that the tendons down the back of legs shrink when inactive. Katie's feet were in a position that could have seen her further disabled if left pointing down. But it was already too late and it would take ten years of physio, two years of wearing plaster, Botox injections and an operation to attempt correction.

There was so much to worry about.

As much as we didn't want to, we had to work. With twenty-eight employees to manage, the pressures were great. We had recently expanded and taken on more plumbers. Anthony had to drive the business and direct the staff. I managed the accounts and calculated the wages weekly. I walked into work and felt like an alien in a different world. Everybody was very kind but I just wanted to complete the necessary tasks so I could return to the hospital. The need to always be with Katie was primal.

The family Katie was staying with before the accident spent as much time at the hospital as we did. They kept us company in the long and lonely vigil, providing a distraction from our struggle. When they were not there I cried constantly for Katie.

I became anxious when she was moved to a neurology ward. Over the previous fourteen days I had grown accustomed to the safety of the machines in the intensive care unit. While she was in ICU I believed she might be cured but when she was wheeled out, still unconscious, I felt her chances of living a normal life were slipping. Reality was knocking to tell me this was all they could do for her; let her lie in a ward. Then, after another week, Katie was transferred again, this time to a rehabilitation hospital.

Emma, meanwhile, continued to struggle through her days and nights. She overdosed twice on her medication and was rushed to an emergency ward. Doctors admitted her and for a while Anthony and I visited two of our daughters in different hospitals.

Fortunately, once it appeared Katie was not going to die, Aimee wanted to return to China and we let her. We didn't want her to miss out on a positive overseas experience. The Qantas airline staff cared for her and she was quickly reunited with her classmates at the end of the flight.

One night, while sitting by Katie's bed, I noticed something significant. She was really hot and had been suffering from overheating for weeks. It was part of the brain injury. We all had to constantly wipe perspiration from her. This night, when I was watching her closely, wiping her down, I saw her little toe wiggle slightly. It was the first time she had moved, apart from biting down on the airway tube, in the four or five weeks since the accident. I told everyone about it. It was very exciting. The following night the next toe moved and the third night the third toe moved. That's how her recovery started and it stayed at that pace for many years. Her brain was like a computer slowly rebooting.

On Katie's sixteenth birthday in July, the nursing staff sat her up, fully supported on the edge of her bed. She was still in a comatose state and could not support herself. When we arrived to visit and saw her in this position, it was a big surprise. Anthony held her and I took a photo of them together to mark the occasion.

After a while, routine set in. Aimee had come home from China and resumed her normal education. She rode with her dad every morning to work and then caught a connecting bus to her secondary school. In the afternoon she caught a train as close as possible to the rehabilitation hospital and then walked the rest of the way, carrying her heavy school bag up a large hill, devoted to visiting her sister every day. We all met at the hospital and later went home together.

Driving to the bank after work one day, I felt the pressure of my life building like a tempest. Our plan to expand at work had disintegrated. Anthony's heart wasn't in it. All our drive and energy had gone, but we still had the new employees. Only ten days before the accident, Anthony had purchased fourteen new work vans, a whole fleet for our company's expansion. The cost was huge – a massive debt. Now our business was grinding to an economic standstill, as the over-heads were immense and production diminished. Among other things, we knew we would have to let the new workers go; another emotional hardship and worry. Going to the bank reminded me of our crumbling financial position, one I had not had to face before.

I pulled up in the car park, utterly depressed and defeated, and went over everything in my mind. The money the Catholic Church offered Emma as part of its compensation scheme was still there. It was an unwanted carrot dangling dangerously before Emma's eyes. Emma wanted to claim it. She was badgering me to accept. I knew it was the drug addic-tion talking but it was hard to keep her off the subject. She was about to turn eighteen, which meant she could soon sign for the payout herself.

And there was Katie . . . her ruined life . . . the distress, travelling into the city every day and the constant heartbreak we were met with. Every part of our life was in decline.

It was all so unbearable.

Then there was the thought of fighting the Church in court.

In these desperate few moments I started to think about our commitment to suing the Roman Catholic Church, one of the richest organisations in the world, with its seemingly endless resources. It was a significant stress. Was it too risky? Would we lose everything? I felt I was falling apart both inside and out.

The enormity of the legal battle ahead of us was the final straw. I couldn't endure it any longer. I picked up my phone and rang Anthony,

'Taking the Church to court,' I began. 'I can't do it. It's all off.'

Without asking any questions Anthony said: 'Okay.'

I said goodbye and hung up. I expected to feel some relief at unburdening myself of this huge emotional and financial worry. But I didn't feel better. I felt the opposite. I sat there thinking. I had never contemplated not holding the Church accountable; it was not an option. My drive from the beginning was to pursue them wholly and totally for what they had done and failed to do.

Over the years I'd only ever had a steely resolve about where the blame lay. I knew every injustice, pain and suffering of our children and ourselves was caused by the Church allowing O'Donnell to stay where he was. I knew every cold and harsh word, every callous act they had thrown our way because we dared to demand their accountability and compassion, would one day be presented to them when we faced each other in a court of law, where they would be exposed for what they were and forced to take responsibility for what they had done.

I had never doubted this.

I had said as much to our solicitor. How could it be otherwise? The world was not round if they, a Church and its priests, people claiming to be Christians, could do these things to children, my children, and just walk away. And now I had given in. I was letting them just walk away. I burst into tears and sobbed, my head pressing on the steering wheel. I had betrayed my daughters and myself.

I couldn't believe the intensity of my anguish. Ten minutes passed. I stopped crying and picked up the phone. I called Anthony. When he answered I said simply: 'It's back on.'

Without asking any questions he replied: 'Okay.'

It was far more horrifying to let them get away with it than to continue the fight. New determination spoke when I got home from the bank. I found Emma in her room.

'There are only two choices,' I said to her. 'You either go back to school or you come and work with us. There's no more staying at home doing nothing.'

Emma became our receptionist. She had a strong work ethic, a friendly phone manner and was helpful to customers. We were delighted.

Katie was placed in the locked-up section of the acquired brain injury ward. I didn't understand why she needed to be in a secure section of the hospital. She couldn't move or utter a sound. But it was in this room that Katie's eyes first started to move. We had learned that one of the first signs of recovery was what the doctors called 'tracking'. Her eyes, staring at the ceiling, would move from right to left and then back again. At first it was a short range of movement. Then, as the days passed, she started tracking from one corner of the ceiling to the other, repeating the action over and over. We thought it was wonderful and instantly wanted more.

Her left hand began to move and it progressed quicker than her toes. We held her hand all the time and began to feel it exploring our fingers and palms. If she touched a ring she gripped it and started wriggling it off the finger. Once the ring was off she would flip it over onto her own finger, then rest her hand. It was as if she was looking for her ring and had found it. It struck me as intelligent and thoughtful but it was all done without facial expressions or sound. She couldn't look at what she was doing. Only feel. Her right hand was inactive, while her left hand seemed to have a mind of its own, without any tangible connection to the body it was attached to.

Katie was soon transferred into the ordinary rehabilitation section. Up until this stage she was being fed intravenously. But within weeks she had an operation, which allowed her to have a food supplement enter directly into her stomach via what was called a 'peg tube feeder', which needed an opening, like a colostomy, at the entry point. It was best not to look at it.

Her comatose state lasted almost four months. She didn't suddenly wake up like I half expected, maybe because I'd seen it happen like that on television. It started with that one toe moving and went from there. To me, her coma ended when she first reacted to something and that was when Aimee brought in one of Katie's Pound Puppies, a plastic toy she had had when she was a little girl. Aimee found it at home, stored away, discarded years ago by Katie. When it was presented to her, she had an emotional reaction at seeing it.

Almost crying, her eyes reddened. She tried to move, eventually lifting her left hand and silently grasping her toy.

It was a beautiful moment.

From then we discovered that she could follow instructions. We said: 'Smile.' And she smiled broadly until we said she didn't have to any longer. Then she stopped just as quickly as she had obeyed. There was nothing in between.

Her improvements were slow and we couldn't help comparing them with other patients in the rehabilitation hospital. Others would come, recover and go. We wondered how long she would have to stay there.

She eventually began to speak. We would say to her: 'Say hello.' And she would reply, 'Hello.' But only in a voice so soft it was barely audible.

The drunk driver who'd hit Katie was brought to criminal court. We didn't attend but the police officer handling the case told us about it. The driver got off on a technicality. I was told that because the policeman who attended the accident scene did not ask the driver if he needed to see a doctor, the case was 'thrown out of court'. Just like that. I did not understand how this minor detail could wipe away the drink driving offence. Katie's accident lawyer told me: 'Don't worry about that now.' So I just kept repeating his words to myself, as I still do.

Emma turned eighteen and continued trying to live as normally as she could.

Not everything was about the cash offer from the Church. Emma wanted to become a nurse, so together we looked into it and found entrance exams were taking place for Division Two nurses. She booked in for two separate university exams and passed both, which meant she was accepted to two different courses. She chose one and looked forward to studying full-time at tertiary level the following year. We saw this as a new beginning for Emma and once more hoped this would be an important turning point in her life. The confidence she would gain might ward off her depression and self-dislike, and we also believed it fitted Emma's nature perfectly.

When Emma was almost four years old, we went on a family holiday to Marysville, a beautiful town east of Melbourne. In the guest lounge where we were staying, Anthony and I were sitting with Aimee, who was six months and Katie, two. Another guest sat on the far side of the large room. The woman was alone and in silence. I watched Emma race around the room, exploring. I hoped she wasn't disturbing others. When she came across the woman, Emma stopped playing and became suddenly quiet. She stood in front of the stranger, who was staring blankly at the floor. Bending down a little, Emma peered up into the woman's face and met her eyes. The two looked at each other for a moment then Emma, with a sad look on her face, put her little hand gently on the woman's knee and patted it. The woman smiled at Emma, who then went happily on her way.

A few minutes later the woman came over to us.

'You have a sensitive child there,' she said. 'She perceived my mood as I am feeling very sad. Your little girl stopped her own playful joy to comfort me. I can't get over how such a young child could show so much empathy. She patted me on the knee in sympathy and made me smile.'

We thanked her and thought our big girl was very special.

With this memory in mind, I believed Emma would naturally be a great nurse and, most importantly, she had chosen to do it herself without any prompting from us.

Also, without any prompting from us, and in preparation for her studies next year, Emma admitted herself into the residential drug withdrawal service again, to get off heroin and methadone. Our hopes and admiration rose even more with this mature and responsible decision.

On Christmas Day 1999 Katie came home. It was lovely to have her back in the house, if only for one day. She was resting on the couch and Anthony was talking to her, while I prepared our lunch. All of a sudden Anthony excitedly called me over.

'Listen,' he said.

Katie spoke in a normal voice. No whisper!

Emma and Aimee heard it too. We were all so excited. It was Katie's old familiar voice. A voice we had not heard for seven months. We all sat around listening and talking to her. It was the best Christmas present. In typical fashion, Katie took it in her stride and didn't know what all the fuss was about. The normal voice stayed for about two hours that day then left. It came and went over the following weeks, until it stayed permanently.

After Christmas came the millennium new year. Katie was in hospital, unable to stay awake late at night but we had seen her during the day. Emma, Aimee, Anthony and I all went to our friends' special celebration. Seconds before midnight, the four of us were standing in a small circle (all the families were in similar groups) joining in with the countdown. When we said 'THREE, TWO, ONE', instead of cheering, hugging and laughing, as all the others were, we all looked at each other and in that split second our pain hit us. All four of us burst into tears. It was so unexpected and sudden, so heartfelt and strong. The dawn of a new time brought home to us the cruel life we had to endure. For that brief moment the runaway train that held us captive halted and we paused to see in each other's faces the hideous, shocking suffering that we recognised in the mirror each day.

Emma began her nursing course with studious determination. Her last regular schooling was in her early anorexia stage, halfway through year 8. We were very proud of her.

Aimee began year 10. Her performance at secondary school was inconsistent. The stress on her was as heavy as it was for us. Katie was learning how to eat again, not just how to use a spoon but how to swallow and digest food, like a baby switching from breast milk to solids. All her meals were softened, mashed and moist. She could not drink – drinking was the hardest to learn. All liquids had to be thickened, even water. I stirred the thickening powder in so the spoon would stand upright by itself in the middle of the cup. While it didn't seem so odd in the fruit juice, it did look very strange in the water. Many a time, even with this aid, she began to cough and choke as it went down the wrong way.

Katie could not cry. The tears would not come and still don't. It was very upsetting to know she was denied this important emotional function. It was just part of her brain damage. But at least she was improving. She was beginning to spend Saturdays at home with us, taking day leave from the hospital. These visits lengthened to take in Saturday nights. She loved being home and hated returning to her ward. We travelled with her in the wheelchair taxi and she screamed the whole way back. It was very traumatic for all of us.

In time, she began to tell the doctors at the hospital that a priest sexually abused her when she was a child. Her memory appeared to be returning but it soon became clear our daughter only recalled things from a long time ago. Her short-term memory never returned to her. To this day, ten years later, she asks the same questions over and over.

About three minutes after asking a question she repeats it, having forgotten the answer. In those early days of recovery, when she was at home she kept asking: 'What date is it?' After months of this, it felt as though she had worn out that part of my brain and it took me some time and effort to recall what day it was. I had to rattle off the whole date – the day of the week, the date, the month and the year. If I forgot to say any part of it, she asked me for the detail I'd left out. I had searched shops without luck for a tabletop calendar to stand in front of her so I could merely point, instead of racking my brain for the detailed date sentence. In the bank I saw the perfect tabletop calendar, the day, the date, the month, all on cards that could be turned over daily to display the answer to Katie's relentless question. The only thing missing was the year, but I thought I could fix that by writing the year on a piece of paper and sticking it on the lower part of the stand. Towards the end of every year Katie almost remembered what year it was, but then it changed and she started all over again. I had never seen one of these date stands for sale. Every time I walked into the bank I saw the calendar and began to think about stealing it. Will they miss it? Would they mind? I asked the teller where the bank bought their date stands. She looked at me blankly and shrugged. I contemplated asking if she wanted to sell it, but thought better of it. Eventually, I settled for an electronic display clock I found with the essential date details – I had to stick the year on the display – and hung it where Katie sat. Now she knows where to look for the date without asking.

She still asks Anthony over and over. 'Can I take over our family business?' There's nothing we would like more but it will never happen. Katie is close to being unable to learn anything new. She can get to know a new person by repeatedly seeing them over a long period but does not remember conversations or activities shared. Amazingly she can learn songs and sing along to the radio; the musical part of her brain is apparently not so damaged.

While Katie forgets what happened three minutes ago, her memories from childhood and before the accident are intact.

It is cruel. Katie remembers her abuse but not current day-to-day things that would help distract her away from her darker past. Our straight-A student has been reduced to a permanent grade five or six level.

It took us a long time to understand Katie's new disabilities. The phone beside her hospital bed was used frequently. She rang ten times a day, sometimes more; telling me or yelling at me that she wanted to come home. I accepted all her calls – not wanting to abandon her. We attended meetings with her social worker, conversation group therapist, music therapist, continence service worker, speech therapist, occupational therapist, chief neurologist, dietician, neurological psychologist, physiotherapist and the team leader. We visited her almost every day, sometimes twice. In the year Katie was in hospital, we missed just six days and were racked with guilt each time, even though a few minutes after we left she had forgotten we were ever there.

During her time in hospital Anthony read *Lord of the Rings* to Katie every night. When she got home I read her *Harry Potter* every night. She returned home for good on 26 May 2000, three hundred and sixty-four days and more than four hundred hospital visits after the accident. It had been a traumatic year but we only ever looked at Katie's progress and were grateful for every inch of it, hoping with all our hearts it would not stop. In the previous twelve months, our business had gone from twenty-eight employees at the time of Katie's accident, down to ten. It was a reflection of our depleted life. But we were still open for business.

A few weeks later we combined a homecoming party with Katie's seventeenth birthday. We filled two hundred beautifully-coloured balloons with helium. Multicoloured ribbons hung from each one and they filled our family room. We invited all our friends and relatives and celebrated Katie coming back to us.

Previously, when Katie was on weekend leave from hospital we let her sleep in her own room and bed, with some trepidation. She insisted. We installed a push-button bell next to her bed, which she soon learned to use. Anthony attached a small light to it so she could see it at night. She would ring numerous times and one of us would get up to her and transfer her to the toilet. As it was nearing time for Katie to leave the hospital and return home permanently, I began to dread the prospect of the hard work involved in looking after her both at night and during the day. She was allowed some carers at home but she didn't want them, and there would be no help at night. Only us.

My fears were reasonable. When Katie settled back into life with us, she rang the bell four to six times a night. We awoke each time and took it in turns to get up to her. This lasted about five years then lessened. It was stressful and tiring.

A neuropsychologist and a neurologist assessed Katie for her accident case with the TAC. She was rated with an eighty-nine per cent disability. Memory is such a necessity that the loss of it rates highly. Katie was confined to a wheelchair unless transferred, couldn't stand unaided, and had little use of her right arm and hand. She writes like a child in grade two.

Emma studied hard all year to pass her nursing course. We were so proud of her and attended her graduation ceremony at a suburban town hall. We heard her name called out and watched as she went on stage to receive her certificate. We then all posed for happy photos. As a graduation gift I bought her a nurse's watch; one that pins on and hangs upside down. Our eldest daughter, who was about to turn nineteen, wore it proudly.

Soon it was 2001. Emma had a successful job interview. She began work as a nurse, took out a loan and bought a car, making repayments from her wages. Things were going well for her.

We had seen our barrister Tim Seccull a few times and had many telephone discussions. Our solicitor, who was originally working alongside Tim, was experienced in handling victims' claims against the Church. He knew how difficult it was to go up against such a rich adversary, but the pair of professionals persisted on our behalf to try to find ways of achieving justice. At this stage, suing the Church still felt like climbing Mt Everest and we were really only at base camp.

The years ticked by and then our solicitor changed jobs. His firm appointed a new lawyer to us – a similarly determined and compassionate solicitor called Michael Jorgensen. He was just like Tim; he had that warmth in his eyes and words. His actions were reassuring and we knew that, together, these thoughtful men would be worthy opponents of the Church if indeed our case progressed and we issued a writ.

Increasingly, that is what I wanted.

For a long time our relationship with Tim and Michael was mostly played out over the phone. There were lots of calls back and forth. I made notes from the conversations, as I did with almost everything that happened to us. I didn't know what Tim and Michael were planning legally. My role was to be persistent and encouraging.

'There just has to be something that can be done,' I said to Michael repeatedly. I held on to that hope, waiting patiently, expecting some positive answers or results.

In preparing our case, we were at times both optimistic and pessimistic, swinging from side to side. Tim and Michael knew the legal reality. At first Tim seemed hopeful. When Michael started, he shared that rosy outlook, but as the men noted the grim legal precedents from around the national court archives, our solicitor grew a little more 'realistic'. Not that his actions ever suggested giving up was an option.

'It's never been done before,' Tim and Michael reminded us often, and then pressed on regardless. Many a time they inspired us with their attitude.

As part of their evidence-gathering, both wanted to go the Sacred Heart Parish to view the church and school hall, so I arranged for a visit.

Meanwhile, a new staff member of the Church's Carelink office contacted us, saying she wanted to meet for a coffee, so we agreed on a time and date. She was very compassionate and asked why we weren't seeing a psychologist. To our resigned shrugs, she said we, including Aimee, should be seeing a counsellor. She told us to send her the accounts. We didn't argue. Up until that point, the Pell Process had refused to pay for our intermittent therapy. We were not 'victims of sexual abuse', according to a letter sent to us by the Archdiocese of Melbourne. So at her invitation, Anthony and I began seeing a local family therapist to help us through our struggles.

In our therapy sessions we discussed our many issues, our irresolvable problems. Katie's plight – her permanent state of disability, the reasons behind the accident – dominated our talks. The trauma from her assaults and accident came back to haunt us for many years and still does. Emma's problems . . . Aimee's difficulties . . . We seemed to almost deal with one aspect of our anger, heartbreak or frustration, only for it to reinvent itself and attack us from a different angle. There was no escaping it; it was our everyday reality.

Aimee also began to see the same family therapist. She was in year 11 and could not get on with Emma, and was frustrated by the constant presence and ever-changing parade of carers for Katie. She was also enduring panic attacks and survivor guilt.

The carers worked at home to cover Anthony and me during business hours. They started at nine in the morning and finished at seven in the evening. After and before that time and overnight, Anthony and I were Katie's carers. She didn't like having carers and believed she could look after herself. She was often irate and yelled at her carers to leave. This was terrible and I felt dreadful about it but the brain injury had removed most inhibitions from Katie. She still says what she thinks and swears often. Regardless, over the years we have had some wonderful young women carers and some of them have become Katie's friends. Many have stayed two or three years with her.

With such angst in the house, we decided Aimee should move out and board at her school. Melbourne-based students didn't normally live in but the school generously allowed Aimee to do so under the circumstances. We were happy she was in a more peaceful environment.

It was a liberal school and one night it hosted a 'Policy on Drugs' meeting and Anthony and I turned up to a room full of chatting parents. The school was thinking of implement- ing a new drug education program, in an attempt to educate students and help them avoid using or experimenting. Many parents had turned up and I thought the teacher giving the lecture looked and sounded a little nervous. I guessed maybe she was new but later I found out why she was so anxious. At question time, the parents, in an orderly fashion and a matter- of-fact way, demanded explanations.

'What does the school think it's doing by introducing a drug program?' said one father.

A mother added: 'What do you expect to achieve?'

The questions were put forcefully. I sat there cringing at the serious tone of these parents' voices and their demands. Now *I* was nervy. Over and over I thought to myself: 'We're going to get into trouble.' I felt a big invisible hand was going to come out of nowhere, and slap us for asking these questions and speaking to a teacher in this way. Then suddenly I realised what I was thinking and how I was feeling. I was scared. It was my Catholic system conditioning.

No big hand was going to hit me.

What a dominant presence the Church had been all my life – and I had only just realised it! It was there all along. But it was so ingrained I didn't even know it was intimidating me. The seeds had been planted so early; they were beyond thought and remained unquestioned. In all the Catholic school and church meetings I had ever attended we were never allowed the freedom of speech that these Anglican parents knew well and took for granted.

I had received a lifetime of Catholic training to be silent. From mass, where we were never asked our opinions or allowed to speak – except to recite the words printed in prayer books – through to church or school meetings as an adult, silence and obedience were expected. We went there to listen and be told what to do. If we didn't like what we heard we would speak in disgruntled tones quietly after the meeting and then obey anyway. I was not used to a meeting where you could argue the agenda and demand explanations from a teacher, or whoever was in charge, no matter what the subject. It was an eye-opener and made me realise just how brainwashed and dominated we had all been in the Catholic system.

We took Katie to a Pearl Jam concert. It was her favourite group. As we were driving out of the underground car park after the show Katie noticed the program on her knee. She picked it up excitedly.

'Oh, Pearl Jam! Can I see them?'

I looked at her with a smile that didn't want to be there. She had forgotten already.

'We have just seen them,' I said, trying to sound positive and help her recall. 'Look.' I pointed behind us to the huge venue we were exiting. When she turned back and saw Pearl Jam's name up in lights her face became instantly distraught and she began crying without tears. 'I can't remember seeing them.'

In her distress Katie asked me to kill her. 'Kill me, please kill me.' I had no words for this. All I could do was hug her.

I had heard this plea before from Katie and it devastated me. I knew she wanted to die before the accident. The O'Donnell assaults made her think life wasn't worth living. Now, being terribly disabled, she felt even worse.

I had recurring dreams. They were wonderful while they lasted in their unreal realm. I could see Katie walking again, free from her twisted body. I was so elated and overjoyed that my girl was whole again, walking happily. Then I awoke and crashed heavily. It was just a dream and the truth was heartbreaking. Anthony had the same dreams. We share the same disappointment.

Holiday respite was something we looked into. The TAC offered various nursing homes or special residential accommodations where we could take Katie for a few weeks to give her and us a break. We checked out the different facilities around Melbourne and regional areas but they were all too sad and we could never leave her at those places. That form of respite was not for us.

A year later we looked into community access holiday getaways for Katie; they sounded ideal so we booked one. When we arrived, there were severely disabled people of all ages. Katie, whose mind and thinking was much the same as it used to be – just less able – was placed into a bus with them. My heart sank. She looked distressed but put on a brave face. She said hello to one of her fellow passengers, who just continued to stare vacantly at her. It was a nightmare. We waved her off but there was no respite for us; only tears, guilt and the memory of Katie's face – she was forever the little girl who wanted to do the right thing and therefore didn't make a fuss as she was driven off on her four-day holiday.

We don't do respite now.

The Catholic Church never understood or indicated it knew how desperate we were. Ever. The Pell Process commissioner Peter O'Callaghan rang to say he was sorry to hear about Katie's accident but no-one from the hierarchy even did that.

The archbishop had written a letter to my family in 1996. The words echoed in my head sometimes, when I felt I was crawling on my hands and knees through the fields of hell.

'I can only trust that through this trial, you and your family might find new depths of faith within yourselves . . .'

Chapter 14
'It's all gossip until it's proven in court'

Father Kevin O'Donnell was such an insatiable sexual predator that his crimes were committed with no obvious cessation from the 1940s until his incarceration in 1995. A solicitor who represented some of the priest's victims through the Pell Process once described O'Donnell as '. . . a two-a-day man'. The term made me sick.

Did he confess these continuous mortal sins, these criminal acts, to another priest each day before he said mass? Not every time, apparently. One of the victims I spoke to said O'Donnell sexually assaulted him at a rural church just before hosting his congregation at the altar. It all happened so quickly and left no time for O'Donnell to confess. Instead, within the hour his filthy hands were handing out the bread in communion.

A priest who knew O'Donnell said it was not usual for sinful clerics to confess to colleagues with whom they shared accommodation. Instead, abusers were more likely to go to a nearby parish to seek absolution. Did O'Donnell talk of his deeds to another man of the cloth? He would have seen it as freeing himself of guilt so he could continue molesting and raping more children (or the same children over and over).

It is barely worth asking the question, for there can be no answer. No-one will ever know how he lived with himself. The secrecy of the confessional is sacred. To break it is considered one of the worst sins.

However, I never thought it was conceivable that the Catholic Church knew nothing about his horrid acts against children. Someone had to know something.

Over the years I have come into contact with many people whose lives have been destroyed or damaged by O'Donnell – from victims named in the criminal court and those involved in our Oakleigh group to others, who have not yet found their voices to make an official complaint. Those victims and their families have told me their stories and I have told them ours.

I have gone out of my way recently to research O'Donnell's history more deeply, paying particular attention to *what* the Church knew and *when*. It makes me wonder how my daughters' lives could have been . . . if only the Church had listened and acted to protect the children, not the paedophile, when the first complaints were made a long, long time ago.

One of the people I met while searching for information was Alan Timmons, the altar boy/cub scout whom O'Donnell trapped in the Dandenong presbytery bedroom, as witnessed by another priest who walked in and said nothing, did nothing.

For Alan, time did no favours. When I met him in 2009 he was married with adult children but, sadly, still suffered nightmares, even though his abuse had happened many decades ago. With tears in his eyes, he struggled to tell me about his treatment at the hands of O'Donnell and, much later, the heartless Church hierarchy. It seemed as raw and difficult for him as it would have been disclosing the events of his horrendous childhood for the very first time in 1992, prompted by Alan and his wife watching a film that dealt with the subject of child sexual abuse. Until then, Alan had never told anyone about his assaults in the 1960s. For thirty years he had lived under the weight of his private shame. The film caused him to break down and cry and he told his wife what the priest had done. After he made that breakthrough, he went back to the Church to make a complaint. He was hoping to find compassion.

Initially he was fortunate. It was a caring priest who responded to his cry for help in November 1992. Father Noel Brady, who was a recently ordained mature-age assistant priest at St Mary's Catholic Church, Dandenong, said it was a house visit he would never forget.

'We went for a walk and Alan told me what happened to him,' the priest remembered. 'He told me he had children, now grown up, who he had never been able to put his arms around. I remember crying with him. I could feel his pain. It still upsets me to think about it. You could sense and feel his pain.'

Father Brady dutifully took Alan's word to the Catholic Church's head office and made a report to Vicar General Hilton Deakin.

The curate felt the Church administrator was less than compassionate. 'I rang Hilton Deakin and he said he would see Alan but it was clear Hilton didn't feel [Alan's] pain.'

Father Brady added: 'I couldn't help but believe him [the victim]. It came out like it happened yesterday. I couldn't see how anyone couldn't feel the same way I did when I heard what Alan had been through.'

The vicar general visited Alan and his wife at their home, to respond to the complaint. The couple said the meeting with the high-ranking official was horrible, that he seemed impervious to claims one of Melbourne's longest-serving priests was a paedophile. Alan, feeling he was isolated once more by the attitude of the Church, was left not knowing where else to go to find justice or peace of mind.

Bishop Deakin recalled the meeting more than sixteen years later, when he was retired. He disputed he was heartless. 'He

[Alan] was a very shattered man. I never offered a view one way or the other.'

What did the former vicar general think, initially, about the accusations against O'Donnell? 'Frankly I didn't know anything about it,' he said.

And what did he do with the information Alan provided him?

'I reported it.'

Who to?

'I don't talk about that. It's due privilege.'

When the archdiocese moved Hilton Deakin to the role of bishop of Melbourne's eastern region at the end of 1992, Monsignor Gerald Cudmore became vicar general. It was very soon after Alan's first complaint.

Father Noel Brady, continuing to try to help Alan, went back to the cathedral within months on the victim's behalf and made the same complaint about O'Donnell, this time to the new Vicar General Cudmore.

Alan was invited to go to the Melbourne cathedral for a meeting. The distressed victim summoned up the courage to go to the Church's headquarters. He took his wife for support. While they were sitting anxiously in a waiting room, another man walked in and sat beside them. It was Father Kevin O'Donnell, Alan's abuser. Vicar General Cudmore had called for him. It horrified Alan, who did not ever want to see the paedophile again. He had taken so much away from the altar boy and left him with a lifetime of regret, shame and guilt. Yet here he was, smiling and apparently without a conscience.

'O'Donnell wanted to be mates,' Alan told me, shaking his head.

The 'mediation' that followed in the cathedral office was disgraceful. O'Donnell fawned over his victim, denied wrongdoing and astonishingly stated that he loved Alan! This unexpected and traumatic encounter made the quivering man and his wife feel much worse. Vicar General Cudmore and O'Donnell stated over and over that Alan was the only person ever to make a complaint to the Church hierarchy about the paedophile's mishandling of children.

It was a lie, a horrible lie.

Alan went home and suffered more trauma. For many years he had kept his secret and it had caused him a lifetime of nightmares. Now he had told the Church and felt more pain and isolation.

It was Jimmy Chambers, another victim from Dandenong, who made the most clearly documented complaint to the Church about O'Donnell's paedophilia – way back in the 1950s.

Jimmy told his scoutmaster that O'Donnell was 'interfering' with him. The boy was refusing to get changed into his green uniform at the presbytery and the scoutmaster wanted to know why. It was because the priest was using these occasions as an opportunity to assault him.

Jimmy is now a grandfather who suffers from post-traumatic stress disorder. He remembers well the time when he made the complaint as a boy. The young scoutmaster and another man went to the Catholic Church headquarters to complain to Vicar General Monsignor Lawrence Moran on Jimmy's behalf.

Vicar General Moran visited the Dandenong parish soon after to speak with O'Donnell, Jimmy recalled.

'We were playing footy outside and when I saw him [the vicar general] coming I got out of there,' he explained. 'I knew he was there because I made the complaint.'

O'Donnell later confronted Jimmy. It was at mass the following Sunday. The priest dragged the child away from his parents and spoke to him with authority and arrogance.

'You reported me to my boss,' the priest said.

'Yeah, I did,' the boy bravely confirmed. 'What's gunna happen now?'

'Nothing,' said O'Donnell, shaking his head.

'What?'

'They just told me to be careful.'

Jimmy was silent.

O'Donnell added: 'Don't tell your mum and dad because they won't believe you. I'm a priest and you're just a child.' Life at the parish and school continued unaltered.

The abuse of Jimmy Chambers resumed until one day, out of the blue, another senior Church official, Bishop Arthur Fox, arrived at St John's, a secondary school O'Donnell founded. Bishop Fox invited Jimmy into a room to question him.

'I know Father O'Donnell has been interfering with you,' Bishop Fox said. 'It's been reported at the cathedral. I'm here to fix it.'

Bishop Fox asked Jimmy about the assaults. 'I want you to tell me who else is involved. Give me some names and I'll get them in here and ask some discreet questions.'

The boy could not give the bishop names because he didn't know about anyone else. The altar boys and scouts didn't talk about O'Donnell's crimes. It was too shameful and they were silenced by fear.

Bishop Fox ended his interview with Jimmy by warning him: 'You should never speak about this to anyone. It would be a mortal sin to discuss it.'

The threat of 'mortal sin' fills Catholic children with fear and horror. For those who have not been educated in Catholic sinfulness it would be hard to appreciate the power of these words, especially when said by a bishop to a child. Mortal sin is the worst sin with dire consequences. When at primary school, we learned from our catechism (a book of Catholic questions and answers), which promoted their doctrine and, sometimes frighteningly, sated our curiosity. 'What does a mortal sin do? It destroys our friendship with God and thus makes us deserve Hell.' And 'What is Hell? Hell is where the

Devil and his angels and all who died in MORTAL sin suffer in the greatest pain . . .'

Jimmy understood all of this and so the bishop's secret was safe with the shaking, frightened sexual assault victim.

The abuse of Jimmy Chambers finally stopped after the bishop's visit, although the priest stubbornly continued to play an active role in his life; buying him things, lending him money. It was all part of his controlling behaviour. Jimmy was relieved that he was no longer being sexually assaulted, but did not know why the attacks had ceased.

'As a child, I don't know what I thought had happened to him. For some reason I thought maybe they did something to his brain,' Jimmy told me one day.

Of course, O'Donnell did not undergo a lobotomy or any other treatment. Instead, he chose never again to assault the boy who had been bold enough to complain to the authorities, so the paedophile concentrated his private predatory attacks on other children.

After making the report and receiving visits from the Church hierarchy – the Vicar General of Melbourne and a bishop, no less – Jimmy thought O'Donnell was cured and mentioned not a word of it for another thirty-five years. But when he finally disclosed his sexual abuse to his family, he was horrified to find out O'Donnell had spent years assaulting his siblings and even his wife's siblings, when they were all children.

Vicar General Moran died in 1970 and Bishop Fox was ninety-one years old when lawyers for Jimmy Chambers questioned him about his involvement in the O'Donnell investigation. He said he couldn't remember.

Jimmy tried to sue the Church for neglect but met a stone-wall of defence. Lawyers for the Catholic Church, when asked about Vicar General Moran's and Bishop Fox's involvement in O'Donnell's behaviour, declared in writing: 'There are no records of any complaint against Father O'Donnell before November 1992 . . .'

The lawyers went on to explain:

Canon law requires that records of ecclesiastical trials dealing with criminal cases concerning moral matters are to be destroyed after ten years have elapsed since the judgement was given. While there is no law regulating the destruction of records or notes about informal complaints, the practice has been to destroy such records after a reasonable period of time if the complaint appeared to lack substance or appear frivolous.

Was a trial held within the confines of the Church as required by canon law? I don't think so. I believe no such hearing was conducted, as is usual with the Church and claims of clergy sex abuse, not just in Australia but also all over the world.

However, there was documented proof of Jimmy's complaint to the cathedral, via the scoutmaster, and I have seen that evidence.

The scoutmaster, Simon Smith (not his real name), lived in Dandenong for a long time. In 1994, months after O'Donnell was first arrested and questioned by police, the Church reached out to Mr Smith to see if he would cause liability problems by publicly recalling the 1958 complaint.

The cathedral asked a priest, Father Tony Guelen, to go and see the scoutmaster as part of an internal investigation. Father Guelen reported back to the Archdiocese of Melbourne in a secret letter addressed to Vicar General Cudmore. It stated that one evening in September 1994 (seven months after police officers interviewed O'Donnell) Father Gruelen went to the home of the scoutmaster where he listened to the witness's revealing and confirming account of the 1958 sexual abuse complaint against Father Kevin O'Donnell.

The scoutmaster confirmed to the priest that he and a second scout leader had presented the boy's complaint to the proper authorities at the Cathedral where they were welcomed and listened to. He described how he later learned from the boy that a representative from the Cathedral had been out to see Kevin O'Donnell and that the assaults had stopped.

The retired scoutmaster then detailed how earlier that year (1994), he had received a phone call from the victim asking him to attest to events that had taken place in 1958. But the scoutmaster did not want any involvement.

Having secured the knowledge that the witness had no intention of testifying against O'Donnell in court, Father Gruelen, the parish priest, left.

In his confidential report back to Vicar General Cudmore, he commented that he hoped his report would assist the future course in regard to the Kevin O'Donnell case.

This revealing Catholic Church internal investigation document shocked me. It is a rare peek inside an institution that is not nearly as naive as it makes out. It is also a letter without heart. The language is disturbing. It is proof that the Catholic Church knew about O'Donnell's offending thirty years before he attacked our daughters. And it suggests the archdiocese was seeking assurances that the former scoutmaster was not going to speak publicly about the 1958 complaint.

Jimmy Chambers still lives with debilitating nightmares; repetitive unwanted visions of his childhood. He also bears guilt for not doing more. He feels he should have stopped O'Donnell from molesting other children.

Of my daughters and all the other ensuing victims Jimmy said: 'I feel as though I let them down. People tell me not to be stupid to think like that but it doesn't help. It's how I feel.'

But what more could he have done? He was a mere boy; a courageous one who achieved a complaint that went straight to the top – to the hierarchy of the Church – and they did nothing with that knowledge, except to warn the child rapist 'to be careful'. The child could do no more. O'Donnell was God's agent on earth and Jimmy's own parents valued the Father's word more than their son's.

Jimmy didn't let children down – the Church hierarchy did that all on its own.

Other complaints were made to the cathedral but the paperwork regarding those incidents remains hidden from the public.

Bill Nelson, the repeatedly assaulted former altar boy who first went to the police about O'Donnell early in 1994, had also complained to Church authorities about the priest in 1984.

After emotionally staggering through his early adulthood, Bill decided he needed help and a relative suggested he required counselling. He went to see a nun, who was a family friend. The Sister, on hearing of O'Donnell's behaviour, wrote a letter to the cathedral, outlining Bill's complaints, demanding a response. The letter she wrote was addressed to Archbishop Frank Little. He never responded.

If the hierarchy had taken action against O'Donnell in the mid-1980s my precious Emma and Katie would have been saved, along with many other children. It did not surprise me to hear that Archbishop Little (who was later knighted) didn't respond to the nun's complaint. Archbishop Little's record of dealing with paedophile priests was shameful. His method was to move the offenders from parish to parish, which led to more children being molested.

The earliest complaint against O'Donnell that I know of was prior to 1949. Peter Taylor, the boy whom O'Donnell had molested in the sacristy and tried to assault in the water at the beach, was not the only victim of young Kevin O'Donnell. Peter's friend's brother was assaulted and reported it to his parents, who complained to nuns at a primary school called St Joseph's in bayside Chelsea. O'Donnell was briskly moved to Seymour, one hundred and fifty kilometres away. Nuns cannot remove a priest. Only the hierarchy has the power to carry out a transfer, as in this case. Did the nuns go to the business manager of the archdiocese, the vicar general, or the archbishop to lodge their complaint? That was the procedure. How and why else was O'Donnell promptly relocated?

The hierarchy had so many chances to do the right thing. That is why I hold the Catholic Church hierarchy responsible for my family's situation and have so fervently pursued justice. It is why I wanted our barrister and solicitor to continue preparing to sue the Church.

The morning arrived that we were to visit Sacred Heart Parish with our barrister Tim Seccull and solicitor Michael Jorgensen. Both wanted to inspect the hall and church, where O'Donnell had repeatedly raped my daughters. Michael was called away at the last moment, which left Tim and me to go over the horrible scene.

Tim arrived at our home at nine in the morning. Our domestic day had already begun, with Katie's physiotherapist working on her, as he had done for the previous twenty-two months, trying to restore to her the simple ability to walk. When our barrister arrived it was the first time he had seen Katie since the accident.

We had told Tim about Katie's struggles after the accident, of course, and he needed no reassuring that our day-to-day life was challenging. But seeing our disabled girl going through so much effort just to move her legs, first thing in the morning, struck him as profoundly sad. He wasn't a barrister at that moment. He was a family man, with young children. Up until now his attitude regarding suing the Church had been one of defiance.

'It's going to be very tough,' he warned. 'But it's the right thing to do and therefore it must be done.'

Seeing Katie in her fragile state just hardened his resolve. And he was about to be further inspired.

We drove to the presbytery and I picked up the keys from my church contact.

Tim didn't just want to see where O'Donnell committed his crimes. He was looking for so much more. Having already determined that the Church could not be successfully sued as a single entity, he was examining the entire block for clues pointing to liability.

'I want to get back to basics,' he said, scanning the presbytery, where O'Donnell lived; the cottage, dark and secretive; the school grounds that O'Donnell patrolled; the classrooms, from which O'Donnell selected children; the church and the hall, where the priest took those children – my beautiful daughters, Emma, aged five, and Katie not much older.

The barrister was asking himself questions as he went. Where did the assaults actually happen? Who am I going to sue? Who's responsible? He stood in different spots and took in the angles of the buildings, twisting his head, as if he were winding back the clock and watching O'Donnell lead Emma to her peril.

Where did the children have to walk? Who could see them? How open was it? Who knew? Where were the teachers, the principal? If the Church isn't liable, who is? Who owns this piece of property?

There were no theatrics from him. He was simply strolling around, constructing his case from the ground up.

We walked into the hall, unlocking the doors as we went, then along the narrow corridor that led to the shower room. Tim scoured every interior detail. He wanted to know the colour of the walls . . . light-brown brick . . . how many doors there were . . . the position of the handles on those doors . . . the distance between the hall's entrance and the stage . . . anything that witnesses might be asked about in court one day. And he was constantly looking for some sign of ownership, a plaque or a sign attributing the building to someone, something. In the hall, he noted the fans hanging from the uneven ceiling, the light streaming in from the high windows, the smooth floorboards, a little less scuffed than the stage.

We left the hall and headed along the corridor to the shower room. Tim went inside and continued his inspection. He seemed to be listening too. Perhaps he could hear the far-off laughter and squealing of children in the playground. Tim wasn't the only one looking for evidence.

This time I was determined to search the shower room, not just stand near the entrance. Since my last visit, five years earlier, I had pieced together many parts of the story – what happened and where. This was the room where the atrocities against Emma were committed. I would search it. I knew what I was looking for.

I walked inside. I searched previously hidden spots, corners, shelving brackets and behind shelves. I was looking for something small, soft and colourful. It could be crammed into a small space. It had a small black 'E' on the right-hand side, written with a laundry marker pen in my writing. It was Emma's missing underpants. I looked and looked but could not find them. I was searching for proof – the undeniable truth – to show the disbelieving Church.

But the underpants were not there. I knew O'Donnell would have been a fool to hide them in there but I had to look.

I thought about how Emma had suffered. No wonder she had nightmares. I became aware of them when she was eight years old. About four times over a twelve-month period, I recall waking in fright, startled and alarmed as the screams of my daughter reached my ears. Rushing into her bedroom, I would turn on the light and could see she was half awake, sitting up in the bed, terrified, her wide and fearful eyes meeting mine, and each time blood was running from her nose into her mouth. I don't know why she was bleeding. I calmed her down while holding tissues to her nose, myself sharing her horror at this out-of-control night terror. I asked but she never said what the nightmares were about. I could not tell what was more devastating for her; the horrors in her nightmare that would cause her to scream or the horror of finding herself bleeding.

Only a few years later the devastation of seeing her own blood was taken to a new level when she had her first period. It sent her into a withdrawn state of mild shock, despair and a heightened sensitivity. It took her hours to tell me what she was distressed about, even after I correctly guessed. She finally confirmed she had her period. I could not understand where her reaction came from, as she had already learned about this change that would occur in her body. I now believe what triggered her shock was the horror in her mind that dated back to the initial assault against her, when she was in prep. But she said nothing of this and only months later, after reading of O'Donnell's offences, and understanding what had been done to her, became anorexic. At age sixteen she insisted her GP inject her with a drug that stopped her period occurring at all. It had been a constant monthly reminder of her childhood rape. She never allowed herself to go off that medication to have another period.

The screaming nightmares ceased after some time, but the non-screaming nightmares never left her. They even invaded her waking hours in the form of 'daymares'. She revealed these to me only in her adult years; how she relived the assaults as if they were happening before her eyes and she was powerless to stop them, just as she had been as a child. All she could do was watch.

Tim was now taking photos. The barrister was suddenly like a forensic police officer, methodically capturing the room's dimensions and contents, as if there had been a murder or armed robbery. Years earlier that room should have been declared a crime scene; just like the sacristy, the confessional, the presbytery and who knows how many more safe lairs in our parish buildings.

Finished there, we walked to the church. Inside were several people who were talking in front of the altar. I led Tim past them, to the other side of the church, near the sacristy door. It was the room where Katie's sexual assault had taken place, the one assault I knew about, as described in her diary. We spoke briefly then entered. Several minutes later we exited and once again stood in the main church area, chatting. A woman I had never seen before approached us and challenged our presence in the church, asking what we were doing. Unlike my old Catholic self, I would not be intimidated. I confidently stood my ground. Tim and I stayed until we had finished what we had come for.

Later, Tim mentioned that he'd spent his examination of the parish taking mental notes of its atmosphere.

'I wanted to get a sense of how the girls felt,' he said.

The shower room didn't repulse him but he said it was chilling. More than that, however, he felt the weight of responsibility on his shoulders growing heavier. He realised the enormity of the fight on his hands, but also the importance riding on it.

I thought it was an interesting concept; a legal man, who relies on evidence and facts, taking in the 'atmosphere'.

In the course of the morning, Tim broadly described another instance of Church abuse he had encountered, telling me about the now-adult victim but referring to him as a child. He did this several times. It spoke to me of Tim's passionate awareness and commitment. By speaking of the 'child' he was holding his client in the reverence that person truly deserved – it was not the adult who was sexually assaulted but the child. It is something both Anthony and I feel and believe is needed – an emphasis on the degradation of the delicate being called 'the child'. Obviously Tim did the same, to maintain and hold on to his passion for innocence and ultimately justice for what was taken away, forever lost. Again I was deeply moved by his compassion and insight.

I can now see Tim was steeling himself for the task ahead and for us. For all the victims who would be watching and waiting to see how we fared.

'It's going to be very tough . . . But it's the right thing to do and therefore it must be done.'

Our solicitor, Michael Jorgensen, missed visiting Sacred Heart but was hard at work investigating and researching our case in other ways. He asked me for names of people I thought might have information about O'Donnell during his time as a priest. It would give the solicitor some background about the cleric's career, his personality and habits, but also the opportunity to ask questions that could possibly unearth surprising and helpful answers. It was an extensive list. Michael rang and spoke to all the people I suggested and interviewed most of them. I helped him track them down so he could make contact. It was a frustrating and arduous exercise. One of the people from the list was interstate, some had shifted, some refused to speak – it was a big effort for Michael.

Father John Salvano was one who agreed to be interviewed. He was the assistant priest at Sacred Heart from May/June 1991 until O'Donnell's mysterious retirement in August 1992. Father Salvano was easy to find because he was still serving the Catholic Church at a neighbouring parish. I listed his name because I heard from a friend that the assistant priest had become worried about O'Donnell's relationship with children during the time of their working partnership in the presbytery. If true, it meant O'Donnell was left in charge of children even after yet another complaint was made, this time from someone who lived with the paedophile. Another priest, no less.

Father Salvano gave a statement to Michael Jorgensen. Anthony and I have since visited him – ten years after his statement – to hear his remarkable insight into the behaviour of Father Kevin O'Donnell and the inaction of the Catholic Church hierarchy.

The curate lived with the paedophile priest at the Sacred Heart Presbytery for more than twelve months. Father Salvano witnessed O'Donnell's volatile career-ending days with a mixture of fear and disbelief. It's an understatement to say the old man's behaviour disturbed the younger priest. From the start, the two did not get on. Father Salvano quickly worked out his senior partner was not the welcoming type. In fact, he was cranky and living recklessly. Father Salvano was a slight man, almost timid in his speech. O'Donnell was a bold intimidator, who flipped into a rage when someone or something ticked him off. He was particularly cruel to his dog; he used to yell and swear at it continuously and would kick the poor thing quite viciously in the belly.

'GET OUT!' he would scream at Laddie, by now old and battle-weary.

Father Salvano said that within months of his arrival the dog disappeared. 'The housekeeper told me that O'Donnell took the dog for a drive and it didn't return.'

Most of the other strange things that Father Salvano saw happen around the parish involved O'Donnell's 'golden-haired boys'. They were mostly young teenagers who spent nights at the presbytery; dining, hanging around and perhaps even sleeping there. The presence of the children intimidated Father Salvano, who assumed they were from dysfunctional families.

'O'Donnell would not go anywhere without children,' Father Salvano said. 'He would let children drive his car, notwithstanding they didn't have a licence. They had unfettered access to the house and one of them even had a key to the safe. In fact, the pecking order at the house was O'Donnell, the boys, the housekeeper, the dog and then myself.'

By August 1991 Father Salvano and O'Donnell were at war with each other. Whenever the younger man asked questions about the number of children at the presbytery, O'Donnell became enraged, swearing and threatening violence. He once punched Father Salvano and another time grabbed him in a headlock. His point? 'Don't question me.'

Father Salvano regularly saw money given to the boys; anything from ten or twenty dollars to hundreds. One boy was given thousands of dollars to buy a car, Father Salvano said. He assumed O'Donnell was taking the cash from Sunday mass donations. In return, the old man was allowed to endlessly hug and stroke the children.

Ironically, the first priest to complain to the cathedral about the 'priests at war' situation at the Oakleigh parish was O'Donnell himself. He went to the vicar general, claiming his assistant wasn't pulling his weight around the parish. It was a ridiculous charge, an obvious attempt to rid himself of a wary adversary. Meanwhile, Father Salvano began noticing children at the house early in the mornings, making him suspect they had slept the night at the Catholic Church property.

In early 1992, before the school year commenced, Father Salvano went to Vicar General Hilton Deakin with his own complaints. The priest told his superior that he was concerned about the abnormal behaviour of O'Donnell, the money, the boys and their apparent sleepovers.

'I told him I thought O'Donnell was emotionally dependent on the children and that the children had unusual and unlimited access to the presbytery,' Father Salvano recalled.

Vicar General Hilton Deakin listened to Father Salvano and said he would come up with a solution to the problem but needed time to consider it. He told the priest to return in two weeks. When Father Salvano went back to the cathedral he was offered alternative accommodation. The Church didn't say it would attempt to change O'Donnell's lifestyle, but rather offered his assistant a way out of the presbytery.

'I didn't want to move because I wanted to have some sort of control over O'Donnell's behaviour in relation to the boys,' Father Salvano said.

Hilton Deakin, from his retirement home in 2009, said he remembered Father Salvano coming to him about O'Donnell but did not recall the details of his grievances.

Father Salvano had a better memory of their meetings. He said the vicar general told him: 'Don't worry about it because O'Donnell will be retiring later in the year.'

O'Donnell would not have chosen to retire – losing access to the children he was still sexually active with. But the cathedral readily accepted his mandatory resignation at age seventy-five. Shamefully, he continued serving part-time after his retirement, in at least two other parishes. He was old but seemed inexhaustible, eager to continue mixing with parishioners and their children.

The cathedral should have banned him from being on Church property on Father Salvano's complaints alone. Instead, the hierarchy continued to accommodate him, again and again.

Leaving the abusive priest where he was in Oakleigh because he was about to retire was a disgraceful act. They could have saved many children new or further trauma. These conversations took place before the 1992 school year commencement so the hierarchy could have saved the five-year-old preps from being exposed to a paedophile's ever-marauding hands and never-sated sexual appetite. We know he was taking children under seven out of classes up to his very last days at the school. The Church bosses could have saved the whole school of three hundred or so children another eight months of sexual assaults by the 'two-a-day man'.

Back at Sacred Heart's presbytery, Father Salvano's dismay deepened when he discovered O'Donnell's collection of guns. In the 1970s, the adventurous booming-voiced clergyman was famous for packing a rifle in his car boot. Now, he had many more weapons and wasn't hiding them. Father Salvano estimated there were about fifteen rifles and ammunition lying around the house at any one time.

The curate was aghast at the sight of the guns and got rid of them, despite fears that O'Donnell would lose his temper again. Thankfully, for Father Salvano, the gun owner didn't raise the matter. Maybe he didn't fancy the cathedral being forced to rule on a priest's right to bear arms.

Father Salvano said of his relationship with O'Donnell: 'When we weren't fighting we didn't speak and would never eat meals together. If he was in the presbytery I would leave to do duties outside. If he was at the school at the same time as I was, then I would retreat to the presbytery.'

In 1992, before his golden jubilee and subsequent retirement, O'Donnell did go out of his way to speak to his assistant. He introduced Father Salvano to a teenage boy whom he had invited to live with them.

Father Salvano declared he was going straight back to the vicar general to complain again. When he returned to Oakleigh, after visiting the cathedral in the city, the boy was nowhere to be seen and the issue was never again brought up. But Father Salvano's concerns about O'Donnell's behaviour persisted and he made several trips in a short period to speak to the men running the Melbourne Archdiocese, Vicar General Hilton Deakin and Archbishop Frank Little.

The hierarchy, as usual, was not moved enough by O'Donnell's putrid behaviour or recklessness to sack or remove him. Nor did it share suspicions of his criminal treatment of children with the police or parishioners.

Fortunately for Archbishop Little, now under increasing pressure from Father Salvano to do something, O'Donnell reached retiring age. He was belatedly moved away from Oakleigh.

I discovered while researching this book the truth about what happened after O'Donnell was retired from Oakleigh. He returned to his old parish headquarters at St Mary's, Dandenong, and lived in a unit near the church.

Father Tony Guelen, the same priest who had reported back to Vicar General Cudmore on the Jimmy Chambers affair, was running the parish and was O'Donnell's carer, under Church guidelines for retired priests. Father Guelen wasn't opposed to O'Donnell's presence. They'd previously worked together and Father Guelen said he never suspected his senior colleague of being a paedophile. 'We never saw anything wrong with him,' Father Guelen recalled. 'Children were here often, yes. One of his strengths was that he was good with all sorts of boys.'

Incredibly and outrageously, O'Donnell began con-celebrating (officiating with another priest) mass on Saturdays at St Mary's. The only cleric opposed to O'Donnell doing this was Father Noel Brady, an assistant priest at the parish. Father Brady was hearing complaints of sexual assaults from O'Donnell's victims since November 1992. He was the first priest we know of to take these complaints to the archdiocese.

O'Donnell's living arrangements came to a head one day when an altar boy innocently asked Father Brady: 'Have you ever been round to Father O'Donnell's [unit]?'

'Have *you* ever been around there?' Father Brady fearfully asked the twelve-year-old.

'Oh yes, he pays me to go around there and cut his lawn.'

A stunned Father Brady reported this to the cathedral. He said he spoke to 'the appropriate authority', only to be instructed: 'It's not happening on Church property . . . we're not responsible.'

'Those were the exact words,' Father Brady recalled, still distressed by it to this day. 'Well I knew what O'Donnell had done and I wasn't prepared to let this boy be another victim.' Father Brady went to O'Donnell's unit and firmly told him: 'That boy is never to come to your place again.' The old man didn't argue.

Father Brady told me Vicar General Hilton Deakin was aware of the complaints mounting against O'Donnell but took no action.

The now-retired Bishop Hilton Deakin said he recalled Father Brady coming to him. He said the curate priest 'had a view about things' but stressed: 'I didn't know anything about it.'

Eventually, Father Guelen asked O'Donnell to pack up and leave the area, due to fears of adverse publicity if he stayed where he was. But there were no hard feelings between the former mentor and assistant. Father Guelen was later the executor of O'Donnell's will and spoke at the paedophile's funeral, even though Father Kevin O'Donnell had by then been revealed to everyone to be one of the nation's worst serial sexual offenders.

Father Brady was compassionate towards victims and continues to promote awareness of clergy sexual abuse in his sermons today.

If only the rest of the Church carried the same attitude. But that is not − and was not − the case. We had to fight and ask questions and demand answers to reach justice. The history of O'Donnell became evidence for Tim Seccull and Michael Jorgensen but they had so much more to consider. Michael and Tim were treading on new legal turf and proceeded slowly and methodically. Most importantly, however, they made their way with determination and passion. It was moving to see them gathering the legal strength to fight on our behalf. The might of the Church was waiting for them but they pressed on regardless.

The 'do-Little' legacy

Archbishop Sir Frank Little served as the leader of the Archdiocese of Melbourne for twenty-two years. His reign came to an end when George Pell took over in July 1996. But the late Archbishop Little's handling of paedophile priests was abominable and should be noted in any discussion about the Church hierarchy's cover-up.

In 1978 a prolific paedophile priest, Father Bill Baker, was in charge of the suburban Gladstone Park parish. The father of one of this cleric's victims found out his son had been sexually assaulted in the presbytery shower, so he took his complaint to the president of the Parish Council, Brian Cosgriff.

When he wasn't a parishioner, Mr Cosgriff was a senior magistrate in Melbourne. He was appalled by Father Baker's actions and decided to take the parent's complaint to the office of the archbishop. He asked a barrister, Brendan Murphy, to go with him as a witness.

The pair expected a fair hearing and a compassionate reaction from the Church leader.

Archbishop Little listened to the complaint about Father Baker before vigorously defending his priest.

'This is a despicable allegation,' Archbishop Little yelled, 'absolutely despicable. How dare you? What about faith, hope and charity?' The archbishop was wild with fury that anyone would accuse one of his priests of sexual assault. He had the magistrate and the barrister led away from the Church property.

Disappointed but determined, the pair of lawmen demanded a second hearing and made an appointment to meet Archbishop Little again at the cathedral in Melbourne. This time, however, Archbishop Little would not even listen to them, refusing to discuss the paedophilia and the dangers to the children of the parish. Mr Cosgriff and Mr Murphy were shown out again.

Brian Cosgriff, a now-retired magistrate, described the archbishop's behaviour as 'reprehensible'. 'It seemed that he didn't want to investigate it. We were left feeling very unsatisfied.'

The claim was not taken to the police because the boy's father did not want his son to go through the trauma of a police interview and a possible cross-examination at a trial, Mr Cosgriff explained.

Archbishop Little may have pretended he was not listening but he did hear the complaint against Father Bill Baker. In fact, he took swift action. He moved Father Baker to another parish. Years later, there were more complaints of sexual assault and another relocation for the paedophile. He continued offending.

In March 1997 another archbishop was notified of Father Baker's behaviour. Our Oakleigh group, during the meeting with Archbishop Pell in our parish hall, demanded that Father Baker, as one of the paedophile priests we knew was still serving actively in a community, be removed. We were met with the angry response of: 'It's all gossip until it's proven in court. AND I DON'T LISTEN TO GOSSIP!'. Two years later, in 1999, after who knows how many more children were assaulted, it *was* proven in court and Father Baker went to prison. More than twenty years after the magistrate and the barrister made the complaint to Archbishop Little, Father

Baker, then sixty-two, was imprisoned on sixteen counts of indecent assault, committed over a twenty-year period, between 1960 and 1979. Judge Russell Lewis, in sentencing Father Baker to four years' jail, said: 'In the past, there have been paedophile priests who have been moved around with the full knowledge of the hierarchy.'

Brendan Murphy is now a Queen's Counsel in Melbourne and one of the leading barristers in his field in Australia. He said of Archbishop Little: 'I've harboured a substantial disrespect for him and what went on and I've got no doubt that within the hierarchy others knew. This wasn't a one-man band. Others would have known.'

Archbishop Little knew Father Baker was a paedophile. Did he know Father Kevin O'Donnell was also a sex offender? Of course he did. He was O'Donnell's superior for seventeen years and in charge of the archdiocese when the complaints came in. We know a nun sent the archbishop a letter about O'Donnell in the 1980s. How many other people complained and were ignored? We will never know for sure, but judging by his reaction to the magistrate and barrister in 1978, his attitude was one of denial and shifting the problem, as per the Church's policies he knew so well.

In 2008, the former archbishop Sir Frank Little died at the age of eighty-two. His ex-private secretary and long-time vicar general, Bishop Peter Connors, was quoted in a newspaper story, saying: 'I had thirteen lovely years sitting opposite him at breakfast every morning. He was a holy man. He loved God and God's people. He was always fearful of hurting priests, and found it hard to correct or reprimand a priest.'

It's a pity Sir Frank, 'his holiness', wasn't as fearful or considerate of the enormous suffering of children.

Chapter 15
The story goes national

Child sex abuse by priests became a global crisis for the Catholic Church in 2002. In the USA the *Boston Globe* newspaper ran a series of investigative stories exposing the local archdiocese's history of covering up the crimes of paedophile priests. It led to criminal convictions, a cardinal's resignation, a Pulitzer Prize for the newspaper, and a seemingly endless stream of victims' complaints and lawsuits. The scandal spread like wildfire across the United States and drove many archdioceses to the brink of bankruptcy, as the Church paid billions of dollars in settlement money. Other costly scandals unfolded around the world.

The Boston scandal was the second wave in the crisis for the United States, which first revealed widespread clergy sex abuse and cover-up in the 1980s, when hundreds of priests and religious Brothers were reported to the Vatican Embassy in Washington DC. The book *Lead Us Not Into Temptation*, published in 1992, claimed the Church spent about US$400 million on victims' settlements between 1984 and 1992. The figure would go up and up and it's still rising at a steady rate.

The book's author Jason Berry found:

> The crisis in the Catholic Church lies not with the fraction of priests who molest youngsters but in an ecclesiastical power

structure that harbours pedophiles, conceals other sexual behaviour patterns among its clerics, and uses strategies of duplicity and counterattack against the victims.

Way back in 1985, the internationally recognised priest and canon lawyer Reverend Thomas Doyle, who was working at the Vatican Embassy in Washington DC, co-authored a ninety-two page report called 'The Problem of Sexual Molestation by Roman Catholic Clergy: Meeting the Problem in a Compassionate and Responsible Manner'. The report – distributed to every bishop in the USA – estimated the Church could face damages of up to 'ONE BILLION DOLLARS' over the next decade. Reverend Doyle warned his colleagues and superiors that the crisis at hand was 'the most serious problem that we in the Church have faced in centuries'. It was a prophetic message that went largely ignored. Reverend Doyle has spent the past twenty-five years holding the Church to account for its heartless treatment of victims, the protective attitude towards paedophile priests, and scandal-minimisation. The Vatican, however, has long appeared more concerned with bad press than the behaviour of sexual abusers within the clergy. Pope John Paul II released a statement in 1993, complaining '. . . it is unacceptable for moral evil to be treated as an occasion for sensationalism'.

Such was the pious siege mentality of the hierarchy all over the world. The same public relations approach and denial exists today.

In Australia, the crisis for the Church didn't materialise through waves of payouts. The difficulties of suing the Church, coupled with confidential compensation agreements – through the Pell Process for victims in the Melbourne Archdiocese and Towards Healing for the rest of Australia – led to a quelling of potential court action and therefore of potentially larger and ongoing out-of-court settlements. The steady flow of complaints from traumatised people was, by the setting up of Church-run schemes, successfully channelled back through the Catholic Church which, I believe, was determined to limit its financial responsibility.

But the Church in Australia did not avoid massive scandals and one of them deepened when, in 2002, Archbishop George Pell was forced to defend, for the first time, his controversial compensation process, six years after it had been rushed in.

Our involvement in the national debate went back to 2000, when I read a newspaper story with the headline 'Sex industry lobby group threatens to expose priests'. A booklet 'documenting four hundred and fifty court cases of paedophilia by priests' was being printed. The story reported that the document named two hundred offender priests, as well as their history of assaults. I wanted a copy.

I made calls and tracked down a contact for the group in Canberra. It was the Eros Foundation, a national lobby group for the adult sex industry.

Several days later I received some copies of its booklet. It was entitled 'Hypocrites: Evidence and Statistics of Child Sexual Abuse Amongst Church Clergy, 1990–2000'. Months later, I rang back to ask for another copy of the booklet and the publisher asked how Emma and Katie were going. We talked some more and he said: 'I know a producer at *60 Minutes*. She would like to hear your story. Can I have your number to pass on to her?'

I agreed.

Several days later, someone from the current affairs television program called. I spoke to one producer, then another. I told them about our private meeting with George Pell, how we showed him the photo of Emma with her cut wrists, of the archbishop's lowly response.

Various phone calls back and forth followed until we agreed to be interviewed on camera. Our disappointing encounter with Archbishop Pell wasn't the central theme of the story being prepared by the national current affairs program, but we didn't know what else the producers were researching.

The *60 Minutes* film crew arrived, along with the producer and a make-up artist. We didn't want to be identified – for the girls' sake – so disguises had to be created. They set about making us look the opposite of how we normally looked. Because Anthony was clean-shaven, wore glasses and had grey hair, they gave him a goatee beard, brushed through a dark hair colouring and removed his spectacles. Because my hair was dark and long and my eyesight was fine, they put a short, curly grey wig on me and gave me some glasses. They gave both of us some cosmetic wrinkles. The make-up session took a long time and at the end of it I looked as though I was Anthony's mother instead of his wife.

As this transformation was happening, the producer told us senior journalist Richard Carleton would be interviewing us. We knew his reputation as a reporter who tackled major issues and it was at that point we realised Channel Nine must have placed some importance on our story.

When Richard arrived we chatted. Then he looked at some paperwork from the Church lawyers and was outraged to see the wording on the pages that accompanied the offer to Emma. The letter from the archbishop and the accompanying letter of offer from his lawyers, who were 'acting for Archbishop Pell', contained the threat that if we took civil action it would 'be strenuously defended'.

Richard Carleton said that in his opinion this amounted to 'hush money'. He photocopied the letter, blacked out our names and included it in the story. Filming took all day and we were told our interview was scheduled to go to air on Sunday 2 June 2002. The day before, however, our story was splashed all over the front page of the *Herald Sun*. The headline boomed: '$50,000 Hush Money – Revealed: Offer from Pell to abused girls' family'. The front page carried a large full-body photo of Archbishop Pell (by then the Archbishop of Sydney).

The first I knew of this was when I unfolded the newspaper at our letterbox; yet another shocking moment at that very same spot. The story and subsequent controversy hit the media like an earthquake. It was reported that the Archdiocese of Sydney was considering legal action to prevent Channel Nine from airing the story. It ensured an even bigger audience tuned in to watch a two-part series called 'Loss of Faith'. We sat and watched it in our family room with about ten friends.

The story featured an interview with convicted paedophile Gerald Ridsdale's nephew, David, a victim of Ridsdale, who claimed he went to then Bishop George Pell in 1993 to talk about his uncle's sexual assaults. He said Archbishop Pell, a family friend, offered him a bribe by saying: 'I want to know what it will take to keep you quiet?'

The archbishop denied the conversation took place. 'Didn't happen.'

I was alarmed to hear Archbishop Pell was a 'family friend' of Ridsdale and his relations. We were led to believe that when he accompanied Father Ridsdale to court in 1993, George Pell did not know the criminal well. But I couldn't stay focused on that upsetting revelation because our part of the story was next.

Unknown to us, Richard Carleton had interviewed Archbishop Pell about our private Oakleigh meeting. We had not seen any footage of the show and were not aware of the content, apart from our own input, so we listened with interest as the interviewer and Australia's most senior Catholic cleric spoke about our plight.

Archbishop Pell was shown a section of *our* recorded interview. In it, Anthony was talking about our meeting in 1997, during which we showed the archbishop the photos of Emma, at confirmation, and with her wrists and arms cut.

Anthony was recalling Archbishop Pell's unchanging face and the cruel comment of: 'Mmm . . . she's changed, hasn't she.' The archbishop, watching and listening to Anthony's recollections, took a sip of water and seemed relaxed.

Richard Carleton said, 'They're not a very happy family are they, Archbishop?'

Archbishop Pell answered, 'No, they've . . . um, they've suffered a lot.'

Richard Carleton was moving the photos in question to one side when the archbishop indicated he wanted to see them. The photos were handed over to Pell. 'They are those photos he (Anthony) was talking about,' said Richard.

Pell acknowledged the confirmation photo but then to our utter and profound shock George Pell denied seeing the other. 'I've never seen the photo . . . with . . . the slashed wrists. I don't believe I've seen it.'

Richard Carleton replied: 'The mother and father say they gave it to you.'

Archbishop Pell: 'I don't believe I've seen that. I have no recollection of that. I mean it's an awful . . . I don't believe I ever saw that.'

At this point I was standing, angry, incredulous, looking at the television. 'He's denying it!'

Anthony had blown that shocking photo up to four times its original size. How could he forget it?

The interview continued and the journalist was keen to make his point about what he called 'hush money' and mentioned the offer of $50,000.

Archbishop Pell replied: 'I offered them nothing. They were free to go into a process . . . run by an independent panel.'

Carleton: 'But I've got a letter here . . .'

Archbishop Pell: 'That's from the lawyers after they'd been through the process, which they were free to enter.'

Richard Carleton produced a letter from the Catholic Church legal firm, warning us that if we decided to sue the cathedral, the claim would be fought 'strenuously'. 'It's from your lawyers . . . "as you know we act for Archbishop Pell". You offered them fifty grand to be quiet.'

Archbishop Pell: 'I offered them fifty grand in compensation.'

Carleton: '. . . to be quiet.'

Archbishop Pell: 'And they chose not to accept that.'

Carleton: 'Words have meaning, sir. You bought their silence, or you sought to buy their silence. "A realistic alternative to litigation that would otherwise be strenuously defended".' He was narrating the lawyer's threat.

Then the archbishop delivered a sentence I will never forget. 'Yes, if they want to go to law we will use the law to defend ourselves.'

Defend themselves from the shattered victims? It's a pity the Church hierarchy didn't utilise the law to pursue their paedophile priests. If they had, none of our fight would have been necessary – children would have been safe in the Church.

Carleton: 'And you swear them to secrecy.'

Archbishop Pell: 'Well, we ask them to keep . . .'

Carleton: 'No, you swear them. You swear them.'

Archbishop Pell: 'There is a requirement that they don't talk about it and most of them are happy not to.'

Carleton: 'Why do you impose this condition?'

Archbishop Pell: 'Because many of them don't want to be subjected to publicity and of course it's shameful to the Church.'

We recorded the program and replayed it later. We watched again and again Archbishop Pell's reaction to Anthony's taped interview, to the photograph, trying to understand how he could deny having seen it. He remembered the first photo. Why would we show him only the happy picture when we were there to level our complaints about the Church at him?

It was many years before I could comprehend what I'd seen on television that night. It took until November 2009.

The release of the Irish Commission of Investigation report into child sexual abuse in the Dublin Archdiocese took a battering ram to the Church's longstanding cover-up of paedophile priests. It also revealed a disturbing but fascinating Catholic Church loophole in the truth, whereby priests are taught to use what they call 'mental reservation', which enables them to 'lie without lying'.

The Commission of Investigation report stated:

> Mental reservation is a concept developed and much discussed over the centuries, which permits a church man knowingly to convey a misleading impression to another person without being guilty of lying.

An example given was:

> John calls [in] to the parish priest to make a complaint about the behaviour of one of his curates [assistant priests]. The parish priest sees him coming but does not want to see him because he considers John to be a troublemaker. He sends another of his curates to answer the door. John asks the curate if the parish priest is in. The curate replies that he is not.

The commission added:

> This is clearly untrue but in the church's view it is not a lie because, when the curate told John that the parish priest was not in, he mentally reserved the words '. . . to you'.

A cardinal explained the concept to the commission.

> Well, the *general teaching* about mental reservation is that you
> are not permitted to tell a lie. On the other hand, you may
> be put in a position where you have to answer, and there
> may be circumstances in which you can use an ambiguous
> expression realising that the person you are talking to will
> accept an untrue version of whatever it may be – permitting
> that to happen, not willing that it happened, that would be
> lying. It really is a matter of trying to deal with extraordinarily
> difficult matters that may arise in social relations where people
> may ask questions that you simply cannot answer. Everybody
> knows that this kind of thing is liable to happen. So mental
> reservation is, in a sense, a way of answering without lying.

Further shameful and deceitful examples of mental reservation
were given. Examples of their lying without lying, used against
victims sexually abused by their priests, used as a tool to hide
from the law and pervert the course of justice, to slow or stop
investigation, or to mislead and confuse with the purpose to
exhaust and frustrate victims already traumatised and silenced
by priests during their childhood.

The cardinal went on to explain his own actions to the
commission stressing '. . . he did not lie to the media about
the use of diocesan funds for the compensation of clerical child
sexual abuse victims'. He told journalists 'that the diocesan
funds ARE [report's emphasis] not used for such a purpose; that
he had not said that diocesan funds WERE not used for such
a purpose'. By using the present tense he had not excluded the
possibility that diocesan funds had been used for such purpose
in the past. According to the victim, the cardinal considered
that there was an enormous difference between the two.

Another victim case highlighted by the Irish report said the
archdiocese issued a 1997 press statement that it had cooper-

ated with the *gardai* (police) where a woman's complaint of abuse was concerned. The woman disagreed. A supportive priest, who acted on behalf of the victim, made enquiries of his own. He approached the archdiocese and was told: 'We never said we cooperated fully' – placing emphasis on the word 'fully' – 'with the *gardai*.' The caring priest gave this information to the *gardai*. If he did not, the mental reservation used in this instance would never have been revealed.

Without reports like the one released in Ireland, I would not have even known about this manipulative tactic, the Church's twisting of reality. Neither I, nor any of the other ordinary Catholics I have asked, had ever heard of 'mental reservation' and without fail every one of them was shocked and then outraged at this dishonest, truth-twisting form of deceit.

As ordinary Catholics, we were not taught this clerical concept. But behind the scenes priests exclusively taught it to each other. Why didn't they teach everybody about it – if they saw it as a legitimate way to lie? We had no such respite from the truth. We were forced to go to fearful confession every week as seven-year-olds to admit our lies and be given penance to seek forgiveness; we need not have bothered.

How many times has it been used against us?

I discovered that mental reservation is a universal tactic that has a long history in Australia. In December 1900 it was a source of scandal for the Catholic Church when it was revealed in a famous court battle, The Coningham Case, involving a man whose wife had given birth to the child of the Cardinal of Sydney's secretary and administrator, who was a priest.

The doctrine was also mentioned in the English House of Commons in the nineteenth century, when Catholics were allowed to be members of parliament for the first time.

The Catholic Relief Act, 1829, says:

It shall be lawful to sit and vote in either house of parliament
. . . upon taking and subscribing the following oath . . . And
I do solemnly, in the presence of God, profess, testify and
declare that I do make this declaration and every part thereof
in the plain and ordinary sense of the words of this oath,
without any evasion, equivocation, or mental reservation
whatsoever. So help me God.

What hope did any of us have? How can we now believe
anything they say? With this new knowledge I have to ask myself
if the priestly mental reservation was applied to Archbishop
Pell's denial of seeing Emma's bloodied photo. I replay the
scene now – he had taken the normal-size photograph from
Richard Carleton and said 'I've never seen the photo . . .',
then mental reservation could finish the sentence with '. . .
I've seen only the A4-size printout'.

His denial stopped Richard Carleton's forthcoming questions of how he could have said such a thing to the parents of
a child suffering so much as a result of the abuse meted out by
one of his fellow priests. It certainly stopped any further questioning, but not about the compensation offer.

The following day we had our opportunity to be heard in
the form of a newspaper article. 'Family slams Pell's denial' read
the headline. Anthony was quoted anonymously. 'He's wrong.
I know we took that picture with us and showed it to him.'

One television station rang and asked if it could send a
reporter and cameraman to record our reaction to the *60 Minutes*
piece. We agreed. Others also called. After the first news crew
arrived and while they were still setting up for an interview, I
went to the front door to find another three television news
crews lined up down our front path. I took out some drinks as
some of them waited hours before we could see them.

As a result of the *60 Minutes* program a bigger debate now
raged across Australia – the 'Hush Money scandal'. There was

much argument about this issue; whether it was a requirement of the victim to remain silent or not. The threat to the victims was if they spoke about the amount they received, the Church could take the money back. To some victims, receiving even very little for lifelong damages was critical. In their broken state, it would be almost impossible to pay the money back.

They were scared.

Archbishop Pell brought a high-priced public relations consultant with him to a carefully managed media conference, saying he made an error during his interview with Richard Carleton.

'I was unclear and imprecise on the confidentiality requirements,' he conceded. 'I was certainly mistaken.'

He came up with the confidentiality scheme and it didn't seem plausible he didn't know its legalities. But the Catholic Church was scrambling. It paid for an expensive full-page advertisement in metropolitan newspapers around the entire country to explain its position.

'Victims are not silenced as a condition for receiving counselling or compensation,' it stated, among other things.

But the next day those same newspapers ran stories quoting a victim who had a silencing clause attached to her payout. Then others produced their 'hush orders'. The Church said its conference of bishops made a decision to take out all silencing clauses from Towards Healing payouts after 2000. But that didn't happen in all cases and the Church was forced to publicly concede this failure. If the issue wasn't causing so many people lifelong trauma it would have been a joke.

The silencing requirement was difficult to understand. To begin the Pell Process, a victim must first fill out an application form, which has a confidentiality clause. It unambiguously reads:

Neither I nor any person acting on my behalf . . . will (save as required by law)
(i) disclose to any person
(ii) rely or seek to rely in any arbitral or judicial proceeding on any communication, statement or information, whether oral or documentary, made or provided in the course of or in relation to the Panel's deliberations.

After going through the process and accepting the compensation offer a release is signed. Is the confidentiality clause signed in the first instance still binding? Was there a second confidentiality clause when accepting the compensation?

A victim I knew who had been through the Pell Process rang the Church lawyers and said: 'I believe I can now tell people how much I received from the Church without the worry of you taking the money back – as I am free to talk about it according to your newspaper announcement.' He wanted to make sure. The lawyer he spoke to on the phone replied, 'No, you cannot disclose how much you received.'

So what could the victims do? Speak out? Better not.

International media picked up the issue and our story. I saw an online news item on the *Boston Globe* website and read it with interest, to see how it was reported in America.

'SYDNEY – The city's Roman Catholic Archbishop said in a broadcast aired yesterday that he offered $28,000 settlement with a family for the alleged sexual abuse of its children by a local priest.'

Twenty-eight thousand? It took me a minute to realise the sum had been changed to US dollars. It seemed a pittance. And that was the maximum Archbishop Pell allowed the compensation panel to offer.

In the maelstrom that followed the *60 Minutes* story, the Church released payout figures from the Archdiocese of Melbourne. Another front-page headline screamed:

'CHURCH'S SHAME FILE'. It turned out that in the six years from 1996 to 2002, the Pell Process paid one hundred and twenty-six victims an aggregate of $3 million in compensation for the crimes committed by twenty-two priests and religious brothers. Talk about a pittance. That worked out to be an average of nearly $24,000 to each victim – less than half of what they could offer. I didn't even want to calculate what that was in US dollars.

And that's before victims had to pay hefty legal fees.

It was shameful tokenism from one of the richest organisations in the world – for lifetimes of shattered dreams and disabilities that they failed to stop. The Church paid, and still pays, the very least amount it can get away with. The maximum has only recently (2008) been raised to $75,000 but I would bet few, if any, people are awarded anywhere near that. The weaker, more isolated, more intimidated into silence the victim is, the less the ex gratia payment is . . . and, don't forget, you sign away your rights to sue.

This injustice from a Church outrages me. I recall certain victims I have seen over the years who've been treated in this way. They are terribly isolated – some are unable to read and write due to the atrocities heaped upon them as children. They were frightened of the priest who set upon them as defenceless children, and they are still afraid. The buying of their silence is complete. Not a word. Nobody hears their stories because they don't want to risk the Church coming back at them.

After all, whose advice do they take? Even the archbishop who came up with the compensation scheme couldn't get it right when questioned.

Meanwhile, these victims live half-lives. Spent is their payment, which has gone nowhere towards improving their state. Once the paperwork is signed there is no comeback. How can a Christian Church be like this? How can the hierarchy of the Catholic Church be happy to take advantage and rip off such unfortunate people?

What do they think God thinks of them?

But now that the Church claims it does not offer hush money, I can reveal the compensation sums received by just four of the boys assaulted by Father Kevin O'Donnell. It was made clear to me during my research that only very few select victims were offered anywhere near the maximum payment.

Alan Timmons, the boy who was assaulted for years in Dandenong and then lied to by the Church that he was the 'only one', tried unsuccessfully to sue the Church. He was so traumatised and tired of the legal brick walls being placed in his way that he gave up and submitted himself to the Pell Process. The Church-appointed commissioner investigated and found O'Donnell did sexually assault Alan. The panel asked the victim what his legal bills were. He said he owed his solicitor $17,000 for representing him. The Catholic Church duly awarded Alan a payment of $19,000. Confused, strung out, desperate and exhausted, he accepted the paltry offer and signed away any future legal rights . . . for $2,000 in his pocket. This final slap in the face would ensure he suffered for the rest of his life.

Peter Taylor, the boy who O'Donnell almost drowned in the late 1940s after a long period of abuse, was a grandfather when he applied for compensation. He was paid $28,000. His solicitor's fees also came to $17,000.

Jimmy Chambers, the boy who confided in the scout-master, who complained to the cathedral in 1958, was one of the first to be badly let down by the Church. His attempts to hold the institution to account through a lawsuit flopped, as all others did.

For his years of methodical grooming and molestation, as well as his lifetime of trauma, he was paid $20,000, still well shy of the maximum allowed under the Pell Process. Lawyers claimed $12,000 from him. The accompanying letter from the Church called O'Donnell's abuse an 'alleged' offence. O'Donnell was in jail by then. He had pleaded guilty. The word 'alleged' should not be used to describe the actions of a convicted criminal.

Bill Nelson, the altar boy who first reported his abuse to a nun was determined to find justice. He went as far as serving writs against the Church. O'Donnell, through a lawyer, sent a letter to Bill Nelson in April 1995, more than a year after the priest confessed to police that he had molested the boy, and just months before pleading guilty in the County Court to assaulting twelve children.

The document states that O'Donnell '. . . does not admit any of the allegations'. It adds that *if* O'Donnell was negligent, the boy was 'guilty of contributory negligence'.

WHAT? The Church was saying Bill was at fault. The defenceless boy, scared frozen in O'Donnell's car or bed, blacking out through terror, was to blame?

The lawyer's intimidating letter listed the ways in which the boy was negligent in his duty.

(a) Failing to take care for his own safety;
(b) Failing to make any complaint in relation to the alleged conduct;
(c) Failing to seek assistance;
(d) Failing to report any such alleged conduct.

The threats and legal stonewalling worked. It almost always did. Bill Nelson, suffering post-traumatic stress, gave up his seemingly endless and unforgiving legal fight and signed up for the Pell Process. Guess what? The Church suddenly conceded that O'Donnell, one of its most senior priests, *did* assault the boy.

It gave him $30,000.

I've often wondered at the cruelty of these amounts. Each payment was an opportunity for compassion missed.

A chance to help turn around a past injustice. I didn't understand. How broken did they want people to be before they would be generous within their own limited scheme? It was once mentioned to us by a victim – who went through the Pell Process – that two or more members sitting on the compensation panel were representatives from the Catholic insurance company. That could explain it.

Those sums of money were, and are, disgraceful. Every one of the hundreds of cases that has gone through Church-run compensation schemes should be reviewed by secular authorities, and legislation enacted to make all contracts signed during the Pell Process and Towards Healing open to reappraisal, allowing them to be dealt with justly – outside the church.

But the Church will fight kicking and screaming at the very suggestion it should hand over its power. Maybe that's why Archbishop Pell said, in his final answer of the *60 Minutes* interview: '. . . of course it's shameful to the Church.'

'Shameful' is nowhere near a big enough word. But then Archbishop Pell didn't always choose his words well. Another answer the archbishop gave during his interview with Richard Carleton stuck in my head and still worries me. Again, it was the language he used. It was completely wrong.

'Is it homosexual sex or heterosexual sex amongst the clergy that's the biggest problem?' Mr Carleton asked.

Archbishop Pell didn't answer the question but offered this response: 'Most paedophilia involves young girls. With the Catholic clergy more of it involves younger men after puberty.'

'. . . *younger men after puberty* . . . ?' What did he mean?

Archbishop Pell was referring to illegal *paedophilia* sex. The 'younger men after puberty' were under sixteen years of age. So he was talking about thirteen-, fourteen- and fifteen-year-olds. Calling them 'men' conjures images of adult males – consenting adult males.

Why didn't he say 'boys' or 'young teenagers'? Doesn't he see them as children? Why did he mention puberty? What does 'after puberty' have to do with the sexual assault of a minor? Does using these words make the offence disappear? Less serious? Did he not know about all the priests in prison for assaulting and raping *little children*? My girls were five and not much older.

The *60 Minutes* program did what the Catholic Church failed to do – it helped victims. It raised awareness of clergy sexual abuse and gave some people a voice, encouraging two hundred brave sufferers to make new complaints. As a result, twenty more perpetrator priests were exposed.

This is what happens when the veil is lifted, if only for a short while. Reverend Doyle, the compassionate canon lawyer and priest from the United States, once wrote: 'When clergy sex abuse is sealed under wraps, it festers and breeds; when it is brought into the light of day, it withers.'

The hush money controversy died down but Archbishop Pell lurched towards another scandal. On Wednesday 21 August 2002 yet another newspaper headline read: 'Sex-abuse allegations force Pell to stand aside', with another photo of Archbishop George Pell.

'Australia's most powerful religious leader, George Pell, yesterday stood aside as Catholic Archbishop of Sydney to allow an investigation into claims that he sexually abused an altar boy more than 40 years ago.'

The cleric made public the accusations in a statement the day before.

The allegations against me are lies and I deny them totally and utterly. The alleged events never happened. I repeat, emphatically, that the allegations are false. An independent inquiry to investigate these allegations has been set up. The inquiry will be conducted, I understand, by a retired Victorian Supreme Court Judge. For the good of the Church and to preserve the dignity of the office of archbishop, I will take leave from today as Archbishop of Sydney until the inquiry is completed.

The independent hearing was established by the National Committee for Professional Standards, a body set up by the Australian Catholic Bishops' Conference. The in-camera inquiry into the victim's claim proceeded and the presiding judge made the decision that despite the fact he felt the complainant was speaking honestly, 'bearing in mind forensic difficulties of the defence occasioned by the very long delay, some valid criticism of the complainant's credibility, the lack of corroborative evidence and the sworn denial of the respondent, I find I am satisfied that the complaint has not been established'.

The inquiry, in contrast to its build-up, received minimal media attention due to the terrorist bombs in Bali, which exploded, killing almost 200 Australians, a few days before the finding was handed down. George Pell resumed his full duties on 15 October 2002.

Even though it now seems forgotten, the judge said he believed both parties gave the impression they were speaking the truth. In my mind this equated to neither guilt nor innocence. But in the case of Archbishop Pell, the finding did not diminish his standing in the eyes of his superiors in Rome. Not long after the scandal, he was promoted from Archbishop of Sydney to Cardinal of Sydney, giving him the power to vote for future popes or, indeed, one day become pope himself.

Chapter 16
Bad company,
diminished choices

Emma's career in nursing was short-lived. After just twelve months, drugs once again took control of her life and skewed her decision-making. A change in her prescribed medication quickly made her body weight balloon to eighty-five kilograms; the extra thirty kilos would never leave her. She hated being overweight and the self-confidence she was slowly gaining fell apart when she looked in the mirror. Upon recognising her faltering state of mind, Emma booked herself into a rehabilitation clinic. It prevented her from falling headlong into the daily abuse she was trying her hardest to resist, but it was proving more than difficult.

In January 2002, Emma tried something else to ward off the hovering hungry demons of addiction. She was working for a nursing agency when she suddenly decided to take a short-term position at a nursing home in Alice Springs. Maybe getting away would help, she thought. The agency flew her there but she did not relax into the new lifestyle; rather she found the Northern Territory instantly intimidating.

Her first reaction to the isolation and loneliness of living in the city in the desert was to drink alcohol heavily. She also started taking too much of her medication. The agency, thankfully and kindly, brought her home within six days.

Three months later, still staggering emotionally, Emma was readmitted into the psych unit. Then the staff caught her shooting up heroin in one of the wards. The psychiatrist was furious and threatened to report Emma's drug use to the Nursing Board, which would certainly end her career. It was such an awful possibility and Emma became distraught. She believed nursing was the only worthwhile thing that she had achieved. Now, with deregistration hanging over her, she tearfully discharged herself and departed the clinic. The unit staff let her go on to the streets with her few belongings and all her medication – a month's worth.

Night had just taken over from day and it was chilly outside. My daughter's thoughts were also dark and cold. A couple of hours later, at about ten o'clock, I received a phone call from Emma saying she was 'going out'. I didn't understand what she meant. I assumed she was no longer at the clinic because of the background noise but she would not elaborate.

'Where, exactly, are you?' I asked, but she did not answer.

'I'm going out,' she repeated and hung up.

The well-worn panic button in my mind went off and I tried to figure out where she might be. There was a lot of background chatter on the phone, as if she was in a pub. I thought about the small upstairs bar around the corner from the clinic. I had noticed it previously but had not been there or even spoken about it to Emma. It was the only picture which jumped to mind so I quickly told Anthony about the unnerving conversation and we ran to the car. I knew we had to find her before she could harm herself. The lack of detail she offered was worrying me, as well as the fatalistic sound in her voice. We drove straight to the hotel and bounded up the stairs, scanning patrons near the entrance, around the bar and even in the toilets. She wasn't anywhere to be seen. Anthony and I then raced back to the car and drove to the nearby clinic.

'What happened to Emma? Where is she?' I breathlessly asked the duty nurse.

We were told why Emma was discharged and I became even more distressed when I heard what she had taken with her. 'You sent her off into the night – upset – with a month's worth of medication? Why didn't you ring us?' I demanded to know, expecting no answer.

I'd had enough. Couldn't they guess what was going to happen? All they had to do was call us. Emma had no car, no money for a taxi. How would she get home? We left in a state of desperation.

'Where is she?' We drove slowly back past the bar from where I thought Emma made the call. I told Anthony to drive down a little laneway that we were passing. He edged the car around the tight entrance and we started crawling stressfully along the alley. It looked like a place someone might come to die, I thought bleakly.

We peered into every dark corner and doorway on both sides. The headlights drew parallel with the second-last building in the lane, which, by its design, demanded closer inspection.

'Slow down for a second.'

The facade staring back at us had a metal emergency stairway cut into the building, parts of it protruding into the light, the rest receding into the blackness. It made a menacing alcove, with a thousand different shadows. We strained our eyes to see a small, white rectangular object lying on the ground. It was a used and discarded tablet pop-pack card.

'Look, there!' Anthony stopped the car.

We jumped out and rushed over to the shadowy alcove. The tablet dispenser was empty. There were more tablet cards strewn around the concrete ground – many, many more – all

empty. Our bulging eyes scanned left and right, then we saw
her . . .

'EMMA!'

Our daughter was crammed under the lowest steps, looking
at that instant like little more than a bundle of clothing. She
must have crawled under there, then wedged herself in tightly.
She was semiconscious; no-one would have seen her hidden
there until daylight, still hours away. Anthony and I half-
dragged her from under the stairs by her arm before helping
her into the car. I quickly gathered all the tablet cards – there
were dozens of them – and the medicine boxes they came out
of. Emergency doctors would need to know what she had
taken, and how much.

Now in the car, we made a short dash back to the clinic,
looking for someone to help us.

'I think you should drive her straight to an emergency
hospital,' a staff member recommended.

In our frenzy we did so but we should have called an
ambulance. The first hospital we headed for had no emergency
section. Others that came to mind also were without an emergency service. We changed course for the Monash Medical
Centre, with one of the largest emergency departments in the
city. It seemed like a long drive even at high speed.

Emma kept falling unconscious and I knew it was vital to
keep her awake. I kept rousing her, talking to her, shaking her.

Even with a clear run along a four-lane highway, the mercy
dash dragged on and on. Vital time was being lost, taking
Emma's chances of surviving with it.

'EMMA. WAKE UP. OPEN YOUR EYES. LISTEN TO
ME. Almost there . . . almost there.'

Her eyelids were too heavy and I could no longer wake
her. Finally we arrived, pulling up in the ambulance bay at
the emergency department, a place familiar to us. We showed
doctors the empty medication boxes. She was admitted and

saved. I later counted the missing tablets Emma had taken that night. She swallowed over one hundred and fifty. She had come so close to dying . . . so close to not being found.

The following day I visited Emma, still unconscious in the emergency room. I tried to wake her, thinking she was asleep, but I couldn't. I left and called back on the phone hours later, at eleven o'clock. I listened as a nurse gave Emma the receiver. 'Hello?' It was a weak greeting followed by the sound of the phone falling to the ground. My daughter had passed out from the effort of saying one word. She had barely recovered the next day, when she was discharged.

Emma never worked again as a nurse.

Tim Seccull and Michael Jorgensen served writs on the Melbourne Archdiocese in our multiheaded case in October 2002. It was a satisfying feeling knowing that matters were proceeding. We had to then wait for Tim and Michael to run the case on our behalf, but we had more pressing day-to-day problems to solve.

Emma, now fully recovered from her overdose four months earlier, left home after we caught her using drugs at our house. We had previously warned her not to do this and even threatened to move her out if she continued to disobey our rule. Anthony and I had Katie and Aimee to consider and we always said Emma was welcome to stay but the drugs were not. Things around our home disappeared – to the pawnshop, presumably – and then reappeared on pension day. Sometimes missing things never reappeared. We had kept threatening expulsion from home, although never enforced it because we didn't want to lose her. But this particular day when we caught her yet again she came to us and said: 'I know I have to leave.' We didn't stop her.

She moved into a flat in the inner-city suburb of St Kilda with a new friend. I kept in contact with her and a few weeks later, during a phone call, Emma said she wanted money for things she needed around the unit, essential and normal things – a table, curtains, pots and pans . . .

'Things that would cost about $5000,' she explained.

Emma was so excited about filling up her new home and it all sounded perfectly reasonable. She then also reiterated how the money (still available to claim) from the archdiocese would be handy. 'I really need it, Mum,' she said.

Over the years, since the $50,000 compensation offer was made, I persuaded Emma to not claim it by giving her our money instead. I told her I would give her the same amount if she waited for our lawyers to mount a civil case. We both had nothing to lose. She would get her $50,000 from me – slowly over time, as she needed it – and if we had no success in suing the Church then she could take the compensation offer and repay me what she had already spent.

I had been giving Emma money since she was a teenager. She began smoking when she was fourteen, around the time of her second admission into the adolescent unit. We provided everything for Emma but I drew the line at cigarettes – she had to buy those herself – so the money I gave her in lieu of the Church compensation bought smokes. Later, it covered car registration and insurance, petrol, bills and eventually her car repayments.

Those repayments were no longer being met because of her need to purchase drugs. We said we would not give her money to buy heroin. I gave her small amounts of cash or made payments myself for things like bills. I kept records of what was spent and tallied it up every now and then. It was tedious but it worked. Now she wanted $5000 for her new life in the spartan flat, with the reminder that if we didn't give her the money, she could go to the Church and claim the compensation.

We discussed it at length and she had me convinced she would spend it wisely, so I transferred the money into her account. Several days later I had not heard from her and couldn't get through on her mobile phone. On the weekend I went to see her.

'Where are all the things you were going to buy?' I asked, looking around the small flat, seeing nothing new. None of the items she was so excited about buying were there. She offered no reply. When I looked at her I could see there was something up. 'What's wrong?' I asked. She had a sheepish look on her face. Then I realised.

'Are you buying drugs with the money?' She nodded.

I should not have used present tense. My daughter and her new friend had *spent* the entire amount on heroin and other drugs in a week. It was all gone. I should have known better. A doctor later said to me it was a wonder she survived the volume of drugs she had gone through during that seven-day period. That was the last time I gave her a large sum of money.

Anthony and I attended a friend's daughter's twenty-first birthday party. We had known the family since our girls were in kinder. After the speeches, the lights were dimmed and photos of the birthday girl's life were shown from infancy to adulthood. The pictures were lovely to see and brought back sweet memories. Suddenly a photo of a birthday party long ago appeared on the screen. It captured a happy group of beautiful girls in their best party dresses. Emma and Katie were among the children smiling back at us. I froze. The photo was gone as quickly as it appeared. More photos of delightful times took its place but I was left in a time warp. It was a picture I had not seen before of my little daughters, when they were happy and whole. The image of our untroubled past hit me like a sledgehammer – the tears were as instantaneous then as they are now as I am writing this. I wanted to break down with the force of emotion that was ripping me apart inside but I held on, surrounded by happier people. Only a few seconds earlier I had been one of them. It was confusing. This was not a sad occasion. But it was. Anthony was standing beside me and I looked at him to see he was in the same state I was in. We held hands and remained where we were standing . . . in the darkness, hoping the lights would never come back on.

At the end of October, while still in the flat, Emma took a medication overdose and cut her wrists, climbed into her car, started driving and had two separate minor car accidents, only minutes apart. Three days later she took another overdose and had a third minor car accident. Again, no-one was hurt but cars were damaged. Anthony set about sorting it all out with the other drivers, insurance companies, repair mechanics and police. It was a nightmare, but so was the rest of our life. We fixed Emma's car too. Some months later, she had another accident. This time we left her car damaged; what was the point of repairing it once more? It was clear by now that Emma was off the rails. In desperation, we convinced her to come back home.

It was her twenty-first birthday. On 6 November 2002 we took her out with the rest of the family but we were not happy with her. Apart from dinner, we did not give her a birthday present.

We tried to come up with a new solution to her reckless behaviour. I tried to get her into the rehabilitation clinic, Odyssey House, but she was refused entry because she self-harmed. I felt like getting in my car and simply driving and driving forever without stopping, leaving with just the clothes on my back, telling no-one I was going. The temptation was great and I thought about it often. It was a soothing fantasy I never acted upon.

Meanwhile, Katie continued her struggle to function day to day. She had a fall in a shop and when her carer brought her home, Katie had her first epileptic fit. We were called home to the horrible sight of our beautiful daughter twisted uncontrollably, distorted and suffering. We called an ambulance and she was admitted to hospital for a couple of days. We couldn't know it then, but that was just the beginning of many serious falls and epileptic after-shocks with hospital admissions that Katie would suffer.

On this same day, Aimee came home from boarding school and departed the country for wintry England, to stay with her aunt. Her relationship with our troubled Emma was more than she could take and Katie's situation distressed her. We wanted Aimee to escape the nightmare that was once home. Our youngest girl had finished year 12, and even with a high 'Consideration of Disadvantage' she still achieved only a low tertiary entrance score, affording her few career opportunities. It didn't seem to matter. With so much distraction, she had done very well just to get through her final two demanding years of secondary school.

Aimee felt caught in the middle. One day, she and Emma had a terrible argument. The pair was often in opposition – Emma received too-lenient treatment from Anthony and me because of what she'd gone through. This day was worse. Their argument escalated, neither sister backing down. It ended with Emma threatening harm to Aimee and my fearful youngest daughter locking herself in her room, music blaring to drown out the yelling. A couple of hours later, I tried to get Aimee's attention through her closed door but no amount of knocking or banging received a response. I went outside the house to her bedroom window. Still, I couldn't see her. When I climbed in the window I found she had gone. There was no note. She didn't return and was missing overnight. The following day, fighting rising panic, I called the only friend of Aimee's I knew who didn't live at home with her parents. After saying hello, I cut straight to the question. 'Is Aimee with you?'

I had a cold sensation in my stomach as I felt the pause and waited for a response. After a moment, the friend replied:

'Yes.' I relaxed and asked to speak to my daughter. Aimee told me about the threat and how I had not defended her. We sorted things out and she came home later that day.

So, with such tension enveloping her, it was no wonder Aimee was enthusiastic about an overseas break. She planned to study childcare in 2003 but for the time being she just wanted out. Against the prospect of our family's ongoing, hectic day-after-day trauma, she imagined London's busy streets would be a peaceful getaway.

The new year ticked by and brought fresh hope with it. It didn't seem to matter what was happening; the change of digits on the calendar seemed to offer the possibility that the days were about to brighten. Emma began seeing a new specialist. The sessions went from weekly to fortnightly but they were positive, given Emma at least liked the psychologist, whose expertise was working with sexual abuse victims.

In March 2003, after more troubles, she was admitted to Monash Medical Centre's psychiatry unit. After twenty days there she overdosed on her medication and was transferred to a medical ward. I told the doctors Emma was not coming back home so they discharged her into an aged care home just a few kilometres away from the hospital.

I began writing to the vicar general, Monsignor Christopher Prowse, asking him if the Church could help provide Emma with accommodation. It was an impulsive and desperate request, and one I quickly abandoned after Anthony and I discussed it further. We would look for another housing option ourselves.

We found her a housing program but there was a waiting list and she could not move in for three months. I sought advice from the Church counselling section, who 'could do nothing', and then decided again to contact the cathedral administrator. After all, the Church caused this mess in the first place. I wrote to the vicar general, this time finishing the letter and asking for assistance in finding three months' accommodation for Emma. It was backed up by a two-page letter from our family therapist – paid for by the Church – outlining the situation and Emma's needs.

Thirteen days later the vicar general responded saying she should claim the ex gratia payment, which would help with her accommodation costs.

No offer of help or accommodation, no 'sorry' for the trouble we have caused or the hell you are going through, no pity – just take the money! Their $50,000 was going to save the world . . . What was to happen to Emma after the money was spent? How long did they think it was going to last? With Emma's disrupted education and drug addiction, would she ever have another job? Another profession? Would she ever support herself? Ever come off the drugs? Ever be able to afford to buy a house? Ever reach that or any other dream?

The extreme wealth of the Church made its heartlessness harder to fathom. Months earlier, the *Herald Sun* newspaper had tried to track the Church's assets in the State of Victoria. Records found that four Roman Catholic dioceses held more than six hundred and thirty land titles. The investigation found the Archdiocese of Melbourne was the largest in the nation. It ran three hundred and thirty-one schools, churches and houses for more than three hundred priests, hundred of brothers and more than a thousand nuns. The church owned nursing homes, colleges and conference centres, the story revealed.

The question was stated: How rich is the Roman Catholic Church in Victoria?

Vicar General Christopher Prowse answered: 'We don't discuss those issues publicly.'

The newspaper estimated assets worth more than $1 billion. I would have thought somewhere in all its properties, charities and hospitals, or given its devotion to the sick, the poor and the needy, the Church could have found the means to help accommodate a twenty-one-year-old woman for twelve weeks.

So the rest of society had to help Emma cope. Her one-week emergency accommodation was extended while the women's shelter tried to find her a permanent home. The shelter was able to eventually locate a nice new unit in Oakleigh – near us – where she lived for a couple of months until something else became available. I visited her regularly, as I always did when she was away from home. She was lonely.

The drug addiction Emma had was an obstacle we couldn't overcome. We tried to steer her away from taking anything from heroin to unnecessary prescription pills. But it didn't work while Emma was living with us and, as painful as it was, we had to understand we could not control her actions. In the hope she would turn away from drugs we had to let her live the life she created for herself. She told me drugs were keeping her alive.

'If it wasn't for drugs I would have killed myself a long time ago, Mum.'

Emma reminded me she had been taking different kinds of drugs since she was five, given to her by Father O'Donnell. I had no answers. I felt so alone in my guilt of what had happened to her through my blind faith in the Church and priest.

The following is one of the earliest suicide notes she wrote.

I feel scared and frightened. I want to keep to myself and not be noticed. It seems quite impossible, so for that reason I mustn't live. I'm dead anyway. Not physically but in every other way. Over the next week I will end it all. I can't stand life any more and don't feel safe. Safe from the world. Safe from me. I feel in great danger of everything and can't go on. I will miss my family and friends and love you all. Don't be sad. It's all for the best.

Good-bye

She left several notes like that.

My daughter's life and behaviour reflected back on me and I too was trapped. She was a slave to the drugs and I was a slave to her in trying to save her. In so much of my life I felt I could not move. Like Emma, I felt blackmailed and imprisoned by what had been done to her. It was as if the abuse she suffered placed a big steel cage over both of us. We could see out sometimes but we couldn't go anywhere; the iron bars were too strong. As time enveloped us, Emma and I became like one being in that cage. I was trying to live for the entwined pair of us – thinking, seeing, acting, fixing faults, predicting pitfalls, jumping at shadows and then peering back into the shadows to what might be coming next.

And I was racked by unrelenting guilt the whole time. Of not looking after my children – even though I did. Of missing vital clues – when they were impossible to see. Whenever I did rescue the girls it was always too late and only ever temporary.

In June, as the cold months took hold of us and the large leaves fell from trees in the yard beyond our suburban verandah, Anthony and I decided we needed a break. We left for Scotland, to visit my ancestors' island of St Kilda. Before we departed, Emma began protesting, playing up, tightening the screws. I did not write any of it down. I just wanted to flee.

But I was pursued for most of the trip. The great oceans I placed between us could not defeat her mobile phone and I could not abandon her by turning mine off.

My mum and brother dropped in to visit Emma regularly while we were away. I found out much later that Mum had a feeling one day that something was wrong with her granddaughter and so rushed around to see if she was coping. Emma had overdosed on her medication and was unconscious. Mum called an ambulance and Emma was admitted into hospital. Two days later she was discharged into a new psychiatric clinic and stayed there until we returned home. Mum did not tell me of the overdose until we arrived back in Australia.

There was more turbulence ahead. It turned out Emma was using heroin during that entire period in the clinic. I thought she would have saved some money because she was contained in the clinic, but she had found a way to spend her disability pension each fortnight during her outings. Staff from the women's shelter found Emma more permanent living quarters in the form of a housing commission unit, which she was now sharing with a woman named Lu.

Lu was a few years older than Emma but I immediately considered her a very caring person and the two of them, over time, became close friends. We welcomed Lu into our lives. I visited them weekly and Emma popped in to see us at home. We also stayed in touch over the phone.

Nonetheless, Emma continued to overdose; twice in the next two months. Then she fell in with bad company. A new person was placed in one of the housing commission units in Emma's block. He was in his thirties and just out of prison, on parole from drug-related charges. They met, chatted and became friends.

He must have been delighted because Emma had a car. She could be useful.

Their aim was to attain money to buy drugs.

Emma and the man drove along urban streets looking for houses to break into. Once they had a specific target they forced their way in and pinched anything of value. The felon had a contact, a 'fence', who gave them cash for the stolen goods. The pair would blow their windfall on drugs and hit the streets again, looking for more houses in which to force entry.

They went through this cycle for a couple of months but it was hardly a well-thought-out series of heists, given that

Emma was driving her own registered car. A resident noted her numberplate detail one day and reported it to the police. Officers went to her doorstep, knocked and arrested both of them. Game over.

On Boxing Day 2003, a police sergeant rang us at home with the news. It was a courtesy call to inform us that Emma had been arrested and charged with the series of burglaries.

Any Christmas joy disappeared.

Because it was her first offence, Emma was released. Her partner in crime went back to prison, as he had breached his parole conditions. The volume of drugs Emma consumed before she was arrested was large. Afterwards, she was severely strung out. Going from a lot to nothing brings a big fall. She saw in another New Year's Eve as close to death as she could imagine.

For Anthony and me, Emma's arrest was almost the last straw. Our family was like an active volcano and the pressure inside was immense. We were all feeling it. I wrote on a scrap of paper some things each of us had said in that month; it was January 2004. The random quotes were telling. They were close to being unbelievable, even at the time.

Aimee, who had given up studying childcare after one year because she didn't like it, said: 'I'd rather be dead than living our life.' This was the second time she had uttered that thought.

Emma said: 'I'd like someone to come up behind me and shoot me in the back of the head.'

I said to Aimee in an argument about Emma: 'I wish I wasn't alive.'

Anthony said, for the second time: 'It would be easier just not to be here.'

Then came Katie. About fifteen times over the past three years Katie had cried and asked me desperately and passionately to 'Please kill me'. In January 2004 she took her self-hatred to a new intensity. As I was helping her out of the car, which was parked on the street in front of our home, she yelled at me repeatedly: 'Kill me! Kill ME! KILL MEEEE!' It was loud, aggressive and shook me for a long time. I didn't know how to respond.

Anthony's mum Joyce collapsed at home that same month; my husband found her during a visit. She was semi-conscious and had a high fever. He called an ambulance and she was rushed to hospital, where she was stabilised and nursed back to health after a week. We were talking about putting things in place for her return home when she suffered a stroke, the type elderly people have when they have been inactive or bedridden for too long. It caused irreparable damage and she did not regain consciousness. Over the next week Joyce declined. Anthony spent many hours with his mum. He asked nursing staff to ring him any time if they thought she was about to die. He wanted to be with her.

They rang and he went in.

When he was too exhausted to stay awake he slept in the chair beside her. When he was able to keep his eyes open, he watched her die.

Later, he told me that he listened to her breathe.

'It was just like she would have listened to me breathing as I slept as a baby.'

His words brought tears to my eyes; he had always been a good son. Joyce was eighty-four when she died and at fifty-one years of age Anthony was orphaned. We arranged and attended the funeral, laying Joyce to rest to be with Anthony's dad, Ken.

While Joyce was in hospital, Emma would bring her problems into the ward and we had to deal with those as well. At this time, when we were trying to focus elsewhere, we felt and understood the absolute attention we always needed to give Emma. As always, we were tied to the runaway train, wanting to get off so we could deal with Anthony's mum, yet unable to. Our daughter's needs never stopped. We felt like hostages.

Soon we had another call from the police. Emma had been arrested, this time for attempted armed robbery. It was incredible.

Emma had gone into a shop with a bread and butter knife and asked for money, using her manners. 'Please.'

The brave shopkeeper said no and chased Emma out of the shop, where some bystanders apprehended her and held her until officers came to make the arrest. The police later said she was the politest armed robber they had ever dealt with.

She apologised, and was cooperative and well behaved.

But that didn't matter. Her previous charges counted against her. Now she had committed another, more serious, crime and was sent straight to prison. She rang us to say she was in Melbourne's most intimidating women's jail. We felt like giving up, offered little help and I refused to visit her in prison. Instead, I spoke to her on the phone.

I remember walking around a large shopping centre during this period and having the surreal feeling that I must be the only woman in the whole complex whose daughter was in prison. It must have been shock. I felt detached from the people surrounding me, as if I wasn't part of reality. Things always seemed to get worse; we would go one step forward then three steps backward, never reaching a stable position. But this disaster qualified as many steps backwards. How could we recover from this? Where would it end?

Anthony visited the prison once, taking clothes to Emma. The Legal Aid lawyer, who was to defend Emma, rang Anthony one night and talked about the technicalities of the case. And then he said something that touched our hearts.

He said: 'Don't give up on Emma.' He could see something in her. Maybe it was the fight in her eyes, barely flickering but still there, despite everything.

Anthony then became involved in the efforts to have Emma released from her incarceration. After a month in prison, which she hated, Emma was released on bail into Anthony's custody with the condition she go immediately into a rehabilitation hospital in country Victoria. Anthony drove her there directly.

The lawyer had worked very hard for Emma; he was a gentle man, who kindly held her in esteem. He did his best for her when we were too tired. His name was John.

A month after being admitted, Emma was released from the hospital and attended Narcotics Anonymous meetings all around Melbourne, sometimes twice a day in an attempt to stay off the drugs. She followed that up by going to another detox hospital, and then signed up for yet another detox accommodation unit, but was discharged after a week for drinking a bottle of cough medicine. One step back . . .

Emma was now basically going in and out of detox and rehab facilities trying to stay off heroin. We visited her regularly, wherever she was. She spent six weeks at Odyssey House, where she was meant to stay for a year. It was a major disappointment. Anthony, Katie, Aimee and I had a family discussion and we all agreed that we wanted Emma back home, given her efforts to stay clean.

'As long as there are no drugs,' I said to her. With that single stipulation, we welcomed Emma back into the family home.

Sometimes her criminal partner from the burglaries rang my daughter from prison. I picked up the phone and heard the prison announcement, saying I could hang up if I wanted before the call was put through. So I did. He was the last person I wanted her to talk to.

Emma's sentencing hearings came next. She had to go to court twice in eight days. We accompanied her both times.

The first appearance was before a County Court judge. It was for the more serious crime of armed robbery. She was convicted and given a one-month jail term, which he stated she had already served. The judge gave Emma a two-year parole period, requiring her to report monthly to a parole officer.

The second hearing, for the burglaries, was held at the Melbourne Magistrates' Court. The magistrate took into account all her personal circumstances, including her child-hood assaults, and mercifully did not add to her previous sentence.

Emma was very pleased she did not have to go back to a jail cell. We were all quite relieved; it's funny what makes you happy at moments of distress. But the recording of convictions meant she could not work as a nurse again for at least ten years, or in any other jobs requiring police clearances.

The convictions also prevented her from living in the housing commission unit with Lu. Another young woman took Emma's place while she was in prison but Emma still visited Lu and the housemate, and the three girls became good friends. One sad day Lu found the other girl dead in her room. Emma and Lu were rocked by the death and Lu shifted out of the apartment, no longer able to stay there. Lu and Emma then rented a unit together.

Aimee, having taken a year off study, worked part-time at two jobs and tried to keep busy, although she was suffering from depression.

Katie continued her very, very slow recovery. She had another fall and cut her head, losing a lot of blood. An ambu-lance was called but before it arrived Katie had an epileptic fit, then another two on the way to hospital. She was admitted into intensive care and was induced into a coma.

Anthony and I stood next to her, looking down on our beloved daughter as we had almost three and a half years earlier, when she was in the same state after being hit by the car.

I wondered if I had died and gone to hell.

Chapter 17
The bagman

Emma often wrote things down in her forlorn attempt to heal her mind. It gave her some clarity and peace, if only for the time it took her to think more deeply about how she felt and why she was so depressed.

In 1996, when she was fourteen, she wrote the following.

It started just a few months over a year ago. When it was all over the newspapers and TV. It was then that I started to remember my traumatic childhood. 'Priest charged with sexual assault' were the headlines. The parish priest from my childhood was being accused of being a pedifoil. I didn't suspect it – I knew he was. From then on the friendly happy person I was gone forever. The school I was going to at the time was across the road from the church. I couldn't stand it. I became very depressed and cryed a lot.

In 1998, she wrote another heartbreaking essay called 'The End of my Childhood by Emma Foster'.

I knew my childhood was over when I was diagnosed as anorexic. I was 13 years old.

Memories started flooding back. As real as if it was happening right now. The day I couldn't eat I pushed the memories away and I tried to ignore the horrible past. I was only eating a meal every one or

*two days. The physical symptoms resembled how I felt inside. Sick,
empty, dizzy, weak. I tried to end it all but it didn't work and as
my weight dropped even more, I was hospitalised.*

*In hospital I was not aloud to walk or stand. I was forced to lie
in bed and face the frightening products of the real world. A world of
fights and injuries. Sickness and disease. Mental illness and suicide.
Right there in that hospital bed my childhood innocence was taken
away from me. Again.*

A psychological report I read with tears in my eyes diagnosed
Emma, in 1999, as having post-traumatic stress disorder, major
depressive order, substance abuse disorder and borderline
personality disorder. She suffered vivid and repetitive
flashbacks of oral sex with the naked priest, the report found.
She struggled with intimacy, fought sleep disturbance and
had a 'low mood most days nearly all day'. She abused drugs
– mostly heroin and benzodiazepines – to block out the involuntary intrusive memories.

My daughter's depression was severe, 'manifesting in chronic
suicidal ideation, intent and plan,' the psychiatric report noted.

I often wondered why she survived all her suicide attempts,
what was keeping her alive. The psychologist wrote: 'the most
important and significant protective factor was her love for her
family and in particular her mother.'

In a way, without dwelling upon it, I'd known this all
along. We would often exchange hugs and the words 'I love
you'.

Most of Emma's notes and diary-type writings were
messy. I could sense how unsteady she was feeling when she
wrote those painful autobiographies. She wrote one letter in
recent years that stood out from the rest, for its neatness and
calmness.

In perfect writing, she wrote the following letter to
Anthony and me.

Thanks for what you are doing. Thanks for always being there with help and support, though I've betrayed you so many times.

I love you both so much. I'm lucky to have you for parents, so grateful. You're both so strong, fighting like this. We'll get them, and hopefully then less people will experience what we've been through.

THANK–YOU

All my love forever

Emma xxxooo

This was my daughter speaking. In those two paragraphs she shone through. The light inside her, somewhere deep down, was glimmering still. I could never give up our fight for her justice.

Our lawsuit against the Catholic Church was levelled at the Archdiocese of Melbourne, individuals within the hierarchy and some Church employees. We'd issued the writs in October 2002, which had been over three years ago, and they had been served the following year, but we'd heard little since. It was now late 2005. The claimants were Anthony, Emma, Katie, Aimee and I. This would be one of the issues.

We already knew the Church's opinion about secondary victims. Anthony and I, while testing the boundaries of the Pell Process, applied for compensation to the Church-appointed independent commissioner Peter O'Callaghan QC. His reply was swift and without ambiguity. He stated that no-one other than victims that had actually been abused could apply for compensation within the terms and conditions of his appointment.

It was with this response echoing in my mind that I was to later learn Mr O'Callaghan made a confidential payment to a resigning priest. The recipient was a cleric, who had, in the 1990s, acted compassionately and spent a lot of his time advocating for the rights of clergy sexual assault victims. During his career, the increasingly 'burnt out' and frustrated Father was also forced to share a presbytery with a 'nasty' senior priest who underpaid him. Eventually, the struggle became too much for the priest, who quit. He said Mr O'Callaghan paid him $50,000 as 'back pay' and for 'stress and strain'.

Mr O'Callaghan confirmed to me in writing that the priest was not a victim of abuse, and that this particular situation was outside the terms of his appointment as the 'independent investigator'.

So the recipient priest was never a victim, yet he was paid by the Church and made to sign a confidentiality contract. I immediately wondered whether it was hush money given to a man who knew too much? But Archbishop Pell had stated he did not buy silence with cash. Mr O'Callaghan saw nothing wrong with the contradiction that parents of victims were not entitled to compensation, but a resigning priest was.

This payout poses many questions about Mr O'Callaghan's role within the Church's employment and, indeed, the credibility of the Pell Process.

How did Mr O'Callaghan calculate the figure of $50,000 – coincidentally the maximum allowed under the scheme – when most of the worst sexually assaulted and raped victims didn't even receive half that amount? Was the compensation panel contacted for its opinion? Were the terms and conditions of Mr O'Callaghan's appointment followed when paying the disgruntled priest?

To my mind, a payment to a priest from Mr O'Callaghan calls into question the entire heartless scheme he administers on behalf of Australia's largest archdiocese. In researching this book and examining the Pell Process more closely, I made a request for an interview with Mr O'Callaghan and it was granted. I visited him in his office in the legal precinct of Melbourne, where he has managed his role as the archbishop's independent commissioner for almost fourteen years. When asked about the payment to the resigning priest, he replied that it was outside the scheme and was confidential.

When pressed, he confirmed he paid the priest for his 'stress and strain' on an 'ad hoc' basis.

Mr O'Callaghan is now seventy-eight years old and has had an impressive career as a man of law. He is much admired in his profession. How did he come to pay out a priest? He clearly did not act alone. Who signed the cheque? Why did the Catholic Church think it should give a confidential golden handshake to a man leaving behind his priestly duties, abandoning the Church, which has a worldwide shortage of clerics?

The former priest, who left the ministry after twenty-five years of service, bravely told me about his payout. He did not think it was inappropriate but he condemned the Pell Process, calling it a cover-up. 'It's appalling,' he said. 'It [the establishment of the scheme] was quite clearly an attempt to control the problem. The money was minor. It was more about controlling the scandal. They [the hierarchy] were petrified of ruining the good name of the Church.'

And so I shake my head at the long-running farce, which purports to 'address the issue in a professional, caring and appropriate manner'.

Thankfully, we were out from under the Catholic Church system and our legal team went forward with our civil claims, in the manner it saw best, against a determined and desperate defence. One of the Archdiocese of Melbourne's lawyers' written arguments, sent to us two years after we began the lawsuit, was that O'Donnell did not harm our girls.

'They [the Church defendants] do not admit that the plaintiff[s] [both Emma and Katie] were subjected to physical and/or sexual and/or psychological abuse while an infant by Kevin O'Donnell.'

Their non-admission was in direct contradiction to the investigation by Peter O'Callaghan, whose findings led to Emma going before the Catholic Church Compensation Panel and being offered the rare maximum of $50,000. And a signed apology was offered to us from the then Archbishop of Melbourne, George Pell.

'I apologise to you and to those around you for the wrongs and hurt you have suffered at the hand of Father Kevin O'Donnell.'

So our civil case continued to move slowly and painfully, despite Tim and Michael's wonderful efforts.

During this time, we occasionally visited the halls and offices of the old, grey cobblestoned part of Melbourne's legal precinct. It was in a legal firm's office building where Katie, who had recovered from her second coma, first talked to me about her assaults at the hands of O'Donnell.

I was pushing her in a wheelchair to a toilet. We reached the door and as I struggled to open it, trying to manoeuvre Katie's wheelchair through, I crouched down. My head was near hers as I stretched out my arm, pushing and holding the door open. She turned her face to me and spoke into my ear.

'He took me into the school hall, downstairs to a room that was under the stage and orally raped me. He told me I was evil.'

I tried not to cry as the obscene picture crashed into my head. I had been in the room she described once, many years ago.

I saw it plainly again – a dark and secluded place, no windows, short walls, low ceiling, a trapdoor that led to the main hall, bolted shut. It was a dark hovel, a daylight-deprived maintenance workshop for the parish. There were ten wooden steps going down. She would have been so frightened being led into that dungeon, with shadowy machinery and tools.

Then the degrading act. I wanted to scream.

Eight years earlier, almost to the day in November 1997, I had guessed the crime that had been committed against Katie. But having it confirmed removed the fairyland hope that it hadn't happened, and hearing it confessed was a shock I could never be prepared for. When I pictured her sweet young face at the time of the rape I crumbled inside. No wonder she sometimes wanted to die.

'I'm so sorry,' I said, when I could speak. 'The only evil is O'Donnell.'

Later, Katie told me O'Donnell sexually assaulted her 'hundreds of times in the hall and the church'. (I hoped this was an exaggeration but, regardless, it must have happened many, many times over the years.) It was mainly in grades 2 and 3; she remembered the teachers. He used to take her out of class and off the playground. He told her she was 'evil' and it remained in her head. She always believed him. She didn't tell any teachers or students about what was happening and nobody ever said anything about abuse to her. The frequency of the assaults is still hard to fathom and I am reminded of the lawyer who described O'Donnell as the 'two-a-day' paedophile priest.

At another moment during our legal process I saw Anthony crying, while looking across the street at the vintage Supreme Court of Victoria. It was not the grand facade that brought a tear to his gaze. He was thinking about what it meant to be a father. Emma had just turned twenty-four. He was remembering when she was born, when he first set his eyes upon her. He held his child in his arms with great joy and a feeling of euphoria and humility for creating a new life, a beautiful life. And then a mere five years later a paedophile priest set upon this precious child. Two or so years later the same thing happened to his second and equally precious little girl.

I walked over to embrace my weeping husband. Katie and Aimee also hugged him.

He mentioned to me that the jousting lawyers in the middle of our civil action were probably fathers, just like him. Not 'Fathers' who weren't fathers – but real, married dads.

Anthony explained to me: 'Those men have to go home to their families and tell their wives and children what they did in this case.' It had been almost a decade since we started seeking justice for Emma. Since she started suffering anorexia in June 1995, Emma had visited doctors, specialists and pathology services nine hundred and six times, not including at least seventy-five outpatient psychology appointments and more than fifty-two admissions into hospital, detox or rehabilitation clinics. She was tired. We were tired. My husband was wondering when and how it would all end. He wasn't the only one.

I often wondered about the cost of Emma's medical treatment funded basically by the taxpayer. The government should implement an advertising campaign to increase awareness of child sexual assault, as it does with other life-threatening dangers, such as smoking, drink driving and speeding. If the associated heartbreak and social breakdown of childhood sexual assault does not touch our politicians, then the cost to society alone should move state and commonwealth leaders to take action and educate the public about the behaviour of paedophiles and the symptoms of abused children. 'The estimated overall cost of 30,009 cases of child sexual abuse to the Australian taxpayer is $2.58 billion, increasing every year.' (The Abused Child's Trust, 2006)

It is difficult to write about the final stages of our attempts to have our day in court without damaging the integrity of that process. Many people were involved and they deserve my respect in that regard. In the end, we achieved a historic settlement.

Irretrievable damage was done to our daughters. So much was lost to them forever and a normal life was never to be regained. But we achieved some degree of justice at last. We were not allowed to call it 'compensation' and we didn't have our day in court but, ultimately, they paid and whatever it was or wasn't called, it felt like a triumph.

The whole legal fight had taken close to ten years. So much stress. Such a frightening period wondering what it would cost us if we didn't reach a settlement. But worse than that was the strangling fear that the Church would not be held accountable for what O'Donnell did, what the hierarchy did.

We were looking for recognition of what they had done to our daughters but also wanted to help Emma and Katie live the best lives they could, after all they'd suffered and all they'd lost, to ensure some financial security that they otherwise would have provided for themselves.

We hugged Tim and Michael and thanked them for their amazing efforts. They had persistently and relentlessly pursued legal avenues to reach justice for those who could not defend themselves – Emma and Katie. At the end of the struggle, they appeared as stressed and strung out as we did.

I still don't understand why we were made to fight so long and hard. Even Mr O'Callaghan QC, the independent commissioner, conceded that the Church knew O'Donnell was a paedophile in the 1950s, long before the predatory priest was allowed to ruin our lives. Mr O'Callaghan told me in February 2010: 'As I understand it and from my investigation . . . I've got no doubt.'

What price would you put on the suffering of your daughters, whose lives were ruined by a priest's sexual assaults? The recipients of such payouts often say that what means most to them is not the money, but an acknowledgement of the betrayal of trust and fault of the Church. But half-hearted apologies from the Church were cheap words. To my family and me, the money does matter. It has meaning and substance for both parties and is part of righting the wrong.

If we had accepted the Church offer of $50,000 it would be gone; spent by our desperate daughter after her eighteenth birthday.

Surprisingly, we ended up learning more about the Pell Process by refusing to sign up to it. Most startlingly, we learned that the scheme saved the Catholic Church millions and millions of dollars. By initially restricting every victim to a maximum of $50,000 (with the average payment less than $25,000) it ripped off every brave victim who came forward. The Towards Healing scheme, that oversaw the response to clergy child sexual abuse throughout the rest of Australia, was no better. It had no cap on payments but was still the Church investigating the Church.

Morally, each victim should be paid hundreds of thousands of dollars. If you multiply a conservative but fairer amount of $200,000 by the four hundred or so victims forced to settle in Melbourne for less than $50,000, the Church has saved itself almost $80 million, and that is in one Australian city alone. In 2008, the Vicar General of Melbourne, Christopher Prowse, said: 'The system has served us very well over twelve years.' No wonder he is pleased.

At least after our common law settlement, Emma could buy herself a house to live in without worrying about scrounging for rent, as well as her self-respect. Katie too could buy a home. She would, after all, need special disability requirements for the rest of her life. Neither of my girls would have been able to provide for themselves otherwise.

We view the Church hierarchy as we do the paedophile – as cruel and possessing a heart of stone. The Roman Catholic Church takes advantage of damaged victims, relying on their brokenness and vulnerability to save money. Only our dogged determination and persistence and the talents and patience of our legal team forced the hand of the great bully. We were pleased this part of our struggle was over. We were just trying to help our daughters survive.

Chapter 18
Emma

When Emma turned one, she received a teddy bear as a birthday present. It was a lovely toy, hand-sewn by a family friend. We named it 'Ted the Bear'. Emma loved her little mate Ted and kept him close always. He slept with her every night of her life.

After the settlement, Emma set about looking at houses to buy. She chose a townhouse that was still under construction; the nearby display homes impressed her greatly and left her in no doubt.

'I've found the house I want,' she beamed.

We wanted to see it before she handed over a deposit and went for a look with Emma and her friend Lu. It was only a kilometre from where her grandparents lived. She led us through a display replica of the house she had chosen – through the kitchen and lounge, then racing upstairs, showing us the bedrooms, bathrooms . . .

She was like a big kid. 'This is the one I love,' she said. It was a pleasure to see her enthusiasm.

Once again, we hoped this significant event in her life would put her on the road to recovery and a healthier future. We allowed her to manage the money she had received from the Church, giving her the freedom to control it with a sense of ownership and an understanding that the funds came because of the injustice that had been done to her. We wanted her to know it was a form of apology and that what happened to her should never have occurred – the payment was a very real proof of this.

After what was a nerve-racking month for me, I suggested I take the funds from her to preserve them until the house purchase was completed. Although Emma managed the money well, she agreed I should now look after it. She was still in and out of psych units and detox but now, at least, had something to look forward to.

The house was finished in a matter of weeks and Emma and Lu moved out of their rented unit into the lovely new home. It was June 2006. The three of us went shopping for furniture. Emma had good taste and chose her decor with an expert's eye. She carefully selected the items and I paid for them with her money. Emma and Lu had fun decorating and making a home together.

Around this time Emma recommenced a childhood hobby of cross-stitching. She attended classes in a local handicraft shop and enjoyed the company of the other women; they would sit and talk while they worked their individual crafts. Emma told them of her life and the trouble she had had and to her delight they remained her friends. She loved the time they shared around the large table. One day she gave me a beautiful bookmark she had made, with purple and green Scottish thistles worked into a white fabric complete with fancy white edging and a purple tassel. Purple was her favourite colour. I used the bookmark only once because I felt it was too beautiful to use; I worried it might become dirty or lost. I told her how special it was and too good to use so it was going in the crystal cabinet as I considered it a family heirloom. She was so proud of her work and so was I.

I visited Emma and Lu every Saturday morning on the way to my parents' house. At other times, Emma would come to see me at work or home. Sometimes she had trouble waking up and missed her psychology appointments so I began dropping in, rousing her and driving her to the counselling sessions. The fact that she actually liked her latest psychologist was a big step forward and worth ensuring she attended. Then we would have coffee together.

Once she moved into her new townhouse, Emma attended only one hospital. It contained both a psychiatric unit and a detoxification unit. From its name I assumed it was Anglican.

It wasn't until one visit, during my daughter's second admission, that she confided in me a female counsellor had made her feel guilty, indicating that Emma was responsible for the sexual assaults she had been subjected to as a child. Incredulous, I questioned her further.

'What did the counsellor say to you?'

'She said: "Why didn't you tell anyone it was happening at the time?" She made me feel I was to blame,' Emma recalled.

My hackles rose instantly.

I replied to Emma: 'I will speak to the person in charge about that counsellor's inappropriate words. What counsellor would say something like that in this day and age, blaming the child?'

It was then that Emma told me the counsellor was a practising Catholic and wore a cross. It was a facility owned and operated by the Catholic Church!

I tried to remain calm but I must have looked furious because Emma immediately wanted to placate me.

'Don't worry, don't put in a complaint,' she pleaded. 'I'm leaving here tomorrow.' The counsellor's remark had forced Emma's decision to leave early, after only one week in the unit.

I wasn't satisfied with ignoring it but I tried to, for her sake. I was just glad her stay was almost finished. Emma's choice of psych or detox units had greatly diminished over the years.

She'd burned bridges at so many places. The big plus with this latest hospital was its location and that she liked the patients and most of the staff. I decided if Emma returned I would then ring and complain about the counsellor. I was amazed that after all these years some people had learned nothing, preferring to blame the child instead of condemning the child-raping priest. My anger smouldered.

Only a month or two passed before Emma was readmitted. I understood she had little choice. I sighed and rang the unit to complain about the counsellor and request that Emma not have any more sessions with this person.

Someone picked up. I began with: 'Can I speak to the person in charge please?'

I was transferred to another voice.

'My daughter has just been readmitted. Last time she was a patient there she had [the person's name] as a counsellor, who indicated Emma's childhood sexual abuse from a priest was Emma's own fault . . .'

The person I was speaking to interrupted. 'That person is not a counsellor.' There was no further explanation, just silence.

I was taken aback and in the gaping silence I thought maybe I'd got it mixed up over time and Emma was talking about the tea lady or the cleaner.

Unsure now, I continued. 'Well whoever it was should not be speaking to patients or even working there with such inappropriate opinions.' I was met with agreement and the matter was left at that.

However, within a year of her new start things began to come unstuck. I discovered Emma and Lu were deep in debt. I looked at their financial situation and found they could not sustain it. Emma's entire Church payment had been spent on her house and furniture. That is what we wanted, no leftovers for drugs, but Emma and Lu had taken out easy-to-obtain small personal loans. They were each on sickness benefits, so finances were tight but they would have managed easily without the drugs expense. For some time Emma had been pressuring me to give her the deeds of the house so she could get a large loan, but we had refused and still held the deed. We knew drugs were once again at the heart of the problem, and could not allow loans to be taken out against the house.

Instead, I paid off all their debts, which of course they were pleased about. They began a pay-back schedule that I thought was manageable for them but it very quickly became redundant. Excuses presented themselves every fortnight, when the money was due. I then decided to reduce their repayments to such a low amount it would have taken them twenty-five years to repay me. I gave them this good news when I took them out to dinner. Of course they were thankful, but it wasn't long before all repayments stopped and the drugs were back in control, with debts once again mounting.

I didn't know what to do. I didn't know how to fix it. Fighting another person's drug addiction is impossible; it is hard enough for the users. For years, Emma's drug-taking had been like a giant tug of war, with us pulling her in one direction and the drugs pulling her from the other. The drugs' pull was stronger – it won every time.

If we thought things couldn't get worse, they did. Emma began taking a new drug – ice. It had an awful effect, turning her into an angry and aggressive person with little patience, and it was hell dealing with her and her problems. I didn't know she was on ice until about three months later, when she decided not to use it again as she didn't like the way it was changing her.

When I did discover the new drug and its damaging effects, I understood why my daughter's mood and health had gone so steeply downhill. Among other things, she began lamenting the loss of memory it caused. While she wanted to forget her childhood sexual assaults, the ice wiped out short-term memory. In that way, she suffered just as Katie did. It was as though Emma too had acquired a brain injury. She became distressed at not remembering what she was about to do, where she was going or what she was saying, often pausing in an attempt to recall things. She stopped taking ice and slowly, over a few months, her memory improved.

But she was never free of heroin or the other reality-erasers she employed full-time.

After the ice experience was out in the open, Emma confided that she had phoned a secondhand furniture dealer after seeing his ad in the newspaper – 'Cash For Furniture'. She arranged for him to come and collect her entire house of one-year-old furniture, which had cost over $5000, in exchange for $500. The dealer kindly advised her against such a decision but she insisted. When he was on his way to her house, Emma changed her mind and rang his mobile to cancel the pick-up. The man told Emma he was glad she'd changed her mind and wished her well.

Emma's twenty-sixth birthday was on 6 November 2007. Anthony, Katie, Aimee and I picked her and Lu up. The whole family then went out to dinner at Emma's favourite restaurant. My mum and dad met us there, presents were given and we all had a fun night.

Despite the smiles on our faces another crisis loomed.

Debts were piling up again to the point that I had reluctantly resumed paying Emma's bills. The alluring tendrils of pleas for help started gradually.

'Just one bill.' Then another. 'Just one more, please? They're going to cut off my electricity if I don't pay soon.'

I reasoned that I was being economical by paying now instead of paying later, with added fines and reconnecting fees. It was a sticky, debilitating quagmire that I could not find my way out of. I knew what I should be doing and saying but could not bring myself to do it. I couldn't withdraw my help.

One of us was always going to be hurt by the ongoing cycle of dependency. I didn't want it to be Emma – she had already been hurt too much. It felt like I was in a tumble-dryer, going around and around, being buffeted and bashed. One inflicted injury after another . . . sexual assault, guilt, love, pity, suppressed anger, blackmail, silencing. I was a reflection of Emma, so we were in it together. I could not escape and turn my back on her.

To her constant pleas for money I only occasionally said no. They were weak protests. We were both addicts.

After her birthday, Emma was booked into a hospital for a rapid detox procedure, which cleans the blood and removes the toxins, reducing withdrawal symptoms. It required only a few days of admission. Emma had spoken of this for a while but as the date drew closer she and Lu started arguing. Lu was to be Emma's support person during the detox procedure, so their plan became lost and the get-cleaner-sooner option was never tried.

Out of nowhere Emma resumed talking about suicide. Over the years she had asked me several times for my permission for her to kill herself. She said I was the only person she stayed alive for and wanted my permission because she didn't want to hurt me.

'If you say I can do it, Mum, I will.' Why did we have to live this awful existence? I never gave her my permission and perhaps she saw the colour drain from my face each time she asked.

But this time it was different. She was not asking my permission. Her suicide talk had a sereneness and matter-of-factness that unnerved me; it was as though she had made up her mind and was at peace. On Thursday 22 November 2007, she came to tell us she was going to kill herself and had come to say goodbye.

Aimee was the rescuer on this day.

Our youngest daughter went out the back of the house with Emma and Lu. The three of them casually chatted on the verandah for longer than an hour. I found out later they talked about many things, including Emma's dream of having a child.

'She wanted a baby girl,' Aimee happily recalled.

It was a relief to watch Aimee and Emma enjoying each other's company, as they had clashed for many years. Aimee resented Emma's drug abuse, thefts, outbursts and addiction-driven dishonesty. Emma had little in common with her youngest sister; it was Katie she bonded more strongly with, perhaps because of their tragic shared history.

On this day of the promised suicide the sisters bonded, as they had been doing for some months. When it came time for Emma and Lu to leave, Emma approached me with apparent ease.

'I want Aimee to have my house.'

This was the second time she had given me that instruction. But this particular afternoon I was disturbed by her attitude. Even after enjoying herself she hadn't changed her mind about killing herself. My head was spinning.

Earlier in the week Emma had phoned me at work and I could hear music playing in the background. Emma stopped talking to me and called out to Lu: 'Oh, that's the song I'm having at my funeral.' Her mind games were taking us to new dizzying places. The past thirteen years had left my thinking and sensitivities far from normal.

After she had left our house, her words and manner ate away at me. I rang Emma's psychologist and left a message early the next morning, Two hours later, when I was at an appointment, the psychologist returned my call and I told her of the situation. She said she hadn't seen Emma for a month and that she would ring the emergency psychiatric Crisis Assessment Team (CAT) at Monash Medical Centre.

Every minute became important to me.

The psychologist rang back to say the CAT team nurse wanted to speak to me. Ten minutes ticked slowly by before the phone rang again. The nurse wanted to know about Emma's 'current status'. I told her as much as I could about Emma's suicide talk and what was different about this time.

'She seemed all organised, had said her goodbyes and seemed at peace about the situation.'

'Because we know her and given her history,' the nurse said, 'we'll ring Emma and assess her over the phone instead of going to see her.'

I felt let down when I hung up. Shortly afterwards, the same nurse rang back. 'We've just spoken to Emma,' she explained. 'She's just used a substance and we asked her to ring us back when she is able.'

I knew that would not happen.

The problem was back in my lap. I was very concerned and kept in contact with both Emma and Lu. Ten days later, on the morning of 3 December, much to my relief Emma re-admitted herself into the Catholic psych unit. Her psychologist had advised her to do so. I knew she would be safe while she was contained. I'm sad to say she always felt better in a unit.

At 2.45 pm the same day, Emma rang to ask if I would pay her phone bill. 'Otherwise it will be cut off.' It was the same old situation. When she rang on my mobile I was trying to get Katie out of her wheelchair and into the car. We were running late for a dental appointment.

Emma's recent drug binge had soaked up all her pension – she had spent it entirely on drugs without paying her bills. She had been irresponsible and now the responsibility was again being laid at my feet, so for the first and only time, after months of urgings from my therapist, I said to her: 'Emma, this is not my problem.' I asked her to ring me back later. 'I'm taking Katie to the dentist,' I added. We said goodbye but she did not ring me back.

Three days later, on 6 December, I rang to talk to her in the unit and see how she was faring. Towards the end of the conversation I asked her a standard question.

'Would you like me to visit you on the weekend?' I expected her to be pleased but she didn't really answer, so I gave her a get-out clause. 'I don't have to if you don't want me to.'

She didn't hesitate: 'I'd rather you didn't.'

'That's fine, we'll catch up sometime.'

This was the first time in thirteen years she had not wanted me to visit her in hospital.

Six days later, Emma rang me from the unit to ask if I would pay her private health insurance, as she had not made the last two payments. The company wouldn't cover her current stay without some more money. Happy to hear from her and without even thinking about it, I said I would pay. She gave me the details and we hung up.

'See you.'

I didn't know it then, but that was the last time I would speak to Emma.

As the busy days of December passed I mentioned to Anthony: 'I don't think Emma is talking to me any more.'

'She'll be all right,' he responded.

'I hope so, she's never been like this before, not wanting visits, not ringing, not wanting to talk to me.'

I tried to look on the bright side and view the situation from a different perspective. 'Well we've never tried this before, if not speaking to me helps Emma get better then that's good. If not speaking to me enables her to get over her problems, then I'm okay with that . . . sort of.'

I was glad she was still in the unit. Hopefully she could sort things out while she was in there.

After not hearing from Emma for almost another week, I asked Anthony to ring her at the unit and invite her to Christmas lunch at home with the family. She said no and told him that she had 'issues with Mum'. We could both only assume she was talking about the money problems, which arose over the non-paying of her telephone account.

Christmas Day came and went without Emma; her present was still under the tree unopened. It remains in its wrapping today. It was the first Christmas we had not all been together.

On 2 January 2008, Emma was discharged from the unit because she and a male patient were found chroming (sniffing paint) together. Apparently they had made plans for this man to stay at Emma's house and he, for some reason, kept ringing Lu at the townhouse to talk about his imminent arrival. Lu didn't want him to come and was upset with Emma for inviting him, and annoyed at them both for having to answer many intrusive phone calls.

So Lu left Emma's house and went to stay at her mother's home. Emma caught a taxi home from the unit to an empty house; her chroming friend didn't stay after all.

Around lunchtime on this same day, Emma rang Anthony on his mobile phone. We were at a shopping centre and she asked if he could ring a local chemist and pay for one month's methadone for her. He said he would, took the details and promised he'd call her back once he'd arranged the payment.

Later that afternoon, while we were still out, Emma rang Aimee's mobile phone.

'I've been kicked out of rehab and Lu is angry with me,' she said. 'Can you do me a favour?'

Emma asked her younger sister if she could go to the detox unit and pick up some things she had forgotten to take with her. Aimee drove to the unit with her boyfriend and then went to Emma's house to drop the things off. When they arrived, Emma spoke to them outside, complimenting the couple.

'Nice car,' she noted to Aimee's boyfriend, and, 'You two look gorgeous.'

Aimee and Emma had continued to grow closer, even while Emma was not talking to me. Emma had recently given Aimee encouragement to study harder. The pair had talked more openly than ever before, even about O'Donnell and the assaults – precious and fragile secrets shared. Emma confided in Aimee a vivid memory from a time before her abuse. She was a toddler in a strange room and climbed up onto a bed to see a woman cradling her baby.

It was Aimee and me.

With this breakthrough in their relationship, my daughters started to make up for lost time. Aimee took some bread and dips around to Emma's house one evening, just to hang out. Emma visited Aimee another night while Anthony and I were away. She stayed but had trouble sleeping without her night-light, which helped her when she awoke from nightmares. Aimee set up a battery-operated lamp and nervously monitored how long it would last. It stayed lit all night and Emma was so appreciative. In the morning Aimee suggested she take Emma with her to drop off an essay at university, to see where she went to school. Emma was enthusiastic but soon took a call from Lu and went home instead.

'I wish she had come with me,' Aimee said later.

Finally, my beloved daughters were relating to each other like sisters. And it was Aimee that Emma turned to in those crisis hours, not me.

'The house is too messy to go inside,' Emma said. So they had a coffee in the garage, sitting and talking a little longer.

Emma's mobile rang. She saw the number: 'It's Dad.'

Anthony had phoned – not knowing Aimee was there – to say he had paid for Emma's methadone. She was pleased. The girls kept chatting. Their discussion had somehow turned to O'Donnell. Emma said she blamed *me* for her abuse.

'A psych nurse at the unit told me that it is the parents' fault,' Emma said to Aimee.

Aimee was angered and defended us. 'Emma, it was *his* fault. No-one else is to blame. That's ridiculous.'

Emma had never blamed us for the abuse before attending the Catholic unit. Aimee argued at length that it was always the perpetrator's fault. In the end, Emma relented and said she supposed it was partly her own fault. It was not true, of course, but exhausted and frustrated, Aimee desisted in the argument. She had to catch a plane to Thailand for a holiday with her girlfriends in just a few hours. The sisters hugged and Aimee and her boyfriend left. It was six o'clock.

It was unusual for Emma to make a call and apologise for things she had said in heated moments. But this time she did. Unfortunately it was common for Aimee to not hear her mobile phone when it rang.

A remorseful Emma left a message for Aimee.

'Hi, Aimee. It's Emma. Sorry I didn't get to talk to you properly before. I just wanted to say I don't blame Mum . . . I'm just really angry at the moment . . . about the way I've turned out. Okay, bye.'

Aimee listened to the message but did not call back immediately. She planned instead to phone Emma from Thailand to make sure she was okay. This she did, but there were no answers. Aimee left descriptions of beautiful beaches and warm weather on the message bank, hoping to conjure some pleasant images in the mind of her strung-out sister.

The following day, 3 January, Lu was concerned about Emma so she rang the police and asked them to send someone to the townhouse. We knew nothing about this. The attending officer made contact with Emma through an upstairs bedroom window. He later said she sounded drunk and told him she didn't want any help. The policeman left.

The next day, Anthony rang Emma to invite her to her grandfather's barbecue birthday celebration the following day. After several unanswered rings, the call went through to her message system so he left the open invitation to come around to our house. We didn't really expect Emma to come and were not surprised when she didn't turn up. I spent the day cooking and hosting the family.

Early in the afternoon of 6 January Lu rang to ask if we had heard from Emma. I told her of our last contact a few days earlier and about the birthday invitation. She told us that Emma's phone message bank was now full, and that she had rung the chemist to learn Emma had not been there at all to get her methadone. I listened and held my breath, knowing that missing two or three days' worth of doses on the methadone program meant going back to the doctor to get a new script – an inconvenience Emma would not usually let happen.

The beginnings of dread invaded my body.

Lu said she was going to Emma's house to see if she was all right and would ring me to let me know what was happening.

About two hours later Lu rang to say she had been to the house and yelled out to Emma, with no response.

'A neighbour and I used a ladder to look upstairs but we couldn't see her,' Lu continued.

I'd been feeling stressed since Lu's first call. Now I felt more so. Lu carefully explained that after she left the house, the neighbour called the police to report Emma as a missing person.

'The police found her,' Lu told me, speaking calmly, but without a hint of joy.

'Where was she?' I asked, a little confused but happy she was found.

'In the house,' came the reply.

With growing fear I asked: 'Is she all right?'

Abruptly, Lu began wailing. 'She's dead, Chrissie, she's dead.'

I couldn't speak and my legs nearly collapsed. Lu was crying and saying repeatedly she was sorry. I had been in the lounge room but as the conversation travelled its frightening path, I'd instinctively headed out and along the hall towards Anthony, who was outside. Then I stopped, not wanting to go out there to give him such hideous news. I started walking around in circles, not knowing what to say to Lu. The shock was so great. I don't know if I said anything. I just walked in circles with the phone to my ear, listening to Lu's sobbing. I felt I should comfort her but no words would come. Suddenly, Lu was gone and her mum was on the phone. She was upset too. I don't remember what she said but I recall declaring I had to go so I could ring the police. I don't know why – maybe to have it confirmed. Not that I needed to because I believed it was true from their voices. I just wanted to get off the phone to tell Anthony so I hung up and stood there.

Emma . . .

'Emma!' I said her name like I'd never said it before.

I looked out the back window. How do I tell Anthony our daughter is dead? He was happily working away in the backyard. I walked out with the phone still in my hand, climbed the few steps and leaned against the pool fence, just looking at him. While his back was to me he was blissfully ignorant of the terrible words I was about to utter – irreversible world-changing words. All this time Lu's anguished voice was replaying in my head.

'She's dead. She's dead. I'm sorry.'

I shook. The words tripped from my mouth as I started to tell Anthony. I related what Lu had said. All the time, he remained with his back to me, continuing to manoeuvre the long vacuum pole across the pool, slowly through the water.

He asked almost the same questions I had asked Lu. He stopped when I reached the final part, the words screaming out at me in my head.

I echoed them into reality.

Instantly distressed, Anthony stormed out through the pool gate, bound for the kitchen.

'I have to ring the police . . . maybe it's a mistake.'

He hadn't heard the proof of Lu's shocked voice. I let him walk into the house. I could not move; I was still leaning heavily on the fence. I put my head on my arms and cried.

After that things were a blur. Life became a blur.

I remember tears. I remember Anthony and I embraced inside the house. It felt like nothing: like cardboard. It contained no comfort.

We told Katie that Emma had been found dead. She was distressed but said: 'Emma is at peace at last.' I looked at her and nodded slowly. It was true. Emma was no longer suffering. She was free. But my mind's vision of her was still crushing me.

Sometime later Anthony rang our friends from around the corner and they came to sit with us. They had lost their baby son many years earlier; theirs was the only company we reached out for and we were grateful to receive it. It was a Sunday and we were Katie's carers for the day so we had to ask our friends to look after her while we drove to my parents' home to tell them. They were distraught.

When we returned home it was time to ring Aimee. We dreaded telling her. Anthony rang the parents of one of Aimee's travel companions and got her mobile phone number. He rang the young woman. She answered.

'It's Aimee's dad. Is Aimee with you?'

'Yes.'

'I'm going to give Aimee some bad news. Can you look after her for me?'

'Yes.'

I could hear my youngest daughter's broken voice through the phone at Anthony's ear. We both tried to console her. She said she would return home straight away.

While she was waiting in Thailand for the return flight, Aimee had an 'E' tattooed on her hip. It was in the same style of capital 'E' that Emma used to sign her name. She came home to an emotional reunion and replayed Emma's last message, still on her phone. We heard Emma's voice and cried again, feeling the worst pain anew.

We waited for some time for the coroner to perform an autopsy and declare a cause of death. Emma's body had been found after two extremely hot days and the coroner recommended we not view her. We'd never see her again.

She was found holding her precious Ted the Bear.

We were told to employ a forensic cleaner to go over Emma's house, and a couple of days later we asked him if we could have Emma's teddy. He said he was sorry but the toy was thrown out because it was beyond repair. We accepted his judgement but felt extra sadness knowing Emma's much-loved bear, the last thing she clung to, her final comfort, was gone.

Anthony and I tried to work out the date of Emma's death. A policeman went to her home on 3 January and spoke to her. He said Emma sounded drunk but she did not usually drink; she had no alcohol in the house and no money to purchase it. I believe Emma sounded drunk because she had taken all her medication and was suffering from the effects of the overdose. That was in the morning. She probably passed away that day, only twenty-four hours after leaving the Catholic detox unit.

The vision of Emma sitting on her bed taking tablet after tablet haunted both Anthony and me. We pictured her distress in our minds, imagining her hopeless loneliness and desperation in those last moments. It will forever cause us pain.

Two days after Emma's body was found, we placed a large death notice in the *Herald Sun* newspaper. We ran it for five days while we waited for Emma's body to be released by the Coroner. It read:

Foster
Emma Louise
6.11.1981–4.1.2008
Our dearest, sweet and
precious Emma,
robbed of her
innocence and whose
shining light was forever overshadowed,
so much so that she was
unable to continue in
this life.
She was beautiful,
caring, compassionate,
loved and admired –
What a loss to all
Our lives!
A troubled life –
Finally at peace.
Loved daughter of
Christine and
Anthony.
Sister to Katie and
Aimee
Granddaughter of
Dawn and Cliff,
Ken and Joyce.

A few days later a journalist from the *Sunday Herald Sun* approached us about Emma's death notice. She interviewed us and on 13 January 2008, a full-page story on Emma's life was published.

I rang Emma's psychologist to tell her Emma had passed away and she was shocked. She dropped in to see us and brought us tears of joy as she related how much Emma loved us, and how highly our daughter had spoken of us during her sessions.

It was five o'clock when Anthony awoke one morning. The funeral was approaching and he had been unable to write the eulogy he wanted for Emma. All of a sudden, however, he was inspired. Now, with his mind bursting, he quietly but quickly made his way through the half-light to his computer – and the words flowed.

His speech was written in one tear-filled session; love, truth and passion tumbling from a father's heart and mind.

In the evening, the forensic cleaner appeared at our door. He had a big smile on his face as he handed to us Emma's teddy, Ted the Bear, complete with his red bow tie and one leg longer than the other. We couldn't believe our eyes. We looked back at this kind man, who was still beaming.

'I went searching for the teddy and found him,' he said. 'My wife has restored him. She put new stuffing inside. He's as good as new.' We were overwhelmed at the kindness and effort of this man and his wife.

'Thank you so much,' I said. 'Ted will sit on Emma's coffin at her funeral.' We later decided to keep the beloved stuffed bear and not cremate him with Emma; the forensic cleaner and his wife had gone to so much trouble. Besides, we didn't think Emma would have liked him destroyed. He now sits beside her ashes. He was always with her. Every night.

The following day our doorbell rang. When I answered, a television journalist from Channel Nine news was standing there. He had learned of Emma's death from the newspaper article. He asked if we would like him to cover Emma's funeral the following day. We said yes, thanking him.

That night we went to the funeral parlour and stood by Emma's closed coffin. It was white. Aimee had chosen it to symbolise the innocence that had been taken from her.

Ever since Emma died I had stepped into the shower every morning and cried. Perhaps it was the isolation, the privacy, the time to think, acting like a trigger. I closed the screen door and wailed with pain. After a few days, Anthony confided in me that every morning he too cried, his tears flowing with the water from the showerhead. We had taken to the same involuntary ritual every day. The funeral morning was no exception.

It had been nine days since Emma's body was found and probably twelve days since her death.

The funeral was held at 10:30 on 15 January 2008. We arrived to find many of our family and friends gathering outside the chapel at the crematorium. I got out of the car and was met by tears and greetings of condolence, hugs and kisses. It was wonderful to see so many people I loved and cared about, all of them with unique memories of Emma and time spent together: good times, bad times, loving times and justice-fighting times.

I continued to speak to people as I made my way to the chapel doors. There were so many faces. I saw our solicitor Michael Jorgensen. We embraced and exchanged a few quiet words. His partner in our legal battle, barrister Tim Seccull, was holidaying interstate. Anthony had rung his mobile and left a message of Emma's death. He returned the call and left a message for us. He was distraught. He was away with his family and apologised for his absence.

I sat with Katie in the front row beside my mother and father, awaiting the service. Lu and her family were also in the front row, on the other side of the centre aisle. The chapel filled quickly; there was no space to move. Those who couldn't find a seat stood lining the walls. They were squeezed in, three people deep. Then we all stood as Emma was brought in, carried on the shoulders of my brothers Ray and Geoff; Anthony's brother Brian; John, an old friend of Anthony's; Anthony and Aimee.

Aimee, her thin frame struggling with the weight, wanted to bear her sister to her last resting place. I looked on in admiration at Aimee's strength of character in initiating her role in honouring Emma.

A celebrant conducted the service, which we had lovingly planned. Katie stood before the mourners and said her farewell to Emma. She spoke very slowly and deliberately and at that moment was not diminished by her disabilities. She spoke with great courage and her words moved effortlessly through the crying crowd.

'Emma, you were a great sister. I could tell you secrets knowing they wouldn't be retold. I think I knew deep down it may end this way but I so didn't want it to.

'Emma – if your spirit is around – know you are already missed and forever will be.'

The celebrant read my written tribute to my daughter. I would never have been able to speak without completely breaking down.

I had written the story of when Emma approached the lonely woman at the guesthouse when she was three-and-a-half years old. I ended with the words:

Thank you, Emma, for your life. Thank you for staying with us as long as you could. Rest in peace our sweet baby girl.
I love you now and forever.

And then Aimee's thoughts were read aloud. The whole room felt like it was drowning in sorrow.

Anthony made his way to the lectern, casting a long, reaching gaze at the coffin, resplendent with Ted the Bear and a photograph of our Emma and delivered the most moving eulogy, one of the finest ever spoken. It was heartbreaking and uplifting at once and few who heard it did not examine the meanings of their own lives and loved ones. Anthony stood straight-faced while delivering the eulogy, out of determination and duty.

Photos of Emma's life from babyhood to adulthood were shown on a large screen. One of Emma's primary school friends, James, collated the pictures we had chosen and put them to music, including the song *Happy Ending* by Mika (a song with sad lyrics, despite its title '. . . *No hope, no love . . . no happy ending . . .*') that Emma had asked to be played at her funeral. James had done a wonderful job.

At the end of the service our family stood in a line to farewell Emma. When I saw her coffin begin its descent into the underground holding bay of the crematorium, I was hit with the horrendous fact that I would never see her again and that her body was going somewhere I didn't know. I was losing her. For the second time my legs almost went from underneath me as I broke down. Anthony's face contorted. It was an awful moment as Emma disappeared from my sight for the last time.

We slowly filed out of the crowded chapel and into the adjoining room. I walked beside Aimee. Anthony was helping Katie to walk. As we entered the next room I looked up and was stopped in my tracks. There, a great wall of silent mourners confronted me. Hundreds of people stood like statues and were looking at us, many still wiping their eyes, all there to farewell Emma. I was overawed. I later found out that many people were unable to squeeze into the chapel to hear the service. They milled outside and strained to listen. More than five hundred people attended Emma's funeral. She would have loved and been honoured to know that so many people cared for her.

For two hours afterwards, I stayed as rows of loving people waited patiently to give me their condolences. Towards the end of this time, I recognised someone I thought could not be there. It was our barrister, Tim Seccull. He had returned from holiday especially for Emma. I made my way over to him and we embraced. I thanked him for coming and we talked.

'After everything . . . here we are.'

We had a light lunch catered for in the room adjoining the chapel but there were so many people the food could not be circulated. A wake followed at our home, where about two hundred people gathered. We arrived late, after finishing at the chapel, to a sea of people both inside and out the family room. This too Emma would have loved. Unfortunately Lu was too distressed to join the wake. I found this out later and wished she had come.

Young people were beginning to tell us that friends were messaging them to say they had seen a video from Emma's funeral briefly appear on the Channel Nine News updates . . .

At six o'clock the people still at the wake gathered in the family room to see the news – about sixty of us were quietly watching. The first story was a large funeral for a celebrity, then another news item, followed by Emma's funeral coverage. It was a warm and honest account of what we had been through with our beautiful daughter. It was two-and-a-half minutes of what felt like justice and understanding for Emma and was a comforting feeling on such a sad day. We shed more tears.

At two o'clock the following morning I could no longer stay awake and left those who could do so to continue enjoying each other's company. The following Sunday, 20 January, the *Sunday Herald Sun* published Anthony's full eulogy.

We then had the awful task of seeing to Emma's house. There were so many memories of her, all her things just as she had left them, it was very distressing. In the garage I found her handbag and papers from the day she came home from the psych unit (the day before she died). There was a 'Community Safety Plan' form from the unit, with questions asking how patients were going to make themselves safe when out of hospital – a plan to be put in place to fall back on if they needed help. One question was: 'Who are the safe people you could contact outside?' There were only three listed – her friend Lu, staff at the unit and patients at the unit. Our names were not there. Not mine. Not Anthony's. In direct contrast, I found paperwork from another detox or psych unit filled out only eighteen months earlier. It listed both Anthony and me as safe people who could help her with 'talking, visits, hugs and financial and legal advice'.

I also found a one-page written account of Emma's experience with the counsellor I was told was not a counsellor at the Catholic unit. In it Emma wrote: 'I am stressed and anxious because I am being pushed to have counselling sessions with a practising Catholic . . .'

I had been thrown off course during my complaint attempt months earlier. The unit manager said the person giving Emma awful and destructive advice was 'not a counsellor'. Now I could read Emma's description of the truth. Emma used the words 'counselling sessions'. She had been in counselling sessions for the past twelve years, so if Emma said it was a counselling session, then that was how it was presented to her and what it was, regardless of the advisor's qualifications.

Questions raced each other in my mind. Who would the Catholic system be using as a counsellor who was not qualified as a counsellor? Emma said it was a 'practising Catholic', who 'wore a cross'.

Emma's recollections of that traumatic session were stabbing me each day. She had written: 'I was shocked to be responded to by "Why didn't you tell anyone when it was happening?" She was being critical.'

Emma added: 'I told her I was five or six. He had the power.' My daughter was trying to repel the accusation thrust at her. 'She made me feel I was to blame . . . she made me feel it was my fault I was abused.'

Again I had to think how this could happen in a psychiatric facility in this day and age. Who had the authority to pose as a counsellor unchallenged in that Catholic facility? Someone who can't believe a priest is capable of such an offence? Someone who holds priests in high esteem and their victims in contempt?

I rang the Catholic unit on a Sunday morning to enquire after a counsellor. The helpful receptionist told me that there was a nun on duty at all times – morning and evening – to talk to patients.

A nun?

I passed all this information on to the State Coroner for Emma's coronial investigation. Fifteen months after Emma's death the Coroner closed the case without answering questions relating to the Catholic unit's practices. Frustrated and unable to let it go, I rang the unit to speak to the person I made my original complaint to. She was still in charge of the facility. I was stonewalled again.

I believe the Catholic unit let Emma down, firstly by allowing the counsellor to make Emma think she was to blame for being raped by an elderly, lifelong-offending paedophile priest and, secondly, the psych nurse on her last admission (that we knew of) telling Emma – as argued with Aimee the night before her death – that the abuse was my fault. This turned Emma against me. What they should have said was the priest should never have touched her. That he was a bad man. Unable to accept that truth, the Catholic system still had to lay the blame somewhere. By blaming Emma, they undermined her already fragile confidence. By blaming me, they took us away from Emma and her ability to rely and depend on us as she had always done. Instead, she no longer wanted to talk to me. Our replacements were the hospital staff and patients, who ultimately were not there and meant nothing to her. I was no longer someone she could come to because, according to them, it was my fault. They removed her mother from her life.

She was left with nobody.

In April 2008 extensive parts of the 13 January *Sunday Herald Sun* article on Emma were read out in the Parliament of Victoria. The Justice Legislation Amendment (Sex Offences Procedure) Bill was being amended and some members used Emma's story to highlight the need for the changes.

Hansard (the official record) page 1040 reads:

> The purpose of the bill is to amend the time frames for special hearings of evidence in sex offence trials involving children and cognitively impaired complainants, impose a lifetime reporting obligation on persons convicted of persistent sexual abuse of a child, and make other amendments relating to sex offences.

It was satisfying to hear Emma's life being spoken about by the lawmakers, but they were not addressing the dire need for intervention into policies of the Catholic Church.

Other governments of the world have been more responsible, albeit belatedly. In Ireland, the Church cover-up has produced government investigations into Church policies and the actions of paedophile priests, bishops and cardinals. Victim campaigner and author of the heartbreaking and inspiring best-selling book *Beyond Belief*, Colm O'Gorman, believes the state must act to hold the Church hierarchy to account.

Mr O'Gorman's lawsuit against the Roman Catholic Church was first highlighted in the BBC film *Suing the Pope*, which led to the resignation of a bishop and the first state inquiry into the Church in Ireland. Mr O'Gorman is now the executive director of Amnesty International Ireland.

I contacted him and asked him what he thought of the Australian approach to dealing with reports of clergy child sexual abuse. He replied:

> I cannot even begin to express the outrage I feel reading your story and reading how the Church in Australia has responded. I have always felt that looking to the Church for an appropriate, just and Christian response was pointless and they had neither the will nor the capacity to acknowledge the depth of their betrayal of those impacted by the abuse they facilitated and covered up.
>
> Where laws allow the Church to dodge responsibility and sidestep legal actions, to deny justice and to avoid being held accountable, then we must work to ensure that governments change such laws and guarantee justice to victims and their families.

Mr O'Gorman was groomed and repeatedly assaulted by a priest and has long fought for justice. He knows the Church's cover-up policy is universal.

He continued:

> The Australian Government has primary responsibility for the protection and human rights of its own people . . . It cannot allow any entity, whether it be a church or not, to dodge legal responsibility and place itself above or outside the law. The state has an obligation to ensure any person whose human rights have been violated has access to legal redress.

His opinion is backed up by article eight of the Universal Declaration of Human Rights. 'Everyone has the right to an effective remedy by the competent national tribunals for acts

violating the fundamental rights granted him by the constitu-
tion or by law.'

At the end of the month, after Emma's name was
mentioned in the Parliament, I heard a protest was to take
place at St Patrick's Cathedral in East Melbourne. It was to
rail against the Church's looming World Youth Day, to be
staged in Sydney. The sacred wooden cross that was travelling
around the world, like the Olympic torch, was coming to our
state. I decided I would attend the protest. The night before,
I made my own placard and travelled alone into the city.

It was a small group of protesters who gathered. Channel
Ten News was covering the event and I was interviewed. I
said I believed that the Catholic Church had failed Catholic
youth, betrayed so many of them. What had the institution
done to young Catholics behind trusting parents' backs?
When secrecy reigned, when the Church hierarchy had the
opportunity to act quietly with justice and integrity, and
had the freedom and ability to choose to save children from
sexual assault by removing offenders, it chose not to. Catholic
youth had been crucified on the 'celibacy' of paedophile
priests. The burning question was WHY? How could they
now pretend they cared for Catholic youth? They had failed
children miserably and now we were supposed to pretend it
never happened, that all is well or that they never allowed
these things to happen.

I publicly protested against these things.

Only thirteen days before Emma's death Anthony and I
retired from our business. We had installed managers to take
our places, believing we would have more time to spend with
Emma. We had also booked a seven-week overseas holiday for
the middle of 2008. We planned to leave for Paris on 9 June
and return to Australia on 31 August. In between, we were
to once again visit the archipelago of St Kilda, a very special
place.

We decided to press ahead with our travel plans. As it turned out, Pope Benedict XVI would be in Sydney for World Youth Day around then, so we were grateful we would not be in Australia at the same time. I could really do without being exposed to all the hype and fuss over the pope. The other side of the world sounded like a good place to be.

We finished clearing out Emma's house and delivered some things to Lu, who was still living with her mum and brother. Nearly four months had passed and Lu was still very depressed over Emma's death. Anthony and I decided we would help finance Lu into a new unit. I spoke to her mum the day we dropped the last few things off, telling her what we planned to do. We did not see Lu that day but her mum was happy with our offer to help and thought it would encourage her daughter to pursue a new start.

Only a few weeks later, Anthony received a phone call telling us Lu was dead. She had taken her own life. It was a deep and painful shock; a sad and terrible loss that such a beautiful young woman was no longer with us.

It was unbelievable they were both gone.

Two days after Lu's funeral, her mother suggested we place some of Emma's ashes in Lu's grave, so they could be together. We agreed. Anthony went to transfer some of the ashes from a container into a small urn. His sound of distress made me turn to him; he looked like he was about to cry. Without speaking, he placed his hand in the container and withdrew a small piece of bone. Our Emma. The shock of this discovery caused us to break down in tears.

Later, Lu's mum and brother, Anthony and I all placed Emma's ashes under the soft clay of Lu's grave. It was comforting to think, in some way, they were together again.

Sometimes I think I see them together in the street. I spot Emma, just for a split second, as my vision passes over a crowd. A familiar something grabs my senses – a similar height and figure, long dark hair – just for a second to give me a fraction of unreal hope. It creates goosebumps of sudden and great expectation. Then reality sharply ceases the intake of excited breath.

It is just my brain getting used to the raw fact that I will never see Emma and Lu again.

Lu died on the Saturday and her funeral was on the following Friday. We departed Melbourne on the Monday.

There were many tears in Paris.

Chapter 19
Aimee

Aimee didn't suffer at the hands of O'Donnell but his deeds and the Church's heartlessness traumatised her. Her grief was complete when Emma died but her personal struggle and symptoms of distress had begun much earlier.

She was nineteen when she awoke to her first panic attack. Her heart was pounding so hard it seemed like it would break out of her chest if it didn't explode. She didn't know what was happening – what it meant. Aimee was sweating and her whole nervous system was blaring in her ears, like a burglar alarm. She was sitting upright in bed, staring hard into the still darkness, trying to focus on something, adrenaline surging at her in powerful waves. She placed her hand on her wrist to read her frantic pulse. Thumpthumpthumpthumpthump . . . Why? It had come from nothing; she had been sleeping. Her feet could be heard scampering across the floorboards of our house to the bathroom, where she vomited with a violence that only added to her anxiety.

Aimee found it difficult to explain to people the experience of feeling so physically and emotionally stressed at once. She didn't have to describe it to me because I had endured panic attacks for years.

My youngest daughter didn't recover quickly from this seemingly random incident in the middle of the night.

She started to dread a recurrence. Like victims of senseless bashings, who spend their days looking over their shoulder, wondering whether they will be hit again, she was always alert to danger. Only she wasn't scared of anyone else; she feared herself.

'I felt like I lost my marbles,' she explained.

Aimee had a boyfriend at the time of the first panic attack and a psychologist said it was possible she had felt comfortable in her relationship, so much so that the wall she had built up around her emotions fell down. I gave her some books I had read about the subject. It didn't help at first and she still couldn't sleep easily. When she went out of the house, she worried she might be struck down by an attack in the car so she became scared of traffic. Increasingly, she was afraid to do anything.

Aimee had been depressed before. Her teenage years were spent with the stress of trying to cope with Emma's suicidal behaviour. We tried to shield her from her older sisters' aftershocks of clergy sexual abuse, but how could we? By the time she suffered her scare in the night, Aimee had given up on the childcare tertiary course and taken a year off study. She worked only casually in two jobs, babysitting and cafe waiting. Most of the rest of the time she was idle and sad. I found out later she thought Anthony and I were hard on her.

'I felt like you and Dad were disappointed in me,' she confessed. It was difficult to hear.

Being a teenager, trying to decide your future, is hard enough for anyone, but she had the added weight of perceived expectation. The pressure on her to be successful in her education, to excel where Emma and Katie could not, must have been immense, even if we did not intend for her to consider our hopes in such a way.

But the depression she suffered before the panic attack was bearable, compared to a condition of constant anxiety.

'I thought life was crap before,' she recalled. 'But after the panic attack . . . it's impossible to explain but I felt haunted . . . I just wanted to go back and be like it was before.'

Once she started to better understand the panic attacks she was able to live without being emotionally paralysed or 'haunted'. 'Rather than retreat (from the fear of recurrence) you have to call its bluff,' she reasoned.

Eventually, Aimee showed incredible bravery to go looking for a new focus. She found a legal practice course at a TAFE. I drove her to enrol and offered to pay for it. 'But if you drop out of this one you have to pay me back,' I said. She agreed and studied for two years full-time. Previously, her performances at school were inconsistent, due to our family life, but in her new endeavour she won accolades for excellence. Satisfied and encouraged by high marks, she studied harder to achieve greater results. At the end of her course, in which she achieved almost perfect test scores, she was held up by the TAFE as a model student, literally. The institution made her part of its marketing campaign to attract new students. She won the course award and received books and cash as a prize. She was also asked to address a conference as a guest speaker. Her confidence soared.

Most of her classmates used their qualifications to become legal secretaries but Aimee did not automatically search for a job. Anthony discussed with her the next move. 'Think about what's important to you,' he said to her. She liked achieving new goals so she applied for a place at university as an arts student. She was accepted. Another year of academic excellence followed. 'I thought it was going to be a step up and I wouldn't be able to get those top marks . . . but I did.'

Aimee applied for a Law degree placement, hoping to study the double degree of Arts and Law.

Weeks later, Emma died.

The day after her mournful return from Thailand, Aimee was given notification she was accepted into the Law course.

Our little girl, who was now twenty-two, decided she was going to be a lawyer. It should have been a moment to celebrate. After all, it was only a few short years since she left high school with a lowly tertiary entrance score.

For a long time, my youngest daughter didn't like her self-destructive sibling. Emma's behaviour dominated our lives. When she stole things to pawn, so she could pay for drugs, Aimee was a silent horrified witness. During the arrests, Aimee was ashamed and disgusted.

In Emma's final months, with Aimee's self-confidence rising, they connected. Both beamed with pride at their new relationship. 'I do have a sister,' Aimee said, smiling. But Emma was a long way down a dark tunnel and none of us could bring her back, not even her little sister.

When Emma left her final message on Aimee's phone the night they last spoke, Aimee didn't call her back until she reached Thailand.

'I wish I had called her before I left,' she cried with me. 'I wish I'd let her know that I do love her.' Thinking of what may have been is almost too much for her to bear.

On 6 January 2008, Aimee was in her overseas hotel when she had a dream. There were no images but a voice called to her. 'I love you. I love you. I love you.' It was her sister Emma, who was either dying or dead at the time. She woke up and was spooked. After Emma's death the dreams continued, but with vivid imagery and no more voice.

'She's alive in my dreams and we have a pure love. It's like nothing I've ever felt in my waking hours. It's unbelievable. She never speaks. We embrace and she's so strong and perfect. I dream about her, as she would've been if she had not been assaulted by O'Donnell – beautiful.'

I see that image every day, when I look at Aimee, my only child not to be taken from me. I see her beauty and more – her abilities and joy, her interactions with people of all ages – and understand now that my other girls are missing, lost forever, never to be returned.

I grieve over the fact that I would have had three girls like Aimee, instead of one, had it not been that a paedophile interfered with our children. We are good parents and Aimee is proof of that. Even in the face of adversity, our youngest daughter is intelligent, confident, funny and stylish. She is still the little girl with the strength of character, but now with a maturity and acumen beyond her age.

Aimee continued: 'In one of my dreams Dad walked up to me and he was holding the hand of a little girl. He said, "Look who's here!" It was Emma.'

It was a big let-down when she awoke from that wonderful slumber.

'I do miss her a lot. I felt I had a sister who I could chat to. I wanted to build on that too, because it had only just started.' Aimee's eyes watered as she told me this. It was like she was looking right through me.

I too have loving dreams about Emma

She is alive and I am so surprised and delighted to see her, I call out her name and hug her laughing and I say: 'You're alive! I thought you were dead.' It is beyond delightful to hold her again in my arms. But then I find out it is not real. The last time she appeared, she was pushing a stroller with her two-year-old son in it.

Aimee's relationship with Katie has been difficult and remains so. Aimee wants to be closer to her remaining sister. She makes Katie laugh but Katie doesn't remember it. She doesn't recall the great day they had together or the joke they shared. Katie's maturity is close to that of the fifteen-year-old she was, when hit by the car. 'It's not a normal relationship [but] I make an effort to appreciate her for what I do have, rather than what we don't have,' Aimee said.

One day Katie, out of the blue, must have sensed Aimee's grief and said reassuringly: 'I do love you.' In her own way, Katie misses Emma too.

It's just so hard for them to fathom how they went from three bright, bubbly children to reach this point.

In recent years, Katie had a boyfriend – one of her carers who fell in love with her. Katie was so happy being in love with this young man but a year later he had to return to his home in India. He could not extend his working visa. 'That was pretty sad,' Aimee recalled. 'We all liked Anjan and Katie still misses him.'

Aimee resumed studying Arts and now Law after Emma's funeral, despite her grieving. She decided to keep hanging in. 'I'm so far behind. Some days my body just has no energy and I can only lie down. My heart aches and everything is so heavy.' She doesn't know what she wants from her professional life. Her number-one ambition is be a mum. Having children is the only way she feels she can experience the true love she experiences in her dreams.

'Since Emma passed away, I've come to know what's important.'

It's more than twenty years since Aimee put her hand out for communion bread from Father Kevin O'Donnell, the day I turned back towards the altar to see him berating her and demanding to know who she belonged to. It is a small victory for me to recall her standing before him, unmoved and unafraid. Now that child, all grown up, can be proud of the way she stood up to the bully in a collar.

'You didn't tell me off, which was good,' she said to me. 'I didn't feel bad in the way he wanted me to feel. I look back and say "Go, little Aimee".'

I do too.

Aimee recalls O'Donnell being a scary man, even though she didn't flinch when he scolded her. The little children knew not to swing their legs in the front row of the church because he would publicly tell them off, she remembered. One day the paedophile went into Aimee's classroom, the same way he stepped into Emma and Katie's classes. She remembers the name of the teacher and that the class was a composite of prep, grade 1 and grade 2 pupils. Aimee was in grade 2, which made it 1992, O'Donnell's retirement year. It was one of the incidents that proved he was still taking children from classrooms only months before he left, after the cathedral was hearing complaints about his behaviour. (We also knew he was taking children from the playground in 1992, and sexually assaulting them as described by Katie in her diary.)

'Can I have a few children to help me,' he asked the teacher, casting his gaze across the bay of young faces looking up at him.

'Do we have volunteers?' the teacher enquired.

All of the children, ten five-year-olds, ten six-year-olds and ten seven-year-olds, raised their hands as high as they could. Some waved and strained with the excitement of being picked.

Aimee put her hand up but was never selected.

She is thankful for that at least. And so am I.

Chapter 20
'Dwelling crankily . . .
on old wounds'

We were perched on the summit of St Kilda's highest peak, Conachair, four hundred and twenty-six metres above the thundering ocean, the breathtaking and frightening cliffs beneath us diving sharply down into the sea. There were no barriers.

The National Trust for Scotland had allowed our travelling party the unique privilege of staying three nights on the double World Heritage Site. My ancestors lived on the isolated archipelago for many centuries but abandoned it in 1930. Now, only workers and tourists come to witness the strength of nature and the surviving evidence of astounding human endurance.

My forebears left behind ancient stone structures. Anthony and I had looked at the oldest village and the countless *cleits*; stone huts built to defy the heaviest rains and the harshest winds, spread out like statues with flat, earth-covered roofs, proud evidence of a race that survived through hard work, ingenuity and thousands of small boulders.

It was all so beautiful from where I sat, in the deep, spongy long grass. I overlooked the steep hills and near-vertical leas of another rock island in the distance – Boreray, a magnificent three hundred and eighty-four-metre natural skyscraper. It too was matted with elegant grass, food for the ancient breed of sheep that strolled up and down the cliffs. I was as close to the edge of the world as I could be. I felt comfortable there. I knew what it was like to live on the edge of everything and stare out into oblivion.

But to delight in real beauty, one's mind must be free and mine wasn't. I was thinking of Emma.

I remembered her short and sad life, the years of trauma. I thought of what was done to her and who violated her. I thought of the unexpectedly and impossible-to-comprehend stonehearted men of the Church hierarchy . . . I wondered 'WHY?' about everything that happened the way it did. There were so many 'whys', none of them with answers. We had gone beyond asking but the questions never left us.

The previous evening, the sun refused to dip behind the horizon until nearly midnight. Once it was dark, Anthony began taking flash photographs of the village ruins.

Click . . . click . . . click.

I lay in bed, listening to the powerful silence between his snapshots.

She had died and left nothing. No children. Ruins on an abandoned island surrounded me but even this place lived on, through descendants like me. What was Emma's legacy?

Sitting on Conachair, other thoughts were invading my mind too. There were things happening back in Australia that I could not ignore, no matter how hard I tried.

Thirteen days earlier we met Aimee and her girlfriend in Rome, where the four of us shared an apartment, exploring each day – sometimes together, sometimes apart – and sitting down to share many meals. It was such a relief to see our youngest daughter healthy. Anthony and I then flew to Glasgow to meet my older brother Ray and his wife Linda, who had flown in from Canada. My brother wanted to join us on our pilgrimage.

We drove a hire car to Uig on the Isle of Skye. The following morning, we took a ferry to Tarbert on the Isle of Harris then drove south to Leverburgh from where, the following day, we would take the fourteen-seater heavy seas vessel – complete with seatbelts – to St Kilda.

Reaching St Kilda is no easy task and totally weather-dependent. We were delayed one night and on that night we received an email from journalist (and co-author of this book) Paul Kennedy, who was familiar with our family's ordeal.

He told us the ABC's national current affairs program *Lateline* was investigating a story on Cardinal George Pell.

Pell had sent two sexual assault victims a letter each and dated them the same day. Both victims complained about the same sexually-abusive priest. To one victim, he stated that the Church investigation showed that sexual abuse had taken place and the Church apologised. To the second victim, Cardinal Pell stated the Church investigation had shown that sexual abuse could not be substantiated and that no other complaints had been received about the perpetrator. *Lateline* was questioning the outlandish contradiction and double standards.

Early the following day we went to St Kilda, a place with no communications apart from those of the British Armed Forces. We were off the radar until the evening of the fourth day.

I was left to stew on Conachair about what was happening back in Australia with the Cardinal Pell letters. Then Anthony interrupted my thoughts, as he stood up in the thick coat of St Kilda grass, holding out his hand to pull me up.

'Let's go.'

We took the long walk off the mountain. A pair of huge seabirds with large webbed feet swooped down on us for invading their treeless peaceful existence. We passed stone huts on vicious slopes, trekking until we walked along the village path. We needed to pack our bags.

It was Friday 11 July 2008. After a Scottish 'wobbly coffee' (a coffee with a welcome shot of local whisky), Ray, Anthony and I left the serenity of St Kilda. Linda, my sister-in-law, was a seasickness sufferer, had not come with us, choosing to stay in Leverburgh. The boat ride back was much calmer than the trip over. That evening we ate wonderful potato and oatmeal soup for dinner (a welcome change from our four days of canned food) and Anthony checked his emails.

There were messages from Paul and the *Lateline* program producer, asking us to go to the nearest capital city as soon as possible. The situation with the two letters had escalated and *Lateline* wanted to interview Anthony about our experiences. We felt we had never really spoken out about our circumstances before as the *60 Minutes* story, six years earlier, had us in disguises. So much had happened since and it was an opportunity to raise some real questions for a national debate.

We made a rash but resolute decision to abandon the last two weeks of our trip and return to Australia – not back to Melbourne but to Sydney where the pope was soon to arrive for World Youth Day. We wanted to help those who could not help themselves; the many voiceless victims who were continuing to be mistreated. The time we spent thinking about what had happened to our family had recharged our batteries. We were ready to challenge the Church again. Now that we understood just how deadly the sexual assault of children could be – not just life-debilitating but life-destroying – we could not ignore it or keep it to ourselves. An opportunity was presented to us and without discussing it we took it. Just one exchanged look between us sealed the silent 'okay'.

We first had logistical problems to overcome. Anthony still wanted to see his sister Carol, who was in England, so we caught a flight from Inverness to London, where the ABC had a news bureau. We could see Carol and do the interview on the same day, then fly to Australia. As we began our long journey home, departing the Scottish isles, Anthony wrote his news release to read out on our arrival.

Pope Benedict XVI was also making travel preparations. He was to arrive in Australia on 13 July and rest briefly at the Opus Dei retreat on the outskirts of Sydney.

The flight to London on Monday 14 July was short. The following day the ABC called and asked us to be at its studio by nine-thirty in the morning. Tony Jones, the *Lateline* presenter, was going to interview Anthony via satellite.

At the ABC office I waited downstairs as Anthony was interviewed. After a short time, I was taken upstairs and saw my husband sitting in a small sound room, behind him a poster of Big Ben and the British Parliament. I heard the last few minutes of the long-distance interview and knew Anthony spoke clearly and made his points well. He said we were preparing to fly to Sydney to make a statement. The fifteen-minute interview covered sexual assault, compensation, Church actions and our desire to improve conditions for other victims; if this meant speaking to the pope then we were happy to do so. An apology was not good enough, unless it was backed up by a change in Church responses and attitudes.

We said goodbye to the ABC staff and caught a taxi to Heathrow Airport, boarded our mid-afternoon Qantas flight and headed for home. When booking the flight back to Australia we discovered there was a shortage of available seats to Sydney. Catholics were coming from all over the world to see the pope and seats were almost fully booked. The best connection we could find went via Tokyo – with a nine-hour stopover – followed by a short stop in Cairns, North Queensland. All up, it was a thirty-six-hour commute.

Anthony's *Lateline* interview went to air nationwide during the long first leg of our flight. In Japan, we were so tired we decided to rest in the Qantas airport lounge. Anthony plugged in his computer and email after email rolled down his screen.

Our phones were also full of messages. There were requests to speak to Anthony from media in Australia, New Zealand and Canada. We had not given it a thought but the world press was in Australia for the pope's visit and the *Lateline* interview was having an effect not only nationally but also internationally. Anthony did two radio interviews for New Zealand and one for Canada. He also made many other phone calls and returned emails. Melbourne's *Age* newspaper sent a photographer from the other side of Tokyo to take a picture of Anthony waiting at the airport. It took the photographer three hours to reach us but the photo appeared on the front page of the major newspaper the following day.

We were so busy during the nine-hour stopover that boarding time quickly arrived. Before we left Tokyo, we were told via phone that a bishop, acting as a spokesman for the Church as World Youth Day coordinator, had commented on Anthony's interview.

Bishop Anthony Fisher said we were: 'Dwelling crankily . . . on old wounds.'

It was a hurtful comment that showed his, and the Church's, arrogance and ignorance, and a lack of understanding and compassion for all sexual assault victims and their families. The Catholic Church had known for centuries about clergy sexual assaults against children. It was obvious the Australian hierarchy had learned nothing since the historical cover-up of paedophile priests became a public scandal in the early 1990s. Bishop Fisher was either naive or much worse . . .

And Emma had died just six months earlier.

Every day, Emma was still dead. Katie had been almost completely disabled for the past ten years through drinking to forget her ordeal. Every day, she was still disabled. When did the wounds become old?

During our flight to Australia, Anthony amended his press release to comment on Bishop Fisher's insult. We landed at

Cairns Airport on the Wednesday morning, 17 July. It was five o'clock. My husband printed out copies of his statement to hand out to reporters in Sydney. We wondered how many, if any, would turn up. I went to the newsagency to buy national and local papers. Both had articles quoting Anthony's *Lateline* interview. We departed for Sydney with butterflies in our stomachs. We didn't know anybody in Sydney and hadn't arranged anywhere to stay. We did not know what to expect. No response would have been disappointing, but we had no idea what was about to happen.

Our plane slowly descended over Sydney. As Anthony was gazing down at the expansive city he turned to me and said: 'I'm only one person.' I held his hand and looked out at the city of almost four million people and tried to smile.

Going through immigration, the officer looked at Anthony and his passport.

'Didn't I see you on television last night?' he asked.

Anthony smiled hesitantly and confirmed that he probably had. We looked at each other, feeling conspicuous, not expecting anyone would recognise Anthony from a short interview on a late-night news program. We seemed to walk straight through quarantine and were heading to the public area, still contemplating the customs officer's remark, when we came face to face with a wall of media people – reporters and cameramen from television networks Seven, Nine, Ten, the ABC and SBS; radio station reporters; press journalists and photographers. At least thirty people stood there looking at us expectantly. We stopped in our tracks, looking back at them, not knowing what to do or whether they wanted us. They were blocking our way. Then one of them said: 'Anthony Foster?' And so with some shock we knew they were all there to speak to us. We shuffled out of the way of other passengers and Anthony read the statement he had prepared.

Before starting I would like to address the outrageous comments and attitude of Bishop Anthony Fisher, which we have found to be endemic among people unaware of the impact of sexual assault. The 'old wounds' he speaks of never heal and the victims of sexual assault suffer all their lives.

After speaking briefly about Emma and her death, Anthony's voice was strong as he continued:

There are many, many similar cases of suffering and loss as a result of sexual assaults on children, youth and adults.

The hierarchy of the Church contributed to Emma's death through their actions and inactions. I hold them personally accountable for her death, which they could have prevented.

Cardinal George Pell, the highest-ranked member of the Catholic Church in Australia, had been quoted in newspapers that same week, criticising some aspects of society in the western world. *The Age* reported: 'Speaking about Australia's high rate of youth suicide, Cardinal Pell blamed those who encouraged young people to pursue promiscuity, alcohol and drugs, saying these things were simply a hopeless "prison".'

If Cardinal Pell cared to find out, he would have known promiscuity, alcohol and drugs were all major symptoms of sexual assault in children. In cases involving clergy, it was the paedophile priests condemning youth to living in prisons, both metaphorically and in reality, not to mention pushing many to suicide. The victims' rights group Broken Rites had stated it knew of at least twenty clergy sex abuse victims who had killed themselves to escape their silent suffering – paedophile priests were getting away with murder by way of their victims' suicides.

Anthony continued:

Cardinal Pell does not know what more he could have done. Well – he should have acted justly and fairly towards victims. He should not have cruelly limited compensation. He should not have crushed victims who did not have the ability to pursue justice. Cardinal Pell wonders why there are so many youth suicides. Well – he should look at the actions of the Catholic Church because, in many cases, the cause is sexual assault.

To be truly repentant of what the Church has done to the victims of clergy sexual assault the Church must unite in a uniform response. That response must be based on moral principles of fairness and openness without recourse to the legal system to deny victims' rights.

The Church must respond morally, not legally. To survive, and have the life that should have been, the victims need unrestricted help. It is the Church's responsibility to provide that help on the basis of its moral responsibility and not on the basis of fighting victims in the courts or other forums or by using the law to deny the Church even exists.

The Church, and the pope as its uniting leader, must take this opportunity to prove their character, for without looking after their own victims they can have no authority to make pronouncements on any other aspect of life. To date they have simply proven that they will use all means possible to control the extent of their support for victims or, even worse, to deny any support.

The Church should be deeply ashamed of the actions of offending priests and the behaviour of archbishops, cardinals and religious orders that have limited or restricted compensation for victims.

An apology is not enough.

Limited compensation is not enough.

Limited help is not enough.

The journalists were in no hurry to interrupt or ask questions.

We wish to meet with the pope to help formulate the way forward. It may be difficult and will require changes by the Church but we are willing to help. Together we can ensure the victims of sexual assault are treated fairly and justly so they may have some hope of surviving and participating fully in this wonderful gift of life.

Once the all-in media conference was completed, individual organisations asked for one-on-one interviews. It was an hour and a half before we were finished.

In the crowd we could see two people from Broken Rites, including its spokeswoman Chris MacIsaac. Another non-media person was a representative from ASCA, Adults Surviving Child Abuse. Our family had been members since 1997 and Emma attended the group's meetings in Victoria. She found them supportive (we found them the same after Emma's death) and so we collected money in lieu of flowers at Emma's funeral to donate to the organisation. Seeing on the news that we were arriving in Sydney, ASCA's Executive Officer kindly arrived to greet us and drive us to a hotel. We had not met any ASCA members from New South Wales before and it was comforting to have them and Broken Rites by our sides at such a time.

After checking in at a hotel, we walked to St Mary's Cathedral, where different television crews interviewed us. We answered similar questions. I went back to the hotel while Anthony and a reporter did a small video report with the pope driving along a major city street in the background.

Until we reached Sydney, we had not heard the full context of Bishop Fisher's 'dwelling crankily . . . on old wounds' remark, which he made during a media conference. Back at the hotel we viewed the footage. He used the ridiculous phrase in a direct response to a question about Anthony's *Lateline* appearance.

'Happily, I think most of Australia was enjoying, delighting in, the beauty and goodness of these young people rather than dwelling crankily, as a few people are doing, on old wounds.'

Criticism of the comment was extensive. The newspapers screamed: 'Don't be so cranky: bishop's advice to sex abuse victims', 'A cranky father tells the church: the wounds are still raw and open', 'Outrage over bishop's remarks on sex abuse', 'Fury at "cranky" sex slur', 'Don't dwell on abuse that ruined lives, says bishop'. These headlines preceded editorials – 'A bishop's remark, not parents' grief, opens old wounds,' wrote one columnist. 'Some wounds are too painful to heal,' added another.

Chris MacIsaac of Broken Rites said: 'Cardinal Pell preached at the World Youth Day opening mass about the good shepherd who left the ninety-nine sheep to find the sheep that was lost. This (Emma) was a baby lamb, and did Pell go and look for it?'

Another advocacy group observed: 'The Catholic Church has a lot to learn about the burden of clergy abuse on the lives of victims and those who care for them.'

The World Youth Day chief executive officer was prompted by the scandal to come out and state that Bishop Fisher had 'misspoken'. The Catholic Church official tried to deny the bishop was referring to us, claiming the cleric was the victim of sensationalism.

The issue did not die down, and Bishop Fisher was not publicly seen or heard from during the remainder of World Youth Day celebrations.

A couple of days later, we discovered that the pope was being treated to a re-enactment of the torture-filled lead-up and violent death of Jesus – the Stations of the Cross. It was telecast to a worldwide audience of an estimated five hundred million people. The play, performed at various venues around Sydney, covered the whipping, scouring, thorns piercing the head and agonising death of Jesus while nailed to a cross some

2000 years ago. If that was not dwelling on old wounds, I don't know what is. The Catholic Church hierarchy do not seem to notice they are hypocrites.

After a very late and light dinner, Anthony and I went to bed. It had been over sixty hours since our six o'clock wakeup call in London and I had only two one-hour stints of sleep on the flight. I was tired.

It was only the first of four frenzied days.

I don't know how many media reports we took part in during our time in Sydney. News crews from far and wide were present and eager to gain opinions. Each day seemed to be the same: get up, walk to Hyde Park, media interviews, return late to the hotel and sleep. But then something significant happened.

The pope seemed to make an apology.

It happened on the Saturday morning, 19 July, at a mass for cardinals, bishops, Australian seminarians and selected guests. But it was not for World Youth Day pilgrims:

'Indeed, I am deeply sorry for the pain and suffering the victims have endured and I assure them that, as their pastor, I too share in their suffering,' he said.

His statement did not impress Anthony and me. It was missing something. I wanted to hear him say: 'Indeed, I am deeply sorry for the pain and suffering the victims have endured *because of what we have done . . .*'

Where were these simple words? The pope was speaking on behalf of the Catholic Church, which refused to laicise paedophile priests, even going against canon law to do so. He was also speaking on behalf of the bishops, who followed secret Church rules to avoid scandal and therefore privately shift child molesters and rapists from parish to parish, victims to helpless victims. The pontiff was the overseer of a destructive and manipulative worldwide pattern of abuse.

If another organisation allowed such child abuse to take place – a private company or less influential religious group

– it would be considered illegal and shut down by the state authorities. Carefully worded 'apologies' would not be nearly enough to save it or its leaders from prosecution. In this case, however, with his power never questioned, the pope was comfortable trotting out his token few sentences.

In leaving out these six little words – 'because of what we have done' – the pope was denying the Church's involvement and, following that, any responsibility. Even the pope giving the 'apology' had a past that contradicted his statement.

Pope Benedict XVI has faced criticism that in 2001 he posted an official Vatican document to bishops all over the world, outlining the Roman Catholic Church's secret policies on investigating crimes by clergy, including child sexual abuse. Cardinal Joseph Ratzinger, as he was then, signed the letter, which reinforced Church laws written in 1962 that were 'buried in the deepest secrecy'.

Canon lawyer Reverend Thomas Doyle wrote the following in his book *Sex, Priests and Secret Codes – The Catholic Church's 2000-Year Trail of Sexual Abuse*:

> The 2001 document reflects the same attitude of exclusivity and secrecy that has marked the church's attitude toward clergy sex crimes from the early twentieth century to the present.
>
> The defensive reaction of high-ranking churchmen . . . . reflects a long-standing attitude at the highest level of church authority: denial and blame-shifting. Church leadership now, as in the past, has strongly resisted any attempts to study its own role in the unsuccessful handling of abuse cases.

So the pope's words '. . . *I too share in their suffering*' were not convincing. He shared nothing with me. He had no idea.

Without a sincere, full and therefore honest confession or apology there can be no forgiveness. The pope of all people should know that. It's like a masked man coming up to your car with a crowbar and proceeding to smash in your windscreen. You look at this man, who still has the weapon in hand, and he says: 'I'm deeply sorry your windscreen is broken.' I recognised it as the apology you make when you're not really making an apology.

Two days later the pope was scheduled to leave Australia. After an early breakfast we received messages that he was going to meet with sex abuse victims at a private mass an hour or so before he departed. Details were scant. The media were ringing to see if the rumour involved us.

It did not; we knew nothing about it.

We also were leaving Sydney that Monday morning, 21 July 2008, flying home to Melbourne. We caught a taxi to the international airport, from where the pope was boarding his flight. Anthony's phone kept ringing. Television crews took footage and radio stations wanted live interviews; the press wanted statements.

We later learned that two of the four selected victims for the private papal mass were siblings and for some reason the Church publicly released this detail. It seemed to be a clever ploy by its public relations spin-doctors because a lot of people thought it was us.

'I believe you got to meet the pope after all,' was a common line people used when they bumped into us in the next few days.

I wondered just how many examples of sexually assaulted siblings the Church had on its books, if a supposedly impromptu and random gathering of four victims had two as siblings.

It had been quite an experience and the media people in Sydney – press, television and radio – had been wonderful to us and were a credit to their profession. The debate and analysis they raised was impressive; broadening people's thinking. Our story had gone around the world. My brother read about it in Canada; Anthony's niece heard her uncle's and cousin

Emma's names on her car radio while driving in England. It was reported in Ireland, France, Italy, Germany, New Zealand and the United States and most likely other countries as well.

As well, almost every major news outlet in Australia reported Anthony's offer to meet the pope – anywhere in the world and at any time – to discuss improving the Church's outlook and ways to attain a more compassionate treatment of victims. Only the Catholic Church officials ignored him. It was interesting to observe the Church hierarchy and how determined they were to ignore such a pressing issue.

While at the airport, we saw on television a reporter interviewing Cardinal Pell. When asked about Anthony's unsuccessful request, the cardinal laughed.

'Oh, thousands of people want to see the pope, not all of them can.'

On 3 September 2008, Anthony and I attended a comedy gala event hosted by ASCA, Adult Surviving Child Abuse, where the Emma Foster Memorial Fund was launched and we were interviewed by ASCA patron Ita Buttrose. ASCA accepted the donation from our daughter's funeral and ran money-raising functions, turning Emma's friends' $1500 donation into $80,000. The fund now enables life-freeing workshops to be held around Australia, assisting adult survivors of child abuse to understand their plight and promote healing. Emma would have been so happy to see her name attached to such a great initiative.

The following year, in June 2009, Anthony and I travelled to Sydney to launch a one-minute documentary-style television advertisement for the child protection organisation Child Wise. The ad, created by generous volunteer professionals, was a snapshot of the effects of child sexual assault on our family. It is shown free-to-air on television stations wishing to support this child protection issue. The launch, which took place on the national breakfast television program *Sunrise*, also featured a forty-page booklet that I wrote, relating what I had learned about paedophile behaviours and the symptoms of ongoing sexual assault in children. It was the result of my thirteen years of experience.

Chapter 21
In the end, for the sake of children, we must change

It is frightening to consider how many people are suffering in silence in this country from the crimes committed against them as children by paedophile priests. There are so many who still have not disclosed their horrible experiences. We know that only three per cent (Savi Report, 2004) of children will ever speak about their sexual assaults, some waiting until their sixties or seventies to finally tell someone. It is probable, even likely, that complaints will be made about Father Kevin O'Donnell for the next fifty years. And he is *one* paedophile priest from *one* city.

I know a little about how some of these silent sufferers feel. Emma once wrote about it:

I can't make anyone happy.
I can't make myself happy.
I'm lonely inside.
I lie to myself to try and feel better.
I can't concentrate.
I never have energy to enjoy myself.
I never have energy for anything.
I hate myself.

I hate the way I think and feel.

I feel dirty.

I feel ugly.

I feel worthless and useless.

I feel my whole life is just a boring road to death.

I've isolated myself for too long.

I don't have social skills.

I can't hold friendships.

I have no talents.

I have nowhere to go in life.

I'm afraid of living.

I constantly cry.

No one understands me.

I don't understand myself.

I am not worthy of being here.

I have to rely on medicine to stay slightly normal.

The Catholic Church is an organisation supposed to represent God in our world, through examples of truth, compassion, love and all things good, yet it makes itself invisible to our law in Australia so it cannot be held accountable for the atrocities some of its members commit against children. The Catholic authorities are happy with their invisibility to our law and cunningly corral victims back to themselves to receive a pittance that they dictate and control to contain scandals and retain assets.

When Anthony and I met Sister Angela Ryan, head of Towards Healing, at a meeting one night late in 2008, we asked her how many victims a year came to her office to report clergy abuse. She initially said two hundred then quickly corrected herself, saying two hundred and fifty. When we asked what statistics she kept, she replied: 'None.' It seemed incredible that this national clergy abuse response service did not collate information as an aid to amend Church failings and attempt to stop history repeating itself. Ms Ryan did say, however, that the media reports during the papal visit caused a spike in complaints.

Another momentary lifting of the lid on sexual abuse.

Professor Chris Goddard, Director of Child Abuse Prevention Research Australia at Monash University, stated in an article in *The Australian* newspaper:

> Churches and schools provide limitless opportunities for those who wish to assault children. Child molesters require privacy, power and secrecy. In order to re-offend, the perpetrators need to create a culture that reinforces that privacy, power and secrecy, and an organisation that responds to allegations of sexual assault − if it responds at all − with delay and confusion . . . The creation of confusion is also used by churches to escape the consequences of their action and inactions . . . When churches are shamed into taking action, by media pressure, church leaders portray themselves as victims.

There must be no confusion for us in regards to child molestation and rape. We must all understand that it happens and how it happens to the one in three girls and the one in six boys in this country.

Writing this book has proved to be a great healing process. During this time of writing and during the years of our suffering, I have had the greatest pleasure of being associated with and meeting some of the best people I could ever wish to know. These exceptional people far outweigh those who have caused our heartache. Their love and support have diminished our pain and enriched our lives and we are the better for knowing them.

The struggle is not over and we must all continue to destroy the silence imposed by paedophiles with our discussion, debate and knowledge.

As I write this final paragraph it is 6 November, Emma's birthday. She would have been twenty-eight today . . .

Acknowledgements

CHRISSIE FOSTER

Writing this book has been a life-altering experience.
Placing the words in this book has created an extraordinary journey of highs and lows and accordingly I have extraordinary people to thank:

The survivors who bravely shared with us their heart-wrenching stories at personal cost and tears. Without their strength to speak in 1994, the guilty plea, a prison sentence and exposure would not have followed. And, quite possibly, we would not have known what had happened to Emma and Katie.

My loving family – Anthony, my husband of 30 years who has spent the last 15 of them defending and protecting his daughters. He has cried heartbreaking tears yet chooses to express words of love. As difficult as it has been for him to read our story, he is proud of my writing efforts. Our daughters: Katie – forever curious to know how the book was progressing and ever provided words of encouragement; Aimee – who, from a young age, has lived through so many traumas to become the strong person she is today; and dear Emma – who would have loved to have been part of the writing experience. My family's support has never faltered and their love has never diminished even though revisiting our past has hurt. My mother, Dawn, who broke from Catholic dogma and joined the fight. She was always on her daughter's and granddaughters' side. She has only ever encouraged and supported us making our journey easier. My father, brothers and relatives for all their years of loving care and being with us.

Our community of friends from Oakleigh and other steadfast friends who are always there – always supportive, always loving.

Fr Thomas Doyle, Michael Finnegan, Patrick Wall and Jason Berry from the United States, Colm O'Gorman from Ireland, Prof Chris Goddard from Melbourne, Dr Cathy Kezelman from Sydney, Fr John Salvano and Fr Noel Brady from Melbourne, and many others for their important voices and much-appreciated opinions.

Our publishing agent Clare Forster at Curtis Brown, who saw the possibilities.

Nikki Christer, publishing director at Random House, whose passion has guided our book.

Our editor, Chris Kunz, who really understood and worked towards making our story the best it could be.

Paul Kennedy, my co-author, who, over the years, has passed in and out of our lives and left a thread of solace by providing the opportunity to be heard and ultimately giving voice to the issue of child sexual assault. In an already busy life he took on the huge task of becoming my co-author, something I saw as an honour at the time and remain grateful for. I cannot thank him enough for his professionalism, commitment and tireless effort. Paul's honesty, integrity and sensitivity are what I wanted for the telling of my family's story – he remained the personification of those qualities throughout the writing process. Paul dared to take on the broader picture and as a result, over some months, we interviewed many people, experiencing both heartbreaking and confrontational encounters. Nothing was ever too difficult for him to take on. In the time I have worked with Paul, my respect for him as a person and a journalist have only grown. It has been both an honour and invaluable experience to have worked with him.

We must not forget all those who have maimed or killed themselves in a bid to escape the painful memories of childhood sexual assaults. All the children, now adults, who suffered at the hands of a paedophile. All the children currently suffering sexual assaults. And all the children, who will in the future, fall prey to the paedophile predator.

Children: our joy, our future and our greatest yet most vulnerable treasure.

PAUL KENNEDY

The courage of people who helped make this book possible will stay with me forever.

My admiration and thanks go to the selfless survivors who shared with us their awful memories, to help others. I hope the book allows them to feel less isolated and sleep easier. They deserve it.

It has been a privilege to help Chrissie tell her family's story. She and Anthony are wonderful parents. Their kindness, dignity and boundless fortitude are truly inspiring. I thank them, and Katie and Aimee, for allowing me to be a part of their lives.

To Michael and Joan Kennedy, also great parents – thank you for teaching me to stand up for what I believe in and encouraging me to always ask questions. To my wife, Kim, your comforting love and support are everything to me. And to Jack and Gus, thanks for being my future.

Finally, I would like to pay tribute to Emma Foster, a brave woman, a fighting spirit, who should have been allowed to experience real happiness and a longer life.